VICHY'S LAST CASTLE

VICHY'S LAST CASTLE

PÉTAIN'S PUPPET REGIME IN EXILE AT SIGMARINGEN

PAUL STJOHN MACKINTOSH

Pen & Sword
MILITARY

AN IMPRINT OF PEN & SWORD BOOKS LTD.
YORKSHIRE - PHILADELPHIA

First published in Great Britain in 2025 by
Pen & Sword Military
An imprint of
Pen & Sword Books Ltd
Yorkshire - Philadelphia

ISBN 978 1 03613 154 8

Typeset in INDIA by IMPEC eSolutions
Printed and bound in England by CPI (UK) Ltd.

The Publisher's authorised representative in the EU for product safety is
Authorised Rep Compliance Ltd., Ground Floor, 71 Lower Baggot Street,
Dublin D02 P593, Ireland.
www.arccompliance.com

For a complete list of Pen & Sword titles please contact

PEN & SWORD BOOKS LIMITED
George House, Units 12 & 13, Beevor Street,
Off Pontefract Road, Barnsley, S71 1HN, UK
E-mail: enquiries@pen-and-sword.co.uk
Website: www.pen-and-sword.co.uk

or

PEN AND SWORD BOOKS
1950 Lawrence Rd, Havertown, PA 19083, USA
E-mail: uspen-and-sword@casematepublishers.com
Website: www.penandswordbooks.com

MIX
Paper | Supporting
responsible forestry
FSC
www.fsc.org
FSC® C013604

Contents

Introduction

Siegmaringen?... what a picturesque hideaway!... you'd think you were in an operetta... perfect decor... you're waiting for the sopranos, the *tenori leggeri*... for the echoes, the whole forest!... ten, twenty wooded mountains!... Black Forest, fallen fir trees, cataracts... your set, the stage, the city, so prettily decked out, pink, green, a little bonbon, half pistachio, cabarets, hotels, shops, crackpot stage direction...[1]

Such was the setting where the elite of Hitler's French collaborators and allies took refuge during the final months of the Second World War. The desperation and degradation of those last days of treason and failed empire-building played out against a fantasy backdrop rich with historical ironies. It might almost be a set for Catalani's *La Wally* or Lehár's *The Lord of the Mountains*. Julian Jackson, a leading British historian of modern France, described Sigmaringen as 'a parody of a parody'.[2]

Inevitably, the whole story of the Sigmaringen enclave has been coloured by the 'hallucinatory narrative and unreliable testimony' of its prime literary inmate, Louis-Ferdinand Céline, as Henry Rousso described *Castle to Castle* – although Rousso also deemed it a literary masterpiece. No matter how delirious and eccentric Céline's account was, few doubt that it also was in some sense special pleading – as well as a well-timed bid to capitalize on post-war curiosity about the war years. Even the deliberate spelling of the location as 'Siegmaringen' – as in 'Sieg Heil' – should serve as a warning. Hence the need for some qualifications before tackling extensive excerpts from Céline's work.

As Phillip Watts stated in his own study on the theme:

There seem to be two ways to write about Sigmaringen, the German town where an incapacitated Vichy government landed in September

1944. The first is to cast the town as the site of an operetta, a fantasy world in which the Vichy government is seen as nothing more than a spectacle, a parodic version of its former self. The second option consists in describing Sigmaringen as a ghost town, a phantasmal city with its haunted castle frequented, for a period of eight months, by the shadows of the men who had ruled France for four years.

Watts also pointed out that both these approaches to Sigmaringen served personal and political purposes: emphasizing the Potemkin/phantasmal character of the enclave might make its denizens' treasonous behaviour seem less important and less culpable; and could conceal its real significance in post-war far-right politics and historiography. The triviality of operetta or spook stories was a way of diminishing and relativizing the seriousness of the reality – a reality which still has a serious legacy in modern French politics.[3]

Céline's writing about Sigmaringen tends to shed a spurious glamour on the enclave, as it does on his own prejudices and career. Wading through the verbal diarrhoea of Céline's late prose is one of the more distasteful undertakings of research into Sigmaringen, guaranteed to send you rushing for relief to a stylist like Charles Péguy, who channels the same sort of incessant effusion with infinitely more grace and clarity. Céline's post-war works like *Castle to Castle* are precisely where terms like 'self-parody' start creeping into one's mind, and as a stylist and a self-publicist, he was a far more deliberate and self-conscious manipulator than he is sometimes given credit for in the Anglosphere.

Yet the Sigmaringen enclave is fascinating and bizarre enough without Céline, as a concentrated distillation of French fascism, a petri dish to study the pathogen in isolation. Yes, arguments persist over whether Pétain's regime itself fits the definition of fascism, but the unambiguous and unapologetic representatives of French fascism certainly were there, peddling their own ideas and plans with the benefit of the Marshal as a mute figurehead, and far more influential in what was left of French collaborationism. As Robert O. Paxton emphasized in his magisterial study of Vichy France, the Paris circle of collaborationists in the German-occupied zone led almost separate but parallel political careers to the high echelons of Vichy, and Sigmaringen and its sister refuges in Germany were their last place to shine. Only in this last gasp of collaborationism did the likes of Doriot breathe the same heady air of fantasy, fanaticism and self-delusion as the Vichy governing elite – those few that were left.

Henry Rousso, whose *Un château en Allemagne. Sigmaringen, 1944-1945* (Paris, Ramsay, 1980), was the first extensive study of the enclave, summed it up as follows:

> The study of the 'government' of Sigmaringen and its activity on German soil between September 1944 and April 1945, is *a priori* anecdotal and derisory. It was only an episode with no interest, subject of a sulphurous masterpiece by Doctor Céline. However, it was through this detour that I better understood the madness of certain collaborators, in realizing the total illusion of belief in the future of a French fascism, born of a nationalism pushed to the absurd, at least in appearance, of a victorious German Europe. It was thanks to the analysis of his attitude at the Hohenzollern castle that I perceived to what extent Pétain had clung to a certain idea of legitimacy and to what extent the Germans had used, up to the last stage, the trap of collaboration, understood on the French side as a strategy aimed at retrieving some portion of national sovereignty. In other words, it was a matter, fortuitously, of approaching the subject from the margins, the limits, the extremes, Sigmaringen as a caricature of Vichy France... it is through the 'end' that common sense apprehends history, whether it be in the idea of 'lessons from the past' or belief in 'a tribunal of History'.[4]

As so often, the caricature, the extreme travesty, reveals plenty about the prosaic reality of its subject. A concentrated distillation of French fascism, Sigmaringen also serves as a concentrated distillation of Vichy's residue, and a chance to examine it in its concentrated form. For anyone who wants to look for persistent traces of the same infection in modern France, it also provides a few symptoms and test cases of French fascism, and some prescription on how to manage and control it.

Chapter 1

The Heritage of Sedition

T he ideologies and tendencies finally concentrated in Sigmaringen
sprang from sources deep in the foundations of France's Third
Republic. This chapter does not set out to be a complete survey
of the fascinating and tumultuous history of the Third Republic, from its
traumatic birth in the agonies of the Franco-Prussian War of 1870-71 to its
equally traumatic demise in the Fall of France in 1940. It does aim to chronicle
the early careers of the collaborationists who ended up in Germany in 1944-45,
and the political and intellectual currents which swept them along that course.

The Franco-Prussian War and the loss of Alsace-Lorraine to the new
German Empire deepened the fault lines in French society that finally
helped fracture the Third Republic and bring about its collapse some eighty
years later. Obviously, the Third Republic's crushing of the Paris Commune
compromised its support among the working classes and the radical left, but
the right-wing, royalist, monarchical strains that had persisted throughout
the revolutionary upheavals of 1848 and the Second Empire of Napoleon III
gained fresh wind from the hot breath of revanchism – the bitter desire for
revenge against Germany and recovery of the lost provinces. Revanchism also
fed another obsession prevalent across contemporary industrialized states –
the growing concern with decadence and sociopolitical decay. Contemplating
France's downfall from its Napoleonic heights to its present loss of territory
and prestige, any citizen of the Third Republic might feel just cause to ponder
decadence and potential rebirth.

Naturally, this fragile wounded pride fed overcompensation. The febrile
excesses of nationalism in French far-right circles after the Franco-Prussian
War are typified by this quote from the preface to Catholic novelist and
controversialist Léon Bloy's retrospective volume of war stories, *Sueur de Sang*
(*Sweating Blood*, 1893):

France is so far the first among peoples that all others, whoever they may be, must consider themselves treated honourably if they are permitted to eat the bread of her dogs.

If she is happy, then the rest of the world is sufficiently happy, even if they have had to pay for that happiness with servitude or extermination.

But when she suffers, it is God himself who suffers, the terrible God who has suffered for the whole world, sweating blood.

This is as absolute and immutable as the mystery of Predestination.

This was the kind of virulent chauvinism that informed a whole current of French right-wing thought post the collapse of the Second Empire. It found a ready audience among nationalist and monarchist groups that still cherished earlier grievances, dating back to the collapse of the French monarchy, or right back to the French Revolution.

With no realistic opportunity to do something about the German victory and the seizure of Alsace-Lorraine, such venom was readily turned against all perceived domestic enemies and impediments; secularists, rationalists, the Third Republic itself. As the historian of French fascism Pierre Milza remarked, 'the Republic – in its parliamentary form – gravely disappointed those French who placed their hopes for revenge on it.' For some traditionalists on the right, the Third Republic's flaws – its corruption, its musical-chairs parade of ministries, its failure to out-manufacture and outbreed the German Empire – reinforced their scepticism about the entire intellectual and moral heritage of the French Revolution and the Age of Enlightenment – liberty, equality, the Rights of Man and the Citizen. Others, who simply feared and loathed the egalitarianism and democratization of a modern industrial society, sought refuge in old ideas of hierarchy and authoritarian order. New intellectual analysis ramified the Catholic conservatism and pseudo-aristocratic nostalgia that had never truly reconciled to 1789 in the first place.

The writer and political figure who consolidated these trends, Charles Maurras, was born in 1868 to a Provençal family in Martigues near Marseille – which might earn him a place alongside the other provincial and marginal figures who became fanatical nationalists in their respective milieux, like Lajos Kossuth the quasi-Slovak, or Adolf Hitler the provincial Austrian. Losing his father at the age of 6, Maurras was raised by his deeply Catholic and conservative mother. From 14 he became profoundly deaf, and was educated by Abbé Jean-Baptiste Penon, a notably royalist cleric, who secured him positions with conservative journals in Paris at age 17. In 1888, he met Maurice Barrès, another conservative writer, who published the same year the first volume of his trilogy *The Cult of the Self* (*Le Culte du moi*). Hannah Arendt, in *The Origins of Totalitarianism*, characterized their collusion as follows:

> These men, who despised the people and who had themselves but recently emerged from a ruinous and decadent cult of estheticism, saw in the mob a living expression of virile and primitive 'strength'. It was they and their theories which first identified the mob with the people and converted its leaders into national heroes. It was their philosophy of pessimism and their delight in doom that was the first sign of the imminent collapse of the European intelligentsia.

The two near-mortal crises which the Third Republic suffered during this period helped reinforce Maurras' views on constitutional democracy – and helped create a receptive audience for his ideas. The movement, led by the populist and nationalist General and sometime Minister of War Georges Ernest Boulanger, almost succeeded in gathering enough popular and conservative support for a coup d'état, but Boulanger missed what opportunities he had, and fled France in April 1889. Already that year, the other great scandal preceding the Dreyfus Affair, the Panama Affair, had begun in February, with the winding up of the Panama Canal Company, which had accumulated enormous debts in its abortive effort to build a Panama Canal. In the protracted bankruptcy proceedings that followed, some 800,000 investors, many of them small French speculators, lost their money, while prominent politicians were exposed as having taken bribes from the company to conceal its insolvency. The involvement of a few leading Jewish financiers in the scandal helped stoke the French right's already substantial anti-Semitism. Maurras was briefly involved in Boulangism, and the Panama Affair helped create a disaffected mass audience ready for radicalization in similar future crises. Furthermore, like anti-clericalism on the left, anti-Semitism was one of the few rallying points that the various syndicalist national-socialist, royalist, ultramontane Catholic, romantic traditionalist, atheist, pragmatic authoritarian, and other factions of the right could unite around.

Maurras gathered a broad constituency across these factions by claiming to demonstrate, in his *Enquête sur la monarchie* (1900) and elsewhere, the necessity of monarchy through systematic reasoning:

> The necessity of the Monarchy is demonstrated as a theorem. The desire to preserve our French homeland once posited as a postulate, everything is linked, everything follows from an inevitable process. Fantasy, choice itself have no part in it: if you have resolved to be patriotic, you will by necessity be royalist. But, if you are thus led to the Monarchy, you are not free to veer towards liberalism, democracy or their substitutes. Reason requires it. We must follow it and go where it leads. *Race, selection, continuity*, these redemptive ideas, logically and rationally ordained, impose the reconstitution, restoration and complete reorganization of France.

Maurras' appeal to reason, however questionable, at least helped bring onside a current of time-honoured French rationalism that might otherwise have supported the values of the Third Republic. It also allowed for the kind of quasi-religious dogmatism already obvious in the writing of Léon Bloy. Albeit constrained by consultative assemblies, Maurras' ideal monarchy, uniting the national interest with its own dynastic interest, freed from the whims of public opinion and local interests, would be supremely motivated to govern well, he argued, in the interests of its own line of succession. However questionable this line of reasoning was logically and historically, it did have the advantage of unifying the French royalist right with more modern radical nationalist movements that had no particular attachment to the hereditary principle or the Divine Right of Kings.

Maurras also identified four groups who he held were the internal enemies of his organic conception of France and the French; Freemasons, Jews, Protestants and foreigners. According to Maurras' *Dictionnaire politique et critique*:

The Republic is [the property of a certain number of] families... These families are represented today by forty or fifty thousand Freemasons, one hundred thousand Jews, seven hundred thousand Protestants and some eight or nine hundred thousand aliens [*métèques*], who have imposed upon democracy – a passive and submissive animal – the aggressive spirit by which they are driven.

All of these groups were vulnerable scapegoats for French conservative detestation of industrialization and modern society, which often sought refuge from the challenges and contrasts of modern life and politics in the kind of imagined rural idyll that fostered Maurras' emphasis on regionalism.

Despite his avowed reverence for systematic thought, Maurras took a 'cavalier approach to the evidence of the past, for he used only that which substantiated or buttressed the preconceived framework of his account'.[1] He also professed support for the Catholic church as an integral part of his ideal past, or future, France, despite his personal lack of religious faith, claiming that the Graeco-Roman heritage of traditional Catholicism imposed a necessary discipline on Jewish visions and Christian sentiments.

Maurras and his fellow-travellers found their royal road to wider influence in the Dreyfus Affair. Before its advent, 'anti-Semitism was a dying movement in France by the summer of 1894', chiefly because Édouard Drumont, the influential anti-Semitic author of *La France juive* (1886) had managed to alienate the Catholic hierarchy and many Catholic conservative allies, as well as other groups that might otherwise have supported his creed. His book attacked the monarchy, the aristocracy and the *haute bourgeoisie*, while still remaining broadly Republican in its political stance. His strident emphasis on social causes also attracted some on the political left, while further alienating his supporters on the right. Indeed, he specifically linked modern capitalism to Jewish commercial interests. By virulently attacking the Boulangerist movement in *La Dernière Bataille* (1890), he further succeeded in setting himself against one of the few contemporary right-wing anti-Republican movements with any chance of success. Despite the early success of his journal *La Libre Parole* off the back of the Panama Scandal, Drumont then swung in favour of the anarchists, including the assassin of President Sadi Carnot in 1894, and by the end of the year, *La Libre Parole* was down to a few thousand readers. It took the Dreyfus Affair and the new opportunities for anti-Semitism to erase memories of Drumont's scabrous, indiscriminate rabble-rousing, and to win him a new, wider audience.[2]

In 1899, five years after the wrongful condemnation of Captain Alfred Dreyfus for treason, a conference of right-wing intellectuals formed Action Française, a movement and soon a journal, created in response to the Dreyfusards' creation of the Ligue des droits de l'Homme. Barrès was involved from its inception, and Maurras joined soon after its foundation in June 1899. Under his influence, the journal and the movement, virulently anti-Semitic and nationalist from the outset, became increasingly royalist, and gradually shed their republican nationalist adherents. As the Third Republic grew more militantly secularist and anti-clerical in the wake of the Dreyfus Affair, so Action Française gathered more and more Catholic adherents, including many French Catholic clergy. Even outside the movement's adherents, *Revue d'Action Française* became a widely read and influential journal, particularly among more mainstream conservatives.

Action Française also acquired a militant and increasingly paramilitary wing from November 1908 in the form of the Camelots du Roi (Newsboys of the King), the hawkers responsible for distributing the movement's journal and its sister publications on the streets of Paris. Besides hawking papers, the Camelots du Roi promptly commenced attacks on Republican symbols and figures, academics, theatrical performances, and other ideologically repugnant targets. With the horseshoe effect in full swing, they also reflected, and even found common cause with, an increasingly militant anti-Republican tendency on the radical left, intellectually validated by Georges Sorel.

Initially associated with Marxism and Dreyfusism, Sorel was already moving towards a far more militant position by the early 1900s, articulated in his *Reflections on Violence* (*Réflexions sur la violence*, Paris, 1908). Sorel advocated violence as a positive good in itself, a regenerative agent capable of combating decadence among the working class and the *bourgeoisie*. Against progressive and liberal ideals of compromise, reform, and coexistence, he extolled class conflict and the Homeric hero as agents for the radical transformation of society:

Revolt – against decadence and its manifestations – could save a society from decline, but not without fervour, that activating faith which alone could generate the energy that can move masses... Sorel is proof, if proof be needed, that the fin-de-siècle saw not only a crisis of liberalism – arising from growing perceptions of its failure – but a crisis of its offspring: Marxism.[3]

Motivated by such ideas, Sorel found himself closer in spirit to Maurras, and by 1909 was making more positive statements towards Maurras and his movement, exemplified by the project in 1910 of creating a joint Sorelian/Maurrasian review, *la Cité Française*. Imprisoned Camelots du Roi also found common cause with some anarchists in their shared opposition to the Third Republic – and their readiness to resort to violence in defiance of the legal and political order.

Both factions, however, broadly upheld the Union Sacrée of 1914, whereby the Third Republic went through the First World War supported by both socialists and militant conservatives. Sorel, for all his idolization of violence, opposed support for the war effort, as did the great Socialist leader Jean Jaurès, assassinated by a lone French nationalist on 31 July 1914. However, by May 1917 the spirit of cooperation and common purpose had been badly eroded by over a million war dead, and the French army started to experience mutinies and refusals to fight. The settling of the mutinies was credited to a popular soldier's general and Chief of Staff, soon to be Commander-in-Chief of the entire French army, Philippe Pétain.

Born in 1856 to a peasant family in the Pas-de-Calais, Pétain had a conservative Catholic and military education, rising slowly through the ranks of the still status-conscious army after his graduation from the Saint-Cyr Military Academy in 1878. His opinions during this period were apparently moderately Dreyfusard, and he later reportedly stated that, 'for my part, I have always believed in the innocence of Dreyfus'.[4] On the eve of the First World War, he was still only a colonel. In the spring of 1914 he suffered a bad fall from his horse, and was treated by Dr Louis Ménétrel, father of Bernard Ménétrel, the doctor who was later to be such an influential counsellor in Sigmaringen.

Commencing the war as commander of the 4th Brigade of the 2nd Infantry Division, Pétain was rapidly promoted as hostilities began, and was General of Division by 14 September 1914, leading the 6th Division through the First Battle of the Marne, and Army Corps General in command of the XXXIII Corps by 20 October. During the Battle of Verdun in 1916, he was promoted to Commander of Army Group Centre, comprising over fifty divisions. His participation in the battle was critical, both in his application of his doctrine of firepower, particularly artillery, above all, and his employment of the *'Voie Sacrée'* from Bar-le-Duc to Verdun to ensure continuous replenishment of materiel and manpower during the battle. After the costly, abortive Nivelle offensive of early 1917, he succeeded Robert Nivelle as Commander-in-Chief.

Pétain succeeded in quelling the mutinies of 1917 by a combination of moderate discipline (554 death sentences for mutiny, mostly commuted), rotations of exhausted units, and direct appeals to the troops enhanced by his personal prestige. Some of the factors underlying the mutinies, which 'do provide a startling example of the political dichotomy that has weakened France since Napoleon', such as 'pacifism, stimulated by the Russian Revolution and the trade-union movement',[5] may have helped shape his later attitudes. Subsequently, Pétain adopted a limited and mostly defensive posture as commander, reportedly saying 'I am waiting for the tanks and the Americans'.[6] The final German offensives in the spring of 1918 apparently pushed Pétain close to a failure of nerve: in 1918 he apparently showed a tendency towards defeatism in the face of the initial German victories, concentrating on the defence of Paris instead of maintaining contact with Haig's British Expeditionary Force (BEF), leading Winston Churchill and others to regard him ever after as a defeatist. Prime Minister Georges Clemenceau claimed that he had heard Pétain say: 'the Germans will beat the English in the open country, and after that they will beat us too.'

Ferdinand Foch was appointed to overall command and coordination of the Allied offensives instead, and Pétain executed his final moves of the war under his command. Despite this ambivalent conclusion to his wartime service, Pétain finished the First World War a national hero, and was appointed Marshal of France in November 1918. In 1920, he was elevated to the Third

Republic's highest military position, Vice-Chairman of the Supreme War Council, where he remained until 1931.

Unfortunately, Pétain's shining public image after the First World War concealed a darker side that was to have grave repercussions later.

> Pétain's political ambition in the declining years of his life offers a perplexing problem – one which is properly explained neither by the claims of selfless devotion offered by himself and his disciples, nor by his enemies' accusations of scheming villainy. The explanation comes rather from the strangely twisted mentality hidden behind the famed marmoreal features of the Marshal – from his intense self-righteousness, spurred by a constant feeling that he never received sufficient recognition, and leading to an almost maniacal craving for self-justification... Pétain's frustrated self-righteousness is the leitmotif which runs through his life and helps clarify his later political behaviour.[7]

Perceived slights during the First World War, with the elevation of rival commanders, above all Ferdinand Foch, over his head because of his defensive tactics, left Pétain with lingering grudges and a conviction that his own unrecognized contributions had in fact saved France. This analysis certainly fits with the later revelations of his tenacity in clinging to his facade of legitimacy, even in his last months in Sigmaringen.

Another figure from a lowly background, Pierre Laval was born in 1883 near Vichy at Châteldon to a family of innkeepers and hoteliers. He studied law, while also moving in Socialist circles, and by 1909 was installed in Paris, where he developed a track record as an advocate for the poor, and especially unionist and Socialist activists. He was first elected as a Socialist deputy in May 1914. In 1923 he was elected mayor of Aubervilliers, and joined the government of Paul Painlevé in April 1925 as Minister of Public Works, retaining the portfolio until June 1926. He progressively distanced himself from the Socialists, winning election as Senator for the Seine in January 1927, all the while pursuing a lucrative legal career. In March 1930 he was appointed Minister of Labour in the administration of André Tardieu, and on 30 January 1931 he became President of the Council and head of government.

With the Great Depression in full swing, *Time Magazine* made Pierre Laval Man of the Year for 1931 – the first French citizen ever to receive the tribute. Its 4 January 1932 testimonial labelled him 'calm, masterful and popular'. It continued:

> Swart as a Greek, this compact little Auvergnat (son of a village butcher in Auvergne, south-central France) was a Senator of no party, an Independent... identified with no conspicuous cause or movement, Senator Laval was also too young to be noticeable in France in January 1931. He was only 47 and France likes its Premiers to be over 60.

Laval's cited achievements included modification of the Hoover One-Year Moratorium on Germany's payment of war reparations and a programme of public works to reduce unemployment, passed in December, but most of the emphasis was on 'the complete dominance of Premier Laval' over the Third Republic's volatile and capricious party politics. 'On Christmas Eve the Chamber gave Premier Laval a straight vote of confidence 315 to 255, then adjourned to the second Tuesday in January, leaving the Man of the Year unshaken, triumphant,' *Time Magazine* trumpeted. 'How great is his achievement may be measured by the fact that only four French Premiers since the War have been able to remain in power for as much as one year.'

Laval's Man of the Year writeup also noted that 'France closed 1931 with vastly greater gold stocks than any other European state (the US has half again as much); she could count her unemployed in hundreds of thousands while Britain and Germany counted theirs in millions'. But it also noted that Laval was 'said to have been briefly enrolled at one time as both a Socialist and a Communist, not being sure which way the cat of popular sentiment would jump'. That preference for power over principle, and supple readiness to seek the main chance, subsequently led Laval into far darker company.

Laval's first government fell just after the appearance of his Man of the Year eulogy, when the Senate defeated him over proposed changes to the electoral laws. He returned to office in February 1934, as Minister for the Colonies, in the national unity government headed by Gaston Doumergue following the 6 February riots. In October 1934, he became Minister of

Foreign Affairs, after the death of his predecessor, Louis Barthou, during the assassination of King Alexander I of Yugoslavia in Marseille. After a round of international meetings and treaty formulation, largely intended to isolate Germany, including the Franco-Italian Agreement of January 1935, a visit to the Vatican, and a Franco-Soviet Treaty of Mutual Assistance in May, Laval formed his second government as prime minister in June 1935. Another self-styled national unity government, formed as France's economic situation worsened, this disparate coalition became increasingly controversial as Laval obtained powers to govern by decree to tackle the crisis. Unemployment continued to worsen, while Laval attempted to deal with the international crisis triggered by Mussolini's invasion of Ethiopia in October 1935. The resulting Hoare-Laval Pact, concluded secretly in December with British Foreign Secretary Sir Samuel Hoare, has since been re-evaluated as pragmatic *realpolitik*, but at the time was condemned as soon as it became public, as a betrayal of Ethiopia and of the principles of the League of Nations. Laval's government fell in January 1936, and he remained out of office until the Second World War.

Many conservatives opposed the Third Republic's inter-war diplomacy and military adventures, some at least out of awareness of the terrible human cost of the First World War. However, a statement by Charles Maurras dated 28 September 1935 shows how far from genuine pacifism was anti-war sentiment among France's right. Opposed to sanctions against Italy for its colonial designs in Ethiopia, Maurras called for the assassination of 140 left-wing parliamentarians who were in favour of sanctions:

> Since the guillotine is not at the disposal of good and logical citizens, it remains to say to them: You have somewhere an automatic pistol, a revolver or even a kitchen knife? This weapon, whatever it is, must serve against these assassins of peace, of whom you have the list.[8]

Well before wartime, Maurras was already advocating the murder of political opponents over such mundane issues as sanctions policy.

Pétain's cannon fodder, meanwhile, entered the post-war era as an influential constituency whose attitudes had been shaped, even deformed, by those four years of grinding, murderous conflict. The spirit of the Union Sacrée did not last long into the post-war era:

> When victory and peace seemed to produce disillusionment, then the disappointment was all the worse. To return to the same dreary round of political crises and scandals, the same fears and insecurities about the future, the same apprehension of division and decadence was worse than a disappointment. It was a disaster.[9]

The post-war mood among the heirs of the pre-war Maurrasian far-right is plain in this excerpt from *Revue d'Action Française*, 15 December 1923:

> The damage of 1789-1830 and 1848 was aggravated in this Dreyfusian revolution which ended in the pillage of the churches and national disarmament. By this provisional defeat which it imposed on France, liberal democracy disorganized our army and tore out its eyes: in its newspapers and its courtrooms it pronounced the capital condemnation of fifteen hundred thousand young men of the war to come.

All this happened despite the Third Republic's victory in the First World War. In fact, an influential minority of veterans had been pushed by the war beyond any adherence to an ordinary peaceful society. 'In the Twenties the ideologies of Fascism, Bolshevism, and Nazism were formulated and the movements led by the so-called front generation,' as Hannah Arendt asserted:

> Very few of this generation were cured of their war enthusiasm by actual experience of its horrors. The survivors of the trenches did not become pacifists. They cherished an experience which, they thought, might serve to separate them definitely from the hated surroundings of respectability. They clung to their memories of four years of life in the trenches as though they constituted an objective criterion for the establishment of a new elite.

Trauma symptoms reflecting the alienating, desocializing impact of PTSD on the individual level became unifying ideological tenets on the political level.

Alongside the 'establishment anti-Republicans' in the army, the Catholic congregations, the *haute bourgeoisie* and the remnants of the aristocracy, these new men, the socially marginalized, deracinated, war-torn veterans of the First World War and the Depression, formed the natural leaders and agitators for the Mob in Hannah Arendt's definition – the dregs and trash from every level of society, too often identified with the people as a whole because endemic to every stratum, professional subversives, inveterate destabilisers and sworn enemies of any order, ready for any chance to tear down the walls.

Jacques Doriot, born on 26 September 1898 at Bresles in the Oise Department, northeast of Paris, was a born peasant and son of a smith, who lost his smithy while Jacques was still young, thanks to economic pressures on rural artisans, and took up a series of positions at factories in the northeast. Unlike almost all other prominent fascist leaders, he was distinctively proletarian in origin, with a corresponding common touch that stood him well in cultivating his core working-class supporter base. Although reportedly a keen student and avid reader, Jacques followed his father into factory work, and in 1915, looking for a solid and steady position, he moved to the capital, taking up residence at Saint-Denis with an uncle. Here he apparently encountered serious politics for the first time, and signed up with the Socialists in 1916, but it was the war that pushed him into more serious political engagement. Mobilized in April 1917, Doriot joined up with the 128th Infantry Regiment and left for the front five months later with the 264th Regiment. Attached to various regiments, he was one of the few survivors of his unit when it was almost wiped out at the Chemin-des-Dames in the spring of 1918. He received the Croix de Guerre for carrying a wounded comrade to safety over almost 2 kilometres. After the war's end, he remained attached to the Armée française d'Orient, France's expeditionary force in the east, participating in the suppression of the Hungarian Communist insurrection in 1919, then supporting Gabriele D'Annunzio's coup in Fiume.

Doriot returned to Saint-Denis in May 1920, just as the Confédération Générale du Travail was launching an abortive general strike in support of railway workers. He moved from the Socialists to the Communists, and from 1921 represented the Jeunes Communistes de France, making personal contact with Lenin and other Bolshevik leaders. Head of this youth movement after his return to France in 1923, he began to push the entire French Communist Party (PCF) in a more stridently Bolshevik direction. He was imprisoned in 1924 for publishing articles calling on French soldiers to disobey their officers during colonial conflicts, then was released after his election to the Chamber of Deputies as a representative for Saint-Denis. Doriot became mayor of Saint-Denis in 1931, all the while attempting to gain greater control of the PCF, particularly in the Paris region.

France's political temperature and left-wing anxieties rose after the right-wing riots of 6 February 1934. These came in the wake of the Stavisky Affair, when a Russian Jewish emigre and fraudster, Alexandre Stavisky, was found dead after his exposure for selling false municipal bonds, with the support and protection of numerous political contacts. Taking office in the wake of the scandal, Édouard Daladier, the new prime minister, began his premiership by dismissing or replacing several notable right-wing sympathizers, including Jean Chiappe, then prefect of the Paris police. On 6 February 1934, various far-right parties and groupings assembled to protest Chiappe's removal and do as much damage to the new Radical-Socialist-led administration as possible, among them Action Française, the far-right republican/ authoritarian Jeunesses Patriotes, the Croix-de-Feu veterans' association led by Colonel François de la Rocque, the Solidarité Française league of perfume magnate and would-be political player François Coty, the Union Nationale des Combattants and other veterans' associations, besides various other generally disaffected groups. The demonstrations were suppressed by the police during the night of 6-7 February, with 17 people killed and some 2,000 injured. Daladier resigned in the wake of the riots, and left-wing groups, fearing a right-wing conspiracy to seize power, started to explore greater cooperation, a process which ultimately produced the Popular Front government of 1936. On the right, meanwhile, many were convinced that only Colonel de la Rocque's respect for constitutional legitimacy, and his failure to storm the National Assembly, had prevented a successful right-wing putsch. They started to look towards more extra-constitutional tactics, along Italian and German lines. Some moved into a right-wing terrorist organization dubbed the Cagoule; many others simply abandoned any attempt to take power through constitutional means.

Doriot became one of the main proponents of greater rapprochement between Socialist and Communist movements after the 6 February riots, forming a Comité de Défense Antifasciste with the Socialists, the Radical-Socialists and the Radical Party. But his independent advocacy of this position, in advance of official Comintern dogma, provoked more and more opposition among doctrinaire factions within the PCF. His personality as much as his policies alienated comrades more rigidly faithful to the Moscow party line, especially the Stalinist PCF general secretary, Maurice Thorez. On 26 June 1934, he was formally excluded from the PCF. Propelled by personal animosity, Doriot almost immediately swung to the opposite extreme, and formed the Parti Populaire Français (PPF), taking with him some personal loyalists like the writer Pierre Drieu la Rochelle and the journalist and sometime Communist propagandist Paul Marion.

Doriot's PPF adopted more or less wholesale a clutch of ideas and principles formulated by the anti-Republican writers of the late nineteenth century. 'What was new, and what rendered the PPF unique in the history of French fascism, was the association of those ideas with an authentic working-class movement coming from the Left.' Doriot himself, meanwhile, 'did not come to fascism for new ideas, but to settle old scores'.[10] Ideologically, he had little to contribute to the intellectuals. No great intellectual himself and patchily educated, Doriot was most naturally at home with his working-class Saint-Denis constituents rather than the right-wing intellectuals who clustered around his movement.

Doriot accepted funding from Mussolini's Italy and indulged Italian acquisitiveness towards Nice, Corsica and Tunisia, while continuing to single-mindedly pursue his grudge: 'The Number One enemy of the country is Communism' declared the PPF publication *L'Émancipation Nationale* on 30 December 1938. The Nazi-Soviet Pact left him and the PPF in limbo. Only with the German invasion of the Soviet Union in June 1941 did he lead the PPF into the collaborationist fold, galvanized by Nazi opposition to Communism.

Another veteran of the First World War who moved into left-wing politics only to be expelled from his party was Marcel Déat. A brilliant student admitted to the elite École Normale Supérieure in 1914, he joined the Socialist Party (SFIO) the same year, then volunteered when the war broke out, and served for the next four years, rising to the rank of captain. After the war, he became a prominent Socialist theorist and politician, elected a municipal councillor in Rheims in 1925, and to the Chamber of Deputies in 1926. He was elected deputy for the 20th arrondissement of Paris in 1932, but in 1933 split from the main SFIO movement as part of a more pragmatic socialist group which supported various incumbent governments. Briefly Minister for Air in early 1936, he lost office after the advent of the Popular Front government. Elected deputy for Angoulême in 1939 on an anti-Communist ticket, he published a controversial editorial on 4 May in the prominent independent left-wing journal *L'Œuvre*, entitled 'Why Die for Danzig?' In it, he wrote:

> To start a war in Europe because of Danzig is going a bit far, and French peasants have no wish to die for the Poles... To fight alongside our Polish friends for the common defence of our territories, our property, our freedoms, is a perspective that we can courageously consider, if it contributes to maintaining peace. But to die for Danzig, no.

An outspoken pacifist since the last war, Déat was at least consistent with his previous positions. However, he was also already consistent with the unprincipled *realpolitik* that was eventually to land him in Sigmaringen.

A fellow veteran, Joseph Darnand, never dallied with the Left. A decorated war hero from a peasant background, he made his living in the 1920s in provincial middle management at a furniture business and a bus company, while joining up in 1925 with Action Française. He rose within the organization thanks to the prestige of his war record and decorations, but by 1935 had apparently parted company with the group over its lack of direct action. Subsequently involved briefly with the Croix-de-Feu and the PPF, he abandoned both for direct right-wing terrorism with the Cagoule, forming a fascistic satellite organization, the Chevaliers du Glaive, in Nice. After the Cagoule's failed putsch of 15-16 November 1937, he was arrested in June 1938 but liberated in December.

Fernand de Brinon, the future President of the Governmental Commission in the Sigmaringen enclave, was born in 1885 to a wealthy and well-connected family in Libourne in the Gironde. After studying law, he took up a career as a journalist on the eve of the First World War and duly became an advocate of greater Franco-German understanding. In 1932, through his social connections, he was introduced to Joachim von Ribbentrop, who became his intermediary in building closer relations with the new German government. Ribbentrop arranged an interview with Adolf Hitler, which appeared in *Le Matin* on 23 November 1933, under the headline 'A Conversation with Adolf Hitler: For the First Time, the Chancellor of the Reich Receives a French Journalist: Sensational Declarations'. With considerable emphasis on the circumstances of the meeting, and how he was able to obtain the introduction, Brinon extracted several choice statements from 'this historic document', including 'I have said many times that the fate of Alsace-Lorraine is settled. The people have given their answer', and:

> My country is not a second-rate nation. It is a great nation which has had unbearable treatment imposed upon it. If France intends to base its security on the material impossibility of Germany to defend itself, there is nothing to be done because the time when those things were possible is over. But if it is prepared to find its security in a freely discussed agreement, I am ready to hear everything, to understand everything, to undertake everything.

Brinon continued to cultivate relations with the Nazi government through the ensuing years, visiting Hitler several more times. In November 1935 he founded the Franco-German Committee with the support of several French veterans' groups, as well as Georges Scapini, a blind war hero, and Otto Abetz, a German diplomat. The committee continued to promote Franco-German understanding through visits by veterans, cultural events, and other initiatives, until its dissolution in May 1939 following the German invasion of Czechoslovakia.

Another journalist, Jean Luchaire, born in Siena in 1901 to the writer and Italophile Julien Luchaire, also took the route into journalism with pretensions to exert political influence. His godfather was Horace Finaly, later General Director of the Banque de Paris et des Pays-Bas. In the early 1920s, he frequented cosmopolitan circles in Florence, moving to Paris after the rise of Italian fascism. In 1927 he founded the review *Notre Temps*, supported financially by the Radical Party politician Émile Roche, who withdrew his support in 1928 over Luchaire's appropriation of its funds for his own use. Luchaire then began to accept financial support from France's Ministry of Foreign Affairs. Luchaire, who married young in 1920 and had four children to support, developed from need to greed in his pursuit of wealth. He was distinguished by his passion for luxury and his concern with his public image. Charming and energetic, bankrolled by his clandestine supporters, Luchaire used his contact list to establish a prominent, if not especially influential, position in French social and political circles.

By 1930 he was already involved in the organization of Franco-German friendship events, according to Abetz's post-war testimony, and *Notre Temps'* broadly pacifist and pan-European stance grew increasingly pro-German under Abetz's influence. In the 26 March 1933 edition, he wrote, regarding Hitler: 'Europeans, we must deal with European governments whatever they are... what matters most to us is peace. Freedom is only the most precious of goods conditional on us being alive.' Luchaire developed a reputation for taking substantial subventions, and for keeping a string of mistresses notwithstanding his marriage. The actress Simone Signoret, a sometime acquaintance, described him as 'weak, cowardly, corrupt, handsome, generous'.

As an eventual member of the pocket government in Sigmaringen, Luchaire climbed highest among the many fellow journalists and writers who eventually sought refuge alongside him. Unlike Luchaire, most of them were at least convinced and consistent apostles of the far right, rather than time-servers. 'It was precisely their particular literary and aesthetic convictions and ideals that led them to and supported the anti-Semitic prejudices and extremist political positions they formulated and defended.'[11]

First among them as a literary talent was Louis-Ferdinand Céline, the celebrated pen name of Louis-Ferdinand Destouches, who became Sigmaringen's mythologist. Céline's background provides some insight into the driving forces behind French fascism, while his harangues were some of its most extreme expressions.

Born in a Paris suburb – 'I shouldn't have been born' – scarred by his difficult childhood – 'marked by semi-poverty and above all by the humiliations of a mean-spirited and narrow-minded family life'[12]– Céline sprang from the lower middle classes who provided numerous footsoldiers for late nineteenth century French anti-Semitism. His social stratum, already in retreat before the forces of industrialization, was traumatized by the Panama Affair and other financial scandals of the Third Republic, blamed by many *petit-bourgeois* victims on Jewish financiers – his second novel, *Mort à Crédit*, was from its title onwards a chronicle of debt-ridden suburbanites unable to adapt to the new age of progress. Briefly engaged in various minor commercial occupations, he joined the French army in 1912, and duly participated in the opening battles of the First World War, receiving a wound in the arm in October 1914, and the Military Medal in November, retroactively joined by the Croix de Guerre. Céline's later claims to have suffered a head wound and undergone trepanation were apparently among the many spurious legends he spun around himself. He was transferred to the French visa service at the consulate in London while recuperating and given his discharge in December 1915. He commenced a vagabond existence, haunting the London underworld, working briefly as a plantation overseer in Cameroon, participating in tuberculosis prevention campaigns in Brittany. After the war, he studied medicine, qualifying in 1924, and toured the world as an employee of the health department of the League of Nations. In 1926, he wrote a semi-autobiographical play, *L'Église*, not published until 1933, which showed the first traces of his anti-Semitism, caricaturing the League of Nations as an organization dominated by Jews. In 1927, after the League failed to renew his contract, he was employed at a Clichy dispensary by the Jewish doctor Grégoire Ichok. Engaged in various marginal medical occupations for the next few years, he supplemented his income by producing medical marketing materials, while working on his first novel, *Voyage au Bout de la Nuit*, which made him a literary celebrity with its debut in October 1932.

Voyage au Bout de la Nuit won popularity – and notoriety – for its themes of military and industrial brutality, rot and corruption, its pervasive mordant nihilism, and its groundbreaking style, which abandoned the classical mannerisms and vocabulary of literary French in favour of street slang and the spoken word:

The success of *Voyage au Bout de la Nuit* propelled hitherto unknown Céline to the forefront of the French literary stage and, in spite of his constant complaints to his publisher, Denoël, made him a wealthy man, able to indulge his taste for travel, staying in Europe's finest hotels, and crossing the Atlantic by luxury liner.[13]

Céline produced a second, even more nihilistic, autobiographical novel, *Mort à Credit*, in 1936, while continuing his medical work in the Paris suburbs. Its poor sales and critical panning from Left and Right may have embittered him still further; in any case, in December 1937 he produced the virulently anti-Semitic polemic *Bagatelles Pour un Massacre*, followed in November 1938 by the equally vicious *L'École des Cadavres*.

Here is Hannah Arendt's evaluation of Céline and his anti-Semitism, from *The Origins of Totalitarianism*:

Louis Ferdinand Céline had a simple thesis, ingenious and containing exactly the ideological imagination that the more rational French anti-Semitism had lacked. He claimed that the Jews had prevented the evolution of Europe into a political entity, had caused all European wars since 843, and had plotted the ruin of both France and Germany by inciting their mutual hostility. Céline proposed this fantastic explanation of history in his *Ecole des Cadavres*, written at the time of the Munich Pact and published during the first months of the war. An earlier pamphlet on the subject, *Bagatelles pour un Massacre* (1938), although it did not include the new key to European history, was already remarkably modem in its approach; it avoided all restricting differentiations between native and foreign Jews, between good and bad ones, and did not bother with elaborate legislative proposals (a particular characteristic of French anti-Semite), but went straight to the core of the matter and demanded the massacre of all Jews.

Céline's first book was very favourably received by France's leading intellectuals, who were half pleased by the attack on the Jews and half convinced that it was nothing more than an interesting new literary fancy. For exactly the same reasons French home-grown Fascists did not take Céline seriously, despite the fact that the Nazis always knew he was the only true anti-Semite in France. The inherent good sense of French politicians and their deep-rooted respectability prevented their accepting a charlatan and crackpot.

As for Céline's own words on the matter, from *L'École des Cadavres*:

> Racism first! Racism foremost! Ten times, a thousand times racism! Disinfection! Cleansing! One sole race in France, the Aryan... France is only Latin by chance, in fact it's three quarters Celtic, Germanic... Hitler is a good breeder of peoples, he is on the side of life, he cares about the life of peoples, even ours. He is an Aryan.

No wonder even anti-Semites of the 1930s suspected that Céline's anti-Semitic writings were deliberately exaggerated parody, although all the evidence suggests that they were sincere. Professing no allegiance to any of the pre-war far-right political groupings in France, Céline nonetheless was associated from the late 1930s with the anti-Semitic newspaper *La France Enchaînée*, created by the journalist and right-wing activist Louis Darquier, founder of the anti-Semitic political party Rassemblement antijuif de France, and from May 1942, head of the Vichy Commissariat General for Jewish Questions.

The continuing influence of Maurrasianism on the inter-war generation of conservative writers is obvious in the case of Robert Brasillach. In his teens, he published a eulogy to Maurras in the local paper *Coq Catalan* in the summer of 1927:

> The doctrine of Maurras is the only important doctrine of the City of our time that includes a philosophy. Maurras built the most complete of political, artistic and moral systems... A society must live like a human organism. For this, we must recognize our limits. We must leave to a caste, to a race, the care and study of government where we know nothing. We need a king. This king will be absolute, everything will belong to him. Let us not rebel against this idea.

This kind of uncritical quasi-religious veneration of the head of state was later projected onto Pétain during the Vichy regime, by Maurras himself and many of his followers. Brasillach was a significant player in this process.

> Brasillach became an especially influential voice in literary and political debates at a very young age. He was given the responsibility for the principal literary column, "La Causerie Littéraire", at the newspaper *L'Action Française* at the age of twenty-two. In 1937, when he was twenty-eight, continuing his weekly column for the anti-Semitic, royalist, extremist nationalist newspaper, he also became editor-in-chief of the nationalist, pro-fascist, anti-Semitic weekly *Je suis partout*. Brasillach stopped writing for *L'Action Française* at the time of the defeat, but he continued to direct and write for *Je suis partout* until he broke with the journal – although never with fascism – at the end of 1943... he is the writer who most clearly transformed Charles Maurras's royalist, classical aesthetic of politics into an explicitly modern, fascist politics.[14]

Another notable writer and propagandist at Sigmaringen, Lucien Rebatet, born in the same generation as Céline, was the son of a village notary and university dropout, who started his journalistic career in 1929 as a music critic for *Revue d'Action Française*, after a brief sojourn at an insurance company. His equivalent to Céline's anti-Semitic screeds, *Les Décombres*, published in 1942 by Céline's publisher Denoël, 'had the highest sales of any book published during the Occupation... [he was] one of the most militant and vicious anti-Semites among the French literary fascists'.[15] In 1932 he switched venues to the weekly right-wing review *Je suis partout*, where he worked alongside Robert Brasillach and Pierre-Antoine Cousteau, elder brother of the future oceanographer Jacques Cousteau. The following year, he married a Romanian, Véronique Popovici.

Especially after the advent of the Popular Front government under Léon Blum in 1936, *Je suis partout* became stridently anti-Semitic and anti-democratic:

> Before the war, according to a type of political existence specific to the extreme right, Rebatet surfed the waves of fears and rejections that swamped a country grappling with a European crisis of unprecedented

magnitude, and doubting its institutions as well as its values... *Je suis partout* distilled its little extremist music – without ever publicly declaring itself fascist – and, under the very singular influence of Rebatet, showed signs of Nazi contagion, but did not deviate from the Maurrassian score. From 1938, he witnessed the implosion of the only party that he favoured, Doriot's PPF, undermined by the expansion of the PSF, a large right-wing mass movement that rallied to the republican institutions.[16]

Jean Hérold-Paquis, later a notorious propaganda broadcaster for Radio-Paris during the German Occupation, known for his catchphrase 'England, like Carthage, shall be destroyed!', fitted the typical rootless, criminal profile of a far-right activist. Orphan, high-school dropout, he became a radio journalist for Catholic interests, despite convictions for defamation, fraud, and keeping a concubine in his marital abode. During the Spanish Civil War, he joined the Bataillon Jeanne d'Arc, a Nationalist unit of Francophone volunteers, and became a well-known French-language pro-Franco broadcaster on Radio-Saragosse in the immediate pre-war period.

Despite the later reappearance of these figures in Sigmaringen and its parallel enclaves, they were hardly representative of French opinion or society between the wars. All the right-wing ambivalence towards the Third Republic in the inter-war period, however, did not engender any single fascist party or movement with genuine broad support – outside Doriot's PPF. All of them had in common 'the meagerness of their effectives and the narrowness of their sociological base'.[17] It took the twin debacles of the Fall of France and the disintegration of the Vichy regime to propel them to brief prominence and lasting disgrace.

The PPF was not the only French party to suffer from the upheavals in opinion and political alignment that followed the rise of Nazism and the Spanish Civil War. As Hannah Arendt put it:

In France, Hitler's rise to power, accompanied by a growth of Communism and Fascism, quickly cancelled the other parties' original relationships to each other and changed time-honoured party lines overnight. The French Right, up to then strongly anti-German and pro-war, after 1933 became the vanguard of pacifism and understanding with Germany. The Left switched with equal speed from pacifism at any price to a firm stand against Germany and was soon accused of being a party of warmongers by the same parties which only a few years before had denounced its pacifism as national treachery... Each party harboured a peace faction and a war faction; none of them could remain united on major politician decisions and none stood the test of Fascism and Nazism without splitting into anti-Fascist on one side, Nazi fellow-travellers on the other. That Hitler could choose freely from all parties for the erection of puppet regimes was the consequence of this pre-war situation, and not of an especially shrewd Nazi manoeuvre.

France's factional divisions crystallized around the Popular Front government, formed after the legislative elections of May 1936. Following the 6 February 1934 crisis, left-wing parties were more ready to cooperate to forestall right-wing radicalism and authoritarianism. The three main left-wing parties, the Radical-Socialist Party, the SFIO, and the Communists of the PCF, along with various smaller left-wing groupings, were supported outside parliament by the trade unionists of the Confédération Générale du Travail, the post-Dreyfusard Ligue des droits de l'homme, and other anti-fascist and pacifist associations and organizations. Together they formed the Popular Front government under SFIO leader Léon Blum, France's first Socialist and Jewish prime minister.

The French labour movement built on the momentum of the new government with a series of more or less spontaneous strikes and sit-downs which spread nationwide. These triggered the negotiation of the Matignon Accords, the charter of workers' rights which, together with other laws enacted by the Blum government, brought many entitlements and liberties for French workers for the first time, including a forty-hour working week, fifteen days of paid holiday, the right to organize and strike, collective bargaining, adjustment of salaries, and other measures. The Popular Front had articulated its joint programme before going to the polls, and by and large delivered on it. 'Our goal is not to transform the social regime, it is not even to apply the specific programme of the Socialist Party, it is to execute the programme of the Popular

Front,' as Blum declared during the debates in the Chamber of Deputies on 6 June 1936.

Unfortunately, the Matignon Accords and the Popular Front programme carried political costs that proved harder and harder to manage – a situation with plenty of parallels in contemporary France. For example:

> The forty hours law was also politically expensive because it became a sort of shibboleth of loyalty to the Popular Front, and a focus of attack for the opposition; for such a piece of legislation to be essentially non-negotiable was a heavy burden for France to carry during a fitful and difficult economic recovery.[18]

Furthermore, the 'apparent shift in political power severely shook the self-confidence of a previously republican *bourgeoisie*. Significant elements of the middle classes embraced movements and ideologies overtly contemptuous of French political democracy and in many cases openly admiring of foreign fascist models.'[19]

Blum stepped down in mid-1937 when the Senate refused to grant him wider financial powers to tackle the impact of the Great Depression. That said, the Matignon Accords remained broadly in effect, and some have argued that Blum:

> saw his role as a conciliator. He worked by a dextrous mixture of persuasion and threat to hold the political coalition together and to bring some of the diverse and antagonistic forces of France into some sort of a consensus. By the summer of 1937 it did not seem that he could do this any more.[20]

However brief and incomplete the Popular Front's record in government, its impact on the opposite end of the political spectrum was profound. 'To the right there was the fear and loathing crystallized by the memory of June 1936, bringing conservatives and reactionaries ever closer in a coalition cemented by anticommunism, increasing antirepublicanism and an ever-more-confident and aggressive anti-Semitism,' affirmed Tony Judt, who called the Popular

Front government 'the moment at which those of the Right parted company definitively from the "socialist and Jewish" Republic'.[21] The Popular Front government dissolved the Camelots du Roi and other far-right political associations on 18 June 1936; simultaneously, the Organisation secrète d'action révolutionnaire nationale, soon to be known as the Cagoule, was formed under Eugène Deloncle, a war veteran and former Action Française militant. This engaged in various subversive and terrorist activities, from spreading rumours of Communist conspiracy to army officers, to bombings and political assassinations. At one point, it approached Philippe Pétain as a possible candidate for a future fascist head of state, but he declined to be involved. Police infiltration and government action effectively wound up the Cagoule in November 1937, but many of its members later featured significantly during the occupation of France, some as Resistance members, others, like Joseph Darnand, as leading collaborators with the Nazis.

Many of the contemporaries of Doriot and Déat were increasingly detached from the Third Republic's principles, whether from left or right. Writing in *Combat* in April 1937, Drieu la Rochelle articulated a sentiment prevalent on the right since the nineteenth century but intensified by the experience of the Popular Front. 'The only way to love France today is to hate it in its present form.'

Chapter 2

Fall and Subjugation

Pétain and Laval, the two most prominent – albeit reluctant – political figures in the Sigmaringen enclave, were responsible between them for the demise of the Third Republic. Various political consequences might have followed from the Fall of France, but it seems unlikely that the result would automatically have been the Vichy regime without the actions of Pétain and Laval. The self-erasure of the Third Republic, and its replacement by an authoritarian dictatorship, came about thanks to the prestige and hidden intentions of the one, and the political skills of the other.

A tight focus on the cabals that later dominated the Sigmaringen enclave, though, can create a false perspective on the overall political conditions in the Third Republic on the eve of war. The current forensic diagnosis of the condition of the Republic just before its assisted suicide gives it a reasonably clean bill of health. As one example, from Hugo Coniez's *La Mort de la IIIe République, 10 mai-10 juillet 1940*, published in 2024, states, 'no one imagined that democracy and the republican tradition, apparently rooted in the national conscience, could be so quickly thrust aside.' The Republic had successfully fought its way through several internal crises and a world war. The monarchists were no longer a serious threat to the Republic – if they ever had been. Parliamentary democracy had emerged victorious from the First World War. Few if any of the various candidates in the 1936 legislative elections positioned themselves openly and explicitly against the Republic. The Popular Front seemed to have lost its impetus after April 1938, while both executive and legislature appeared to be governing more effectively and consistently. 'Contrary to received ideas, the Third Republic had begun to pull itself together.'[1]

France's military defeat changed all that. As the Phoney War dragged on following the British and French declaration of war on 3 September 1939,

Pétain became increasingly involved in the political, rather than the military, aspects of the struggle:

> From his Spanish embassy, the Marshal kept in touch with the developments at home, and the increasingly bad news which reached him gave him a sense of his destiny. He became convinced that he was about to be called to perform his greatest task of national salvation, and he prepared actively for the responsibilities he soon expected to shoulder. He kept in communication with Laval and some lesser political figures, took a number of trips to Paris unconnected with his post as Ambassador, consulted important people, including Darlan, in a search for dependable collaborators, toyed with little lists of cabinets he contemplated forming, and finally was to confess his expectation in the dramatic statement to Anatole de Monzie – a secondary French political figure – on 30 March 1940: "They will need me in the second week of May!" This was not evidence of an actual plot to undermine the Republic, but of eagerness to play whatever opportunities the upheavals at home presented.[2]

Current analyses of the demise of the Third Republic focus on the 'devastating and humiliating' shock of the military defeat – ultimately the fault of the military – and the characters and beliefs of the significant political actors: 'nothing implied *a priori* the establishment of an authoritarian regime in vanquished France, especially as the Germans never demanded it… the fate of the regime was decided in a few days, even a few hours, by a handful of individuals.'[3] All the evidence suggests that in 1939, France was morally and materially ready to confront Nazi Germany:

> The Daladier government was arguably the most popular that France had seen for a decade; it enjoyed an unprecedented degree of support from the Radicals to the traditional Right. Although both the Communists and Socialists opposed the government's domestic policy, all of the former at least until 26 August and a majority of the latter supported its foreign policy.[4]

France's shock defeat in 1940, so often taken as a verdict on an entire political system and way of life, is nowadays attributed to much narrower and more strictly military factors – especially the ossification of strategy in the inter-war period. It was the military, not the society or political class, that was unfit to face the challenges of a new war. 'The immediate cause of Vichy was the crushing defeat of 1940... it was not decadence that led to 1940; it is 1940 that has led us to view the late Third Republic as decadent.'[5]

France's War Ministry and military policymakers enjoyed relative stability compared with the Third Republic as a whole, with its frequent changes of ministry, but this tended to ringfence military thinking, and insulate it from parliamentary scrutiny. France had forty-three different ministries between 1919 and 1939, but only four long-serving ministers of war in the period 1932-39. Furthermore, over the same period, only three leading military men occupied the supreme military post, vice-president of the Superior Council of War: Marshal Pétain, from 1920 to 1931; General Maxime Weygand, from 1931 to 1935; and General Maurice Gamelin, from 1934 until defeat in 1940. Weygand also served as Chief of the General Staff from 1930 to 1931, and Gamelin from 1931 until the war. As Robert Doughty's recent study of the roots of this collapse observes, 'only five military officers occupied the most important positions in the army's hierarchy from 1920 to 1939.' Naturally, this condition did not favour flexibility or openness to new ideas.

Worse, the military system that evolved under this structure privileged rigid top-down control which constricted its capacity to adapt and learn on the fly. 'The French preferred rigid centralization and strict obedience... Unfortunately for France, her army was prepared to fight precisely the type of war that Germany wanted to avoid,' noted Robert Doughty. This was more than the usual respect for rank and the chain of command; it was a deliberate strategic doctrine designed to manage the kind of massed infantry and artillery battles of the last war.

Accepted military dogma in the French high command was focused on methodical employment of infantry and artillery, with relatively limited mobility, and aircraft and armour playing at best a supporting role. Innovations such as tanks and air power were recognized and taken up – France went into the war with better tanks overall than the contemporary German models

– but in a context which blunted their impact. In 1934, Charles de Gaulle, then a lieutenant-colonel working in the General Secretariat of the Supreme War Council, published a book, *Vers l'Armée de Métier* (*Towards a Professional Army*), advocating highly mobile mechanized warfare, but this was largely disregarded by the high command. As Robert Doughty has emphasized, 'France prepared to go to war with a doctrine essentially based upon the World War 1 experience modified to incorporate new ideas about motorization and mechanization. This modified doctrine was anything but radically innovative, since new weapons essentially remained tied to old ideas.'

The Maginot Line doctrine of defending France's frontiers with massive fortifications, understandable as a means to buy time for full mobilization, and materially as well as morally necessary when France had about 75 per cent of her coal and 95 per cent of her iron-ore production in her vulnerable north-eastern areas, is treated more forgivingly in current assessments than in the past, when it was used as shorthand for an entire mentality. Some analyses regard it as a useful force multiplier, and a sensible precaution against a hostile neighbour with a much larger population. Its worst qualities came into play when combined with other factors in French strategic doctrine. Pétain's participation in military and government discussions around the fortification of the frontiers before the war had shown him relatively open-minded to the type and depth of fortification, but with a persistent emphasis on preserving the national territory intact and inviolate. Resources and manpower ploughed into the Maginot Line fortifications further committed capabilities to one strategy and limited potential future room for manoeuvre. Finally, when war came, the Germans were unable to capture a single Maginot Line fortress before the Armistice on 25 June, and suffered heavy casualties in the process. However, that result emphasizes the strategy's failure more than its success. The Germans were able to defeat France without capturing a single Maginot Line fortress.

Why? General Gamelin is given much of the blame in modern analyses, completely wrong-footed by the German feint on 10-17 May which drew him into the Low Countries while their main thrust came through the Ardennes, 'one of the colossal blunders in the history of warfare'.[6] The German plan had the advantage of playing to his preferences and prejudices; Gamelin was a firm believer in fighting the battles of the coming war off French national soil, and skewed his operations accordingly, whatever his supposed allies in the Low Countries thought of the matter. His abortive Saar Offensive of 7 September-16 October 1939 had failed to force an early end to the war, and to relieve Poland from German assault. He persisted in his plans in defiance of substantial and repeated intelligence and reconnaissance reports from Belgian, Swiss, French and Vatican sources that disclosed the Germans' true intentions. The paucity of radio communications, from Gamelin's headquarters right on down the chain of command to individual tank units, further compromised France's ability to react to events. At his headquarters at the Château de Vincennes, Gamelin had no radio or telegraph links, and relied on telephone and messenger for accounts of the developing battle. General Weygand immediately corrected this situation when he assumed command on 20 May 1940, following Gamelin's dismissal.

Despite the collapse of the French effort in the Low Countries, and the success of the German push through the Ardennes on 10-11 May, French resistance stiffened after the initial shocks. 'The German victory was not some kind of stroll in rural France, but came about only after very hard fighting that has been lost from sight in most evocations of the "fall of France".'[7] Weygand's appointment may have helped to some degree, but more important was French adaptation to German tactics and recovery of morale after the initial shocks. After the end of May:

> the French armies made a Herculean effort to prepare for a new and more effective fight for France. The German staffs had to craft fresh plans to overcome a fast-reviving spirit. And the German troops met considerably more skilled military resistance. During June the resistance caused the Germans serious losses of soldiers, tanks, vehicles and aircraft – but at a price to the French armies of only 27% of the deaths sustained in May.[8]

Falling back on shorter lines of communication – including France's sophisticated internal railway network – steadily reinforcing, fighting in conditions which increasingly favoured their established infantry-and-artillery doctrine, French armed forces gained a second wind in June 1940 that could well have led to a different result, given the will to sustain them.

The weakest link, however, was neither the units in the field and the junior officers, nor even the government: it was the French high command. Whatever the Vichy regime's attempts to tar pre-war politicians with blame for the debacle, soldiers in the field appeared to have little doubt. Marc Bloch, historian, Resistance hero and martyr, wrote in his caustic account of the Fall of France, *L'Etrange Défaite:* 'There was hardly an officer in my entourage who doubted it; whatever one thinks of the deeper causes of the disaster, the direct cause… was the incapacity of the command.' Through his obsessive pursuit of the Breda variant of the Dyle Plan, attempting to keep the battles off French soil, Gamelin effectively lost the Battle of France in one week. Weygand's succession brought some improvements in French defensive tactics, but too little, too late. The high command, having already lost the Battle of France, were increasingly focused on coercing the government to end it.

On 17 May, during the last days of Gamelin's military leadership, Pétain, aged 84, was appointed Vice-President of the Council in the government of Paul Reynaud, who apparently saw him as a symbolic touchstone of order and security, calculated to bolster French morale. By this time, he was already in touch with Weygand. On 5 June, Reynaud appointed Charles de Gaulle Under-Secretary of State for National Defence and War, with specific responsibility for liaison with the British. From 12 June, Weygand began to press for an armistice, albeit with the proviso of potentially continuing the fight from the French colonies. On 14 June, the Germans occupied Paris. The French government, including most of the National Assembly, fled to Bordeaux. On 15 June, Reynaud proposed a military surrender in mainland France, with the government and National Assembly withdrawing to North Africa to continue the struggle alongside the Allies: Weygand objected strongly to the proposal as contrary to the honour of the armed forces. His efforts seemed calculated in part or overall to push responsibility for the capitulation to the Germans onto the government, rather than the army.

This near-mutiny illustrates how far the schisms in French society had spread into the French high command. Weygand himself 'was a militant Catholic with two *idées fixes*, the pernicious influence of the Freemasons and the scourge of "Godless communism." A self-styled *apolitique*, he had nonetheless a political ideal. Somewhere in the misty reaches of the Moral Order and the Orleanist "Republique des Ducs".[9] The Third Republic's persistent tradition of leaving military planning to the military left the high command to execute their mistaken strategies, effectively without governmental intervention, and left the government with little credibility in military affairs if it did try to intervene. 'The elements of the problem itself made it certain that Weygand's operational and strategical concepts would go virtually unchallenged and that, because of this abnormal situation, Pétain could put into operation his plan for the armistice which alone would give him the "means of seizing the power" he coveted.'[10]

Already a clear ideological fellow-traveller, Weygand became a tool and ally in Pétain's manipulation of the situation: On 13 June, he refused to leave France to carry on resistance overseas even if put in irons; two days later, he refused repeatedly even more insistently, clearly emphasizing that he thought such plans were an attempt by the government to transfer blame. Such a declaration, needless to say, was tantamount to mutiny against the government he professed to serve, at a time of dire national peril. This is not to say that there was a true military conspiracy to lead France to defeat in order to enable Pétain's rise to power – rather, that there was an unfortunate meeting of minds between Pétain and certain echelons in the French high command which made them allies against the actual government of the Third Republic.

Meanwhile, de Gaulle was trying to engineer different solutions. On 11 June, he proposed to General Charles Huntziger that he should take over Weygand's role, but was unable to convince Reynaud to sack Weygand. After discussions with Winston Churchill and the British, he helped engineer a proposal for a Franco-British union to continue the fight if metropolitan France was occupied, but Weygand by this time was tapping Reynaud's phone, and learned of the proposal before it was put to the French cabinet on 16 June. In the event, the offer of union was rejected, and Reynaud resigned.

Reynaud's resignation on 16 June was also triggered by Weygand's implied refusal to step down if the government tried to dismiss him. Pétain was immediately appointed in his stead by President Lebrun, and the next day announced that fighting should stop and that he was seeking an armistice with

Germany. In his radio declaration, he declared that 'sure of the confidence of the entire people, I give to France the gift of my person to alleviate her misfortune'. De Gaulle flew to London, and made his own celebrated Appeal of 18 June, calling for continuing resistance to the Germans by the remaining French forces and the French colonies.

Much post-war analysis and many apologetics have done little to invalidate some of the immediate post-war assessments of Pétain's motives and actions at this point. His own interpretation, that he was offering himself up for France, in an almost Christ-like gesture to atone for her sins, has hardly stood the test of time. Writer and historian Henri Gullemin emphasized in his foreword to one of these post-war critiques, General Jean-Henri Jauneaud's *J'accuse le maréchal Pétain* (1949):

> The responsibility, discreet but infinitely heavy, of Marshal Pétain for the disaster of 1940. Certainty is gradually growing – and the evidence is accumulating – that, far from fearing the military defeat of France, Marshal Pétain considered the event to be favourable to his plans and did nothing (quite the contrary) to prevent it. Because Marshal Pétain had designs, very precise political designs; from 1934, Marshal Pétain had been involved in politics. He had his convictions which can be summed up in a bitter hatred: in his eyes, anything which, in his eyes, bore a flavour of the Left, especially socialist, was Evil.

Gullemin quoted a confidential remark by the Marshal from October 1938:

> "It is under pain of death that we must change domestic policy", but, he added, the French "have not yet suffered enough." The military catastrophe would provide the Marshal with this providential suffering indispensable to the success of his enterprise, thus giving him the opportunity and the means to impose on France the politics he preferred: a variety of fascism, Maurras combined with Salazar. As Bernanos wrote with exemplary lucidity: Vichy was "the triumph of an unpopular minority which, for twenty years, had been seeking its chance in vain and which has finally found it in the national disaster".

Needless to say, Pétain's declaration, while fighting was still under way, hardly bolstered French resistance:

> His rule was to enable him to maintain his vast pretension. From the time he joined the Reynaud cabinet, he was to work for the establishment, then the perpetuation, of his rule with an obsessive singleness of purpose which made him blind to any other necessity; which made him disregard ruthlessly the consequences of his actions, including their effect upon the progress of the war – unless they bore directly on his self-preservation. The existence of his régime was to be the beginning, the end, and the ultimate justification of all his actions.[11]

Weygand, meanwhile, became Minister of National Defence in Pétain's new government, a position he held until September 1940.

Pétain's early declaration, before the terms of an armistice had even been agreed, had one grave consequence which was later an important factor in the Sigmaringen enclave: the capture of a huge number of French troops as prisoners of war – between 1.6 and 1.8 million according to the sources – most of them captured after 22 June as a result of the Armistice, not in battle. These were to prove a useful tool for the Germans to put pressure on the Vichy regime, and in due course led the Vichy leadership into severe errors of judgment to attempt to secure their release. And it was Pétain himself who was primarily responsible for putting such numbers into German hands.

Pétain, now head of government, duly signed the Armistice with the Germans on 22 June 1940 in the forest of Compiègne, in the same railway carriage where the Germans had signed their surrender in 1918. France was partitioned into the Free Zone and the Occupied Zone controlled by the Germans, although at this point, expectations were that the German occupying forces would eventually be withdrawn. On 9 July, the National Assembly voted 624 to 4 for the revision of the Third Republic's constitution – albeit with no particular stipulation about what kind of revision would be made. The next day, Pétain's government put forward a bill granting him full powers, to legislate by decree and to actually draft the new constitution, to be subject only to popular ratification.

Laval, though not involved in the declaration of the Armistice, was the prime mover in the parliamentary negotiations and voting process which led on 10 July 1940 to the end of the Third Republic. Convened in the Grand Casino Theatre at Vichy, the National Assembly voted by 569 votes to 80 'to give all powers to the Government of the Republic, under the authority and the signature of Marshal Pétain, in order to promulgate by one or several acts a new constitution for the French state. This constitution must guarantee the rights of work, the family and the country.' Only 670 of the 907 senators and deputies in office in 1939 were present at Vichy, and the terms of the vote itself dictated neither the dissolution of the National Assembly, nor the removal of the President of the Republic. However, Pétain secured the retirement of President Lebrun four days later. Lebrun, who had signed the text of the constitutional law on 10 July, refused to sign his resignation, but retired, leaving Pétain as head of state.

Senator Joseph Paul-Boncour wrote later in his memoirs that Laval:

> was truly the great architect of those days... Doubtless he could have done nothing if the prestige of Marshal Pétain had not covered him; but this prestige would have had no direct effect on the political operation headed and accomplished by Pierre Laval, if the latter had not put at his service, to dispossess Parliament, the same methods of a long parliamentary practice of which he was a past master.[12]

As just one indicator of his attitude, Laval took part in a ministerial discussion in Vichy in August 1940, regarding France's successful purchase in 1939 of Norsk Hydro's entire production of heavy water to date (180kg), and its removal to Britain in June 1940. Before a full meeting of Pétain's council, including Weygand and Darland, Laval expressed his regrets that the Germans had not got hold of the heavy water instead of 'those English bastards'. As the meeting broke up, Weygand remarked, 'See that gentleman over there. Every time the Germans want to shit in his mouth, he opens wide.' Laval overheard the remark, and a full-blown row ensued, with Pétain waving his arms and crying 'Gentlemen, gentlemen...'[13]

Laval, as so often in his political career, demonstrated careful respect for the forms and procedures of government, enough to give his clique and other parliamentarians some cover of legitimacy, while cynically disregarding their intent and spirit. Measures were taken to hold preliminary discussions in secret and avoid full records of procedure. The final vote was calculated not just to bring a close to the Third Republic but to comprehensively bury it.

Even so, a vote to end the Third Republic was not a vote to decide what replaced it, beyond the vague idea of a new authoritarian state led by the Marshal. Laval has borne much of the blame for the process, but the vote definitely reflected a broad wish for firm leadership during a crisis. The British assault on the French fleet at Mers-el-Kébir on 3-4 July, intended to keep the vessels from falling into Axis hands, definitely fed anti-British hostility, but this hardly was sufficient cause in itself for the creation of an Axis-style authoritarian dictatorship. A caretaker administration to maintain the basics of government while constitutional and other issues were worked out was one distinct possibility. Pétain's actual plans for the kind of state he would create were an entirely different matter. They were enacted the very next day, with his formal assumption of the title of Head of the French State, and constitutional acts granting him powers to decide and execute all executive and government acts without reference to the Assembly, apart from declarations of war. Of course, under their own terms, these new acts were not referred to the Assembly for ratification.

Significantly, Pétain's new regime had no basis of sovereignty beyond that vote by the Assembly – which, of course, ultimately had a basis of democratic sovereignty that was directly contradicted by the new acts. Pétain never sought popular approval for the creation of the Vichy state, which he probably would have won in 1940 if he had held a plebiscite. He was content to rule by decree, with formulation of the promised new constitution on hold, and the Assembly in abeyance but never actually abolished. The constitutional acts of the new regime, as published in the Official Journal, appeared with a formula explicitly recalling king or emperor: 'We, Philippe Pétain, Marshal of France, Head of the French State...'

All the same, the qualified political and enthusiastic popular welcome for the new government under Pétain was palpable. After the war, in his testimony during the trial of Pétain, Daladier declared:

When I sometimes heard members of the government say: "We are implementing the armistice with honour and dignity," deep in my conscience I replied: No, with dishonour and indignity. There should have been a protest, a violent one, in the face of the world, so that the whole world would be aware of it. I am told that there was one. It remained secret, as if it had never been made. At that time, I saw representatives from Alsace-Lorraine, friends of mine from yesteryear, and I said to them: how can you remain inactive? And they answered me: we tried, we prepared something, but "they" told us – "they", Vichy of course – not to do anything, that we would bring even more misery down on the shoulders of those who we wanted to defend.

The French army doctor whose memoirs appeared post-war under the name Gérard-Trinité Schillemans, later appointed as Pétain's doctor in Sigmaringen, recalled the popular mood at the time:

Myself, I remembered the Marshal's visit to Lyon in 1940, of the indescribable enthusiasm that had greeted him, and the hope that he had then instilled in us, after the sad days of June. With the youthful enthusiasm of that time, letting myself be carried away by my imagination, I had dreamed of helping him and even perhaps of finding myself at his side, through the dark hours.[14]

However, neither the National Assembly's vote nor the public mood were specific endorsements of the actual programme that Pétain and his followers planned to introduce. In keeping with his beliefs and self-image, of course, this was not put forward for discussion or approval, but simply enacted, with minimal consultation outside Vichy's corridors of power.

One of the Vichy regime's first acts was the scapegoating of its ideological opponents. 'As the shock of the initial losses swept France, bitter accusations of treason and conspiracy swept the country... In this floundering morass of accusation, some even believed that God had abandoned France because of her sins and the error of her ways. No explanation was beyond belief', as Robert Doughty has noted. Pétain and his followers took full advantage of this national mood by heaping blame on the Third Republic, and on almost every aspect of the political and cultural tradition that had originated in 1789. Léon Blum was arrested on 15 September and detained without trial. The eighty Assembly members who had voted against the measures of 11 July, overwhelmingly Socialists, were removed from office, and in many cases were either imprisoned or fled into exile. Soon, the weight of the state's hostility fell on exactly the Maurrasian classification of internal enemies; Protestants, foreigners, Freemasons, and above all, Jews.

Vichy's so-called National Revolution was the programme of institutional transformation instigated by Pétain, although not always personally directed by him. Its positive values, never fully codified but frequently invoked, included traditionalism, authority, the fusion of executive and legislative powers, hierarchy, social conservatism and cohesion, the family, Catholicism, regionalism and ruralist primitivism – alongside technocratic dirigisme and pragmatic state control. Its negative values included rejection of democracy and equal rights, of political and economic liberalism, of cultural and intellectual modernism, of rationality and materialism, and of perceived marginal and outsider groups – above all, the Jews. For many of its more reactionary constituencies, the National Revolution was a national counter-revolution, to settle grievances that had rankled since 1936, or 1905, or even 1789.

'Work, Family, Country' – a coinage associated with pre-war far-right groups like the followers of Colonel François de la Rocque – replaced 'Liberty, Equality and Fraternity' as the official maxims of the Vichy state; although, with characteristic incoherence, the Vichy regime never abandoned the old Republican tricolour. Georges Scapini, the blind right-wing veteran previously involved with Brinon in pre-war pro-German initiatives, was appointed minister plenipotentiary in August 1940 and ambassador in September, with responsibility for the French POWs in Germany. A consultative National Council of around 200 members, nominated by the head of state and without legislative power, was formed on 22 January 1941. Education, long the Third Republic's instrument for projecting Republican values into *la France profonde* and turning peasants into French citizens, was remodelled to serve the new regime with a purge of suspect teachers, the closure of the state teacher training colleges on 18 September 1940, a new curriculum programme introduced on 15 August 1941, and numerous other measures. Indoctrination of the young was supplemented by the formation of the Chantiers de la Jeunesse Française (French Youth Worksites) on 30 July 1940, dragooning French men aged 21 with programmes of physical education and ideological instruction. Measures promoting family values tried to address France's falling birth rate and supposed moral decline by rigorously tightening divorce laws on 2 April 1941, discriminating in favour of fathers of large families in state job allocation, etc. The media were controlled by the French Office of Information, formed on 10 December 1940 after the nationalization of the information services of the French news agency Havas.

Laval led the first Vichy cabinet under Pétain, with the title of Vice-President of the Council, from 16 July until 13 December 1940, when his failures to win German concessions and his lack of deference drove the Marshal to remove him. He was replaced by Pierre-Étienne Flandin, a veteran of centre-right politics in the Third Republic, who lasted less than two months in office, from 14 December 1940 to 10 February 1941, due primarily to German anger at the removal of Laval. In his stead, Admiral François Darlan, the Vichy Minister of Merchant and Military Marine, took office from 10 February 1941 to 18 April 1942. Vichy administrations were already proving as short-lived as the Third Republic parliamentary governments, whose instability its opponents had condemned so strongly.

Jacques Doriot was briefly a member of the Vichy National Council, where he intrigued with Marcel Déat over plans to form a single party to underpin the new regime. He also intrigued with Adrien Marquet, Minister of the Interior under Pétain from 27 June to 6 September, over plans to install the PPF in power. Once informed, Laval ordered Marquet's removal on 6 September, to be replaced by Marcel Peyrouton. Doriot's efforts to seek power and influence within the new Vichy government went no further, and by October 1940 he was back in Paris in the Occupied Zone.

Variations on Maurrasianism were introduced at almost every level of policy. Maurras himself remained in Lyon rather than moving to Vichy, but he proclaimed himself almost from the start a committed Pétainist, stating in *Revue d'Action Française* of 17 April 1942 that 'we will follow him with eyes closed to the ends of the earth.' Had he simply persisted in this position, he might have preserved his reputation better. But with the German attack on the Soviet Union in 1941, he generalized the situation to embrace the struggle against Communism and saw the actions of the Resistance increasingly in this light. 'We say several times a week that the best way to respond to terrorist threats is to impose a legitimate counter-terror on them. The axiom is applicable to the violence of speech and attitude of which the Jewish hordes are guilty: retaliation.'[15]

As Henry Rousso, the pioneering modern historian of the Vichy period and Sigmaringen, states:

> During its brief existence, from July 1940 to August 1944, the new regime was dependent on the military occupation of the country; at first partial, then total after the invasion of the Free Zone on 11 November 1942. Its room for manoeuvre depended on the role that the Third Reich intended to assign to France in its military strategy and in the new European order once victory was achieved. In this sense, Vichy constituted a response to the geopolitical situation where the French had suddenly been deprived of power over their own destiny. Before the alternative of external dissidence supported by the progress of internal resistance emerged, the new regime initially benefited from the resigned support of French society, the majority of which had accepted the need to end a lost war.
>
> However, the external situation was not enough to explain either the nature or the choices of Vichy. In a few months, without intervention from the occupiers, a charismatic dictatorship was established: the "French State", an authoritarian regime whose legitimacy rested on Marshal Pétain, a figure of the Great War. The latter's seizure of power triggered a cult of personality that was partly organized, partly spontaneous. The "Marshal" was thus able to impose a new political, social and moral order: the National Revolution, which marked a clear break with the Republic and defended the principle of a "national community" from which "unassimilable elements" were excluded: Jews, Communists, Freemasons, foreigners.

And, Rousso adds, Vichy was "the sole case in Nazi Europe of a new regime, established without pressure from the occupier, disposing a certain autonomy in a territory partially left at liberty; its existence prolonged up until the Liberation, and even beyond, a form of civil war which recalled the global struggle between the fascist systems, Communism and the democracies."[16]

In his efforts to build useful relations with Nazi Germany after the Armistice, Laval enlisted two figures who were later to be his virtual overseers in Sigmaringen: Fernand de Brinon and Jean Luchaire. Both were well acquainted with the German diplomat Otto Abetz, who had been appointed in June 1940 by Joachim von Ribbentrop to represent the Reich's Foreign Ministry in Paris alongside the military authorities; Luchaire's secretary had become Abetz's wife. Laval made his first visit to Paris on 19 July and attempted to begin negotiations with the Germans. For a while, this suited both parties, giving Laval a counterweight to the Armistice Commission in Wiesbaden, and Ribbentrop a Foreign Office presence in dealing with France. Abetz was promoted to ambassador in early August, while Brinon and Luchaire liaised between him and Laval. However, various offers from Laval, including a potential share in the French colonial trade and volunteers to join the fight against Britain, achieved little, least of all the main French priorities: an easing of restrictions along the Demarcation Zone between Vichy France and Occupied France; reduction in payments for the cost of occupation; the return of the French government to Paris; and the release of French POWs.

Pétain himself became directly involved after the abortive British-Gaullist attack on Dakar in September 1940, sending emissaries to Berlin, and in October, proclaiming on the radio readiness to seek new alliances and a 'peace of collaboration' – with the tacit understanding that France would want her territorial integrity guaranteed and some degree of considerate treatment. In the course of the brief Franco-German honeymoon, Hitler met Laval on 22 October 1940, and Pétain two days later, at Montoire, just north of the Demarcation Zone near Tours. The meeting was more symbolic than productive; it produced no agreement, and Hitler's excursions also took in Italy, where he discussed partition of French colonial possessions with Mussolini. Nonetheless, through November and early December, Vichy France continued to make plans, overtures and declarations, in the absence of any substantial German concessions. Pétain even announced his intention to move his government from Vichy to Versailles. Ribbentrop vetoed the plan on 3 December.

By mid-December, the failure of the self-deluding policy was obvious, and Laval bore the consequences. On 13 December, Pétain forced the resignation of the engineer of his ascendancy and had him placed under house arrest at his mansion in Châteldon, a foretaste of the treatment both were to receive from the Germans at Sigmaringen. Through threats and bluster, Abetz secured Laval's release on 16 December, and the Vichy-German honeymoon was definitively over, despite persistent French efforts to rekindle the relationship. At first, Abetz refused to talk at all to Laval's successor, Pierre-Étienne Flandin, and it was only with the accession of Admiral François Darlan on 10 February 1941 that relations really began to thaw again.

Marcel Déat, at this stage an ally of Laval but personally detested by Pétain, had attempted to interest the Marshal in forming a single party or movement along German or Italian lines, but Pétain resisted the idea. Instead, the Marshal backed the creation of the Légion Française des Combattants (LFC) on 29 August 1940, to forcibly combine all the former veterans' associations into a single entity loyal to the Vichy regime. Joseph Darnand promptly became LFC head in the Alpes-Maritimes department. Déat was arrested the same time as his patron, but was released soon after, and moved to Paris, where he continued his efforts to create a single pseudo-fascistic movement in France. The nearest that the Vichy regime ever came to creating such a group was the short-lived Rassemblement pour la Révolution Nationale, created in January 1941 to function alongside the LFC, both of them supported by Pétain to head off Déat's ambitions.

Modern analyses have not been kind to apologetics for Vichy as a sort of limited safe zone doing its best to mitigate the Nazi horrors and keep them at arm's length. 'The strategy pursued over four years rested on two elements. On the one hand, it was a question of managing the consequences of the Occupation, of asserting French sovereignty over the entire territory, including the Occupied Zone, of keeping the country out of the global conflict while speculating on its place in the future Europe expected to be German. These objectives were reflected in the choice of a policy of collaboration with the victor. On the other hand, it was not only a question of restoring the authority of the State and the cohesion of the nation, but also of profoundly changing French society despite the defeat and the Occupation, or rather, thanks to the opportunity offered. These two objectives were indissociable. Collaboration with the enemy had to create the conditions favourable for internal upheavals, while the National Revolution made it possible to affirm that France was ideologically aligned with the camp of the Third Reich, and that it was therefore a partner worthy of trust.'[17]

Perhaps most despicable of Vichy's attempts to show itself a good Axis partner was the legislation against Jews, which laid the ground for the later deportations. Few historians now accept the post-war apologetics that portrayed the Vichy regime as safeguarding France's Jewish population against the Nazis. In October 2010, a draft of the law of 3 October 1940, corrected in Pétain's own hand, was revealed. Evidence of his own attitudes towards the Jews prior to 1940 is limited, but it appears that he moved to appease a perceived current of anti-Semitism in France in order to help consolidate his own regime. Laval had already declared to Abetz in July that the new regime, as one of its proofs of goodwill towards Germany, would ensure the removal of Jews from public functions. Blame for the resulting statute was retrospectively shared between Raphaël Alibert, a devoted Maurassian Action Française parliamentarian Vichy Minister of Justice from 12 July 1940, and Marcel Peyrouton, career diplomat and Vichy Minister of the Interior from September 1940 to February 1941. Without proper parliamentary procedure, the drafting of the statute was particularly obscure, but Pétain's own handwritten changes, rare in Vichy legislation, show his close personal interest in it. His intervention in the statute tended towards even greater harshness – for instance, ensuring that 'no Jew whatsoever should be allowed to exercise state judicial or educational functions'.

Pétain himself had no particular record of personal anti-Semitism:

Yet the spirit of Charles Maurras's "integral nationalism" marked the mindset of many in the Marshal's own entourage at Vichy, which lent coherence to the choice of Alibert as the new regime's first justice minister in 1940. Pétain himself, while disinclined to put credence in any abstract ideology, was all too ready to practice Maurras's *antisémitisme d'État*.[18]

In a reply to protests from the Grand Rabbi of France against the law, dated 22 November 1940, Pétain wrote:

> Obedience to the law is one of the essential principles of any state and one of the indispensable conditions of the revival of France which I am pursuing, as you know, with all my strength, appealing to the dedication, and when needed, the spirit of sacrifice of my fellow citizens, in whatever situation they find themselves.

As this suggests, his attitude seemed to be that French Jews were expected to sacrifice their rights and freedom, and if necessary, their lives, for the greater good of Pétain's National Revolution and of France.

The resulting 'Law Bearing on the Status of Jews' of 3 October 1940 barred Jews from any participation in official posts, the law, the military, and the mass media, and announced the drawing up of quotas for the number of Jews in liberal professions. The law also defined Jews in racial terms, rather than confessional status, along the lines of Nazi models. All this was done, however, without any particular external pressure from the Germans. At best, the legislation might have been inspired by an impetus to demonstrate that Vichy France could implement its own policies, rather than have German models thrust upon it, but on balance, it seems perfectly clear that Vichy France, very much at Pétain's behest, set out autonomously to implement a doctrinaire homegrown Maurrasian agenda, including the full gamut of domestic anti-Semitism.

A law of 13 August 1940, again instituted without German pressure, banned secret societies, cracking down on another Maurrasian bugbear, the Freemasons. Resented across Catholic Europe as secretive purveyors of liberal, secularist ideas, the Masons were especially reviled by French conservatives after the *Affaire des fiches* (Affair of the Record Cards) of 1900-05, where the Minister of War, Louis André, in the aftermath of the Dreyfus Affair, had worked with Masonic lodges and government offices to identify and exclude notably Catholic or otherwise conservative officers from promotion, instead advancing fellow Masons and those closest to the secular spirit of the Republic. Masonic influence was relatively mitigated in the aftermath of the scandal

– which did not stop the Maurrasian Vichy ideologues from paying off that particular grudge. Some 14,600 officeholding Masons were identified in print, and the Vichy government put its officials and scholars to work to unearth the hidden Masonic networks, but the results were predictably disappointing. For resident foreigners, pre-war legislation had already paved the way for the kind of draconian discrimination introduced by the Vichy regime. As Hannah Arendt observed:

> 10,000 Italian refugees were enough to postpone indefinitely the assimilation of almost one million Italian immigrants in France... The French government, followed by other Western countries, introduced during the Thirties an increasing number of restrictions for naturalized citizens: they were eliminated from certain professions for up to ten years after their naturalization, they had no political rights, etc.

Out of all the Maurassian paper tigers, only the Protestants escaped with relatively little discrimination or interference with their lives.

The Vichy cult of personality around Pétain had its obvious political value, and parallels in many other contemporary authoritarian regimes, but Pétain may well have embraced it out of vanity as much as expediency. Certainly, the development of his own cabinet suggests as much:

> Pétain's entourage at Vichy came increasingly to consist of men who could be relied upon to uphold and propagate the legend of Pétain's providential mission. Soon, all the old political figures disappeared and were replaced by awe-struck panegyrists, like Dumoulin de la Barthète, or by members of the military – men bred to the unquestioning respect of their superiors – and especially by former subordinates like Generals Laure and Debeney, who were familiar with the hypersensitive vanity of the old Marshal.[19]

In another foretaste of the situation in Sigmaringen, the Germans kept Laval in Paris, evidently as a potential figurehead for a rival government to the Marshal's, and partly to exert additional leverage on the Vichy regime.

In July 1941, despite Vichy France's formally neutral status, a group of activists in both the Occupied and the Free Zones founded the Légion des Volontaires Français contre le Bolchevisme (LVF), headquartered in Paris, an association with military aspirations, organized by collaborationist groups including Marcel Déat's Rassemblement National Populaire (RNP) and Jacques Doriot's PPF, and supported by right-wing luminaries including Jean Luchaire and the Belle Époque Breton nationalist and novelist Alphonse de Châteaubriant. Tolerated rather than supported by the Germans, who refused permission for it to grow its membership beyond 15,000, it was also only given lukewarm and distant support by the Vichy government. Pétain was opposed to its members wearing German uniform, while Laval followed his regular practice towards paramilitary groupings by trying to bring it under his control through a regulation of June 1942. Despite feverish promotion and propagandist claims by its promoters, the LVF never numbered more than around 5,800 active recruits. Its first units arrived on the Eastern Front towards the end of November 1941, where they performed poorly, suffering heavy casualties. Reconstituted in the spring of 1942 with a trickle of new volunteers, the LVF was mostly retired from frontline service on the Eastern Front, and chiefly engaged behind the German lines, where it committed repeated atrocities against Russian civilians.

An early and enthusiastic supporter of the LVF – as well as Doriot – was Louis-Ferdinand Céline, who declared in a 21 November 1941 interview with the PPF's journal *L'Émancipation nationale*:

I didn't wait for the Kommandantur to parade at the Crillon to become a collaborationist... We don't think enough about the protection of the white race. We must act now, because tomorrow it will be too late... Doriot behaved as he always did. He is a man... we must work, campaign with Doriot... This Legion, so slandered, so criticized, is the proof of life. I would have liked to go with Doriot... I tell you, the Legion is very good, it's everything that's good.

Céline may never have been an active member of the PPF, but this certainly goes even further to undermine any defence of his wartime stance as somehow neutral or disengaged.

Meanwhile, in the Alpes-Maritimes, Darnand formed the Service d'Ordre Légionnaire (SOL) in the summer of 1941, as a paramilitary group open to the most militantly pro-Vichy members of the LFC. In December, the organization was extended across the whole of Vichy France, with Darnand moving to Vichy in January 1942 to take national command. Virulently opposed to 'democracy, Jewish leprosy, and Gaullist dissidence', this organization eventually metamorphosed into the hated Milice.

Simultaneously with his appointment as Vice-President of the Council on 10 February 1941, Admiral François Darlan was also made Foreign Minister and Minister of Information, adding Minister of the Interior a week later, and by 11 August was also Minister of Defence. He had already been made Pétain's successor-designate on the day of Laval's removal. He introduced a less ideological, more pragmatic and even technocratic style of government, with little enthusiasm for the initial ideological extremes of the Vichy regime. However, he also backed many of the even more draconian anti-Semitic measures introduced during 1941, including the creation of the Commissariat General for Jewish Questions in March 1941, apparently motivated by the wish to improve relations with Nazi Germany.

Darlan also sought to lever collaboration in foreign policy into amelioration of the Armistice terms, most notably via the Paris Protocols of May 1941, which provided the Third Reich with access to Vichy airfields in Syria to support allies in Iraq, and the Tunisian port of Bizerte, in return for paper concessions regarding release of French POWs and easing of restrictions along the Demarcation Line. Fernand de Brinon was part of Darlan's negotiating party, with Otto Abetz on the German team. The terms threatened to bring Vichy France into the war as an active co-belligerent on the German side, and the Vichy government refused to ratify the texts, seeking more concessions. In the event, the British, having defeated Iraq's pro-Axis nationalists in the Anglo-Iraq war of May 1941, invaded Syria and Lebanon in June, capturing both in just over a month. Darlan's Paris Protocols had lost Vichy France some of the jewels of its Middle Eastern colonial empire, in return for the release of a few POWs.

The Syria debacle brought home to many in the Vichy hierarchy the potential cost to France of continuing close cooperation with the Nazis. On

12 August 1941, Pétain made a radio broadcast which summed up the growing difficulties of his regime, just a year after its institution:

> French, I have grave things to tell you. For several weeks, I have felt an ill wind rising from several regions of France. Anxiety is gaining ground, doubt is taking hold of souls. The authority of my government is being disputed, orders are often poorly executed... It comes above all from our tardiness in building a new order, or more precisely in imposing it. The National Revolution, whose broad outlines I outlined in my message of 11 October, has not yet become a reality. It has not penetrated, because between the people and me, who understand each other so well, there has been erected the double screen of the partisans of the old regime and the servants of the trusts.

Both Third Republic diehards and plutocrats were unlikely culprits for the National Revolution's malaise, but the choice of the latter especially reflected the fact that, thanks to economic realities, the burden of indemnity payments to the Reich, and technocrats within the government wishing to rationalize the French economy and administration, Vichy France was moving inexorably away from the pastoral traditionalist stereotype that Pétain clung to. In typical vainglorious style, he concluded: 'In 1917, I put an end to the mutinies. In 1940, I put an end to the rout. Today it is from yourselves that I want to save you.'

Events almost immediately conspired to make the Vichy regime's situation much worse. Later that month, following the first Resistance assassinations of Germans in the Occupied Zone, the occupiers began the arrest and shooting of hostages in retaliation. This both horrified the French public and discredited Vichy attempts to resume sovereign control of the Occupied Zone. On 27 August, when Pierre Laval, as well as three other notable refugees in Germany in 1944, Jacques Doriot, Marcel Déat and Fernand de Brinon, had assembled in Versailles for a parade to mark the departure for the Eastern Front of the first unit of the LVF, a former Camelot du Roi, Paul Collette, shot and wounded Laval and Déat, as well as two other victims.

The Vichy regime conspicuously failed to rebuff its image after Darlan's accession. Attempts to tar the Popular Front government of 1936 and other figures in the dock for France's defeat, in the Riom Trials of February–April 1942, backfired. Léon Blum and Édouard Daladier proved so effective in defending their own records and throwing the blame for failure to modernize the French army onto the high command and Pétain himself, that the Germans pressured the Vichy regime to halt the process. Darlan, already harbouring doubts regarding Germany's eventual victory, made overtures to the Americans, while the Germans increasingly disdained him. Laval, meanwhile, had cultivated relations with the Germans while in Paris. Eventually, Laval formed his second government under Pétain with German approval on 18 April 1942. Darlan retained the position of Vichy Minister of National Defence and Pétain's successor-designate. Laval appointed other figures on the far right, hitherto not counted in Pétain's counsels, including Abel Bonnard, far-right poet and writer, as Minister of National Education, and René Bousquet, organizer on the French side of notorious deportations of Jews such as the Vélodrome d'Hiver roundup, as chief of police.

On 22 June 1942, Laval gave a broadcast, with Pétain's prior approval, which set the tone for his second Vichy administration and the rest of his collaboration with the Nazis. 'I have the wish to re-establish normal and trusting relations with Germany and Italy', he declared, continuing, 'I wish for the victory of Germany, because, without it, Bolshevism, tomorrow, would take root everywhere. So, as I told you on 20 April, here we are faced with this alternative: either integrate ourselves, our honor and our vital interests being respected, in a new and pacified Europe, or resign ourselves to seeing our civilization disappear.' The broadcast brought consternation in Vichy and helped buttress the Gaullist cause, but Laval refused to repudiate it. At his later trial, Pétain claimed that he had been revolted by the phrase and expected it to be excised, but actual analysis of the documents indicated that he had simply wanted 'believe' changed to 'wish' – with the implication that he was setting up Laval to take the blame for any later condemnation.

In the summer of 1942, Laval collaborated with German roundups of Jews in France, acceding to the participation of the French police in the notorious Vel' d'Hiv' roundup of 16–17 July 1942, which netted over 13,500 Jews of foreign extraction, and adding a further 7,000 Jews from the Free Zone at the end of August. Laval insisted that young children should be arrested and deported along with their families. He subsequently sent a telegram to French embassies worldwide justifying the action, stating that 'the only way to ward off the Jewish peril was to repatriate these individuals to Eastern Europe, their place of origin'. Laval's motives in these transactions appear to have been purely to foster good relations with the Germans and to try to consolidate France's place as a trusted junior partner in some post-war German European order. Correspondingly, in September 1942, Laval authorized the Abwehr and the German security police to pursue suspected Resistance members into the Free Zone.

Whatever the suffering of the Jews under Laval's premiership, the act that alienated almost all of France was the introduction of forced labour in the Reich, Service du Travail Obligatoire (STO). Having worked its first drafts of slave labourers to death, the Reich was looking for fresh manpower for its war industries from all subject territories, including France. Gaston Bruneton, a Protestant industrialist, had pushed for the creation of a French government body responsible for French workers in France, and in April 1942 was appointed head of the Vichy French Labour Service in Germany. Laval followed this with a voluntary scheme in June 1942, bartering three French workers for the release of one French POW, but this scheme proved so ineffective that Laval introduced a compulsory scheme in August, operating across both Free and Occupied Zones, bartering the freedom of the French workers for the opportunity to extend Vichy governmental power across metropolitan France. Militant protests and strikes across southern France forced the government to roll back the scheme, but after its full formal institution from February 1943, STO became a peerless recruiting agent for the French Resistance, and one more nail in the coffin of Laval's reputation.

As the National Revolution unfolded in the Free Zone, a different collaborationist culture developed in the Occupied Zone, especially in Paris. Its political players had far fewer scruples about working directly under the German occupiers than their counterparts and rivals in Vichy. Many were far closer ideological allies. Fernand de Brinon, formally installed in Paris in November 1940 as Delegate-General of the French Government in the Occupied Territories, demonstrated recurrently that his loyalties lay more with the German occupiers than with his ostensible masters in Vichy.

Eugène Deloncle, former head of the Cagoule, formed the Mouvement Social Révolutionnaire in Paris in September 1940 with the approval of Otto Abetz, as a homegrown French fascist party seeking to work within a Nazi-dominated Europe. On 2 February 1941, Marcel Déat founded the RNP in Paris, still seeking to create a French political movement that could work within the Axis. Urged by the Germans, the Mouvement Social Révolutionnaire and RNP merged later that month, but mutual distrust and rivalry divided rather than united their efforts, and by October 1941, the two movements had divided again. This kind of internecine conflict actually suited Abetz, who had been instructed by Hitler to keep France weakened and divided.

On 15 August 1941, following public anti-German demonstrations in Paris, the military authorities banned the Communist Party in the Occupied Zone and decreed the death penalty for its members. On 20 August, equating the Jewish population with Communist agitation, German forces and French police rounded up some 3,000 Jews in Paris for deportation. The launch of Operation Barbarossa on 22 June 1941 brought France's Communists, hitherto largely pacifist towards the Soviet Union's erstwhile German ally, into the Resistance fold, and attacks on German occupying forces multiplied. Executions of groups of hostages in retaliation became regular practice, albeit gradually supplemented by deportations as the Third Reich began to use retaliatory arrest as a cover for implementation of the Final Solution.

However marginal and impotent the collaborationist political groups in the Occupied Zone, they were complemented by the vociferous collaborationist intellectuals and propagandists who later fled en masse to Sigmaringen. Jean Luchaire operated the collaborationist newspaper *Les Nouveaux Temps*, founded in November 1940, as a mouthpiece for Axis propaganda, albeit mostly loyal to the Vichy regime. Among his circle in Paris was his daughter Corinne, already a well-regarded screen actress at 20 years old, who became associated with the collaborationist milieu.

Many more extreme journalists grouped around the weekly *Je suis partout*, which continued its pro-fascist pre-war editorial policy under Robert Brasillach, becoming a prominent mouthpiece for collaborationism. On 14 May 1941, after the first roundup of Jews and other 'undesirables' in the Occupied Zone, *Je suis partout* celebrated:

The French police have at last taken the decision to purge Paris and put out of harm's way the thousands of foreign Jews, Romanians, Poles, Czechs, Austrians, who for many years have been doing business at our expense. On Wednesday morning, the Prefecture of Police executed a major sweep, as 5,000 residents were placed under arrest.

Prominent among the contributors to *Je suis partout* was Lucien Rebatet, who briefly engaged in radio journalism in Vichy before relocating to Paris in October 1940. For Rebatet:

while it is undeniable that his wishes for proscription were largely fulfilled by the discriminatory measures that the French State determined from the autumn of 1940, the escalation that he cultivated in this domain, his virulent criticisms of the regime and his unbridled Naziphilia condemned him to a certain kind of oppositional marginality. Rebatet did not wish to understand that his maximalist positions had no chance of leading an opinion whose lukewarmness he himself denounced and which, from mid-1941… began to free itself from the equivocations maintained by attachment to the person of Marshal Pétain. Alongside this development, Rebatet appears to be constantly out of step: he stigmatized Vichy as early as 1940, when Marshalism was in its triumphant phase, and the more he felt public opinion was hesitant, the more his discourse grew radicalized and risked encouraging public hesitancy. Rebatet probably bears the heavy responsibility of having encouraged vocations and bolstered membership in the Milice or the LVF, but it is certain that his message generally convinced only minds already won over to his cause and resolutely in the minority in the country.[20]

Robert Belot's analysis of Lucien Rebatet's political frustration also stands as a comment on the failure of the collaborationists to develop any unified platform:

Failure, then, of the activist who was to see his efforts tending towards a unification of the collaborationist forces shattered by the twisting ulterior motives of the many leaders of the moment, too inclined to focus on their own petty interests, tussling in their personal rivalries, and, above all, devoid of any popular base or any programme.[21]

However, though he might have been disappointed politically, Rebatet enjoyed a brief literary success with the publication in the summer of 1942 of *Les Décombres*, part autobiography, part political polemic, produced by Céline's publisher Denoël.

Céline himself, comfortably installed in Nazi-occupied Paris, cultivated ties with Laval, Brinon and other prominent French collaborationists, and hobnobbed with the Nazi cultural elite. Although not actively engaged in collaborationist projects like Rebtatet, he periodically denounced some of his former acquaintances and *bêtes noires* publicly as Jews. In March 1942, he attended a lunch organized by Georges Oltramare, a Swiss fascist journalist and future fellow exile in Sigmaringen, to celebrate the fiftieth anniversary of the first number of Édouard Drumont's *La Libre Parole*. Fellow attendees included Pierre-Antoine Cousteau, Jean Hérold-Paquis and his publisher Robert Denoël. He found time to illustrate a new edition of the *Bagatelles* in 1943, showing two Polish Jews in traditional costume, with the caption 'Two Polish Gaullists'. And just in case anyone is led astray by Céline's post-war exercises in misdirection, here is what he was stating, clearly, unambiguously and sincerely, unqualified by any irony or relativism, without any diverting argot or ellipses, in the pamphlet *Les Beaux Draps*, published in February 1941:

A prolific, ardent nation, rises admirably from the greatest military ashes, from the cruellest occupations, but only on one condition, this very essential, mystical condition, of having remained faithful through victories and defeats to the same breeds, to the same ethnicity, to the same blood, to the same racial strains, not bastardized, those which made it triumphant, sovereign, in times of trial and conquest, to have preserved itself despite everything from the fornications of lower races, especially from Jewish pollution, Berber, Afro-Levantine, from the born corruptors of Europe... any Jewish-contaminated country degenerates, languishes and collapses; war does not kill it, it finishes it off.

Never slow to peddle personal grudges or indulge his obsessions, Céline also wrote a complaining letter to the secretary-general of the Institut d'étude des questions juives, a major fount of propaganda linking the Gaullist resistance to Jewish interests. Having gone through the institute's library, he was 'hurt to see that in the library, neither *Bagatelles* or *l'Ecole* appear, while you favour... a miasma of last-minute abortions'. Despite efforts by pre-war and post-war apologists to portray Céline's anti-Semitic diatribes as somehow ironic or parodic, his behaviour and his other statements, public or private, confirm that he was fully sincere – or at least as sincere as the narcissistic self-obsessed nihilist could be about anything. Word and action definitely reinforced each other. Certainly, the rank-and-file Milice who later witnessed his arrival at Sigmaringen expected a great prophet of fascism – and were very disappointed at what they saw.

Ironically, it was Darlan, Pétain's trusted successor, the keen ally of the Axis in Syria, who helped end Vichy France's limited autonomy. He visited Algiers to see his hospitalized son just before Operation Torch began on 8 November 1942, and local Resistance fighters working alongside the Allied invasion force captured him on the night of 7-8 November. Under Allied pressure, Darlan called a ceasefire for Vichy forces in North Africa on 10 November. Hitler's immediate response was the invasion of the French Free Zone on 11 November 1942, extending German dominance over Vichy France to full occupation. After this invasion, Darlan brought Vichy forces in North Africa over to the Allied side, to fight against the German units invading Tunisia. The Vichy armed forces and police offered no resistance to the German occupation of metropolitan France, but the Vichy navy successfully scuttled most of the remaining fleet at Toulon on 27 November, keeping them out of Axis hands. Stripped of his titles by Pétain, Darlan stayed on as Allied-back High Commissioner of France in Africa in the teeth of de Gaulle's opposition, until his assassination by a young right-wing anti-Vichy activist on 24 December 1942. Vichy France henceforth was nothing more than a puppet government facilitating a German occupation, just like the other occupied territories across Europe. National Revolution institutions lingered on, but the Vichy experiment, such as it was, was effectively at an end.

Chapter 3

The Marshal Stumbles

By 1943, French collaborationism was operating in a very different climate from the exhausted acquiescence of 1940. The entry of the United States into the war, the loss of France's colonies, the breakdown of the Nazi-Soviet Pact, the fierce Russian resistance on the Eastern Front, the German occupation of the entirety of metropolitan France, the increasing privations of the population, made worse by STO, all combined to discredit the Vichy regime and the National Revolution, though Pétain himself retained personal prestige. Despite shrill proclamations of inevitable German victory from the most diehard and extremist collaborators, few among the population now believed in any future European order with France a junior partner of the Third Reich; rather, Germans and domestic collaborators alike invoked more often the menace of triumphant Bolshevism. The Vichy government continued to operate from Vichy under full German occupation, though with no real autonomy or control of its own territories. Brinon remained in office as its liaison and representative in Paris.

STO and its consequences had the most immediate effect in radicalizing popular resistance to the regime. 'It was the STO which transformed the Maquis, the guerilla arm of the Resistance, into a veritable army. Estimates of numbers fleeing the STO into active resistance reach 100,000.'[1] Enacted into Vichy law in February 1943 at Laval's instigation, STO was implemented by Vichy police and officials rather than the occupation forces, inevitably delegitimizing the regime even further. Altogether, some 600,000 French workers were estimated to have been caught up by the STO and the earlier voluntary labour schemes, joining the roughly 2 million French POWs still in German hands. In September 1943, Jean Bichelonne, who held ministerial rank in the Vichy Ministry of Industry and was already heavily involved in the administration of STO, negotiated agreements committing major French industrial facilities and their workers to the service of the Reich. Gaston Bruneton, meanwhile, had his status elevated in February 1943 to General Commissioner of the General Commissariat for French Labour, as the massive increase in the number of STO workers expanded his responsibilities.

Allied to his pro-German moves in the war economy was Laval's facilitation of anti-Semitism. The onetime socialist and self-styled philosemite showed a very different face in his new administration, thanks partly to his grievances from his dismissal in 1940. Laval's own anti-Semitism, hitherto implicit and allusive, became explicit once he was back in office in April 1942, expressed as revenge on the Maurrassian elements of Pétain's entourage, who had plotted his dismissal on 13 December 1940. An opponent of these explicitly anti-Semitic counter-revolutionaries, Laval took up, along with power, their language on the Jewish question. At the Council of Ministers of 3 July 1942, which prepared the roundups in the Occupied Zone, Laval no longer resorted to the petty cautions that had characterized his anti-Semitic outbursts until then:

> We must distinguish between French Jews and the refuse sent by the Germans themselves. The intention of the German government would be to create a Jewish state in Eastern Europe. I would not be dishonoured if I were to one day send the countless foreign Jews who are in France to this Jewish state.

Abetz reported to the Gestapo that, aside from some formal distinctions between French and foreign Jews, Laval had no strong ideological convictions regarding the Jews – and no moral scruples about sacrificing them in the service of good relations with the Reich. He also understood clearly what their actual fate was and sought advice from the Germans on the agreed terminology to sustain the fiction of a new Jewish home in Eastern Europe. Almost the only divergence he showed with German policy was in the summer of 1943, when he resisted German attempts to denaturalize Jews granted French citizenship between the wars, more with an eye to probable German defeat than any moral considerations. When the Germans occupied the former Italian Occupied

Zone after Italy's surrender in September 1943 and indiscriminately rounded up Jews, his protests were minimal and mostly revolved around infringements of French sovereignty.[2]

Laval also instigated the creation in January 1943 of the Milice Française, introduced in response to German demands for greater security on French soil. With Pétain's endorsement, he absorbed Darnand's SOL into the new organization, and made Darnand its secretary-general and effective operational chief, while remaining nominal head himself. The initiative served to reinforce a regime that no longer had even the rump Armistice Army granted it by the Germans, discredited domestically as well as internationally by Operation Torch.

> In accepting the creation of the Milice, Laval saw a response to those who accused him of weakness. He could answer: you see, I myself have created a force capable of fighting against the adversaries of Collaboration and the National Revolution. It's not just the troublemakers in Paris who are capable of taking action.[3]

In principle an organization for maintaining public order and defending the government, the Milice inherited in practice most of the precepts of Darnand's SOL and was conceived as a political as much as a paramilitary force, another attempt at creating a single national extreme-right movement in France to reinforce the faltering National Revolution. Both Laval and Pétain gave it their full support. In an address dated 19 April 1943, Pétain announced to the French people:

> I have placed the French Milice under the direct command of the head of the government. I want you to help in its development because it must constitute the indispensable force to lead the fight against all covert powers... the Milice, comprising above all young and dynamic elements, must be invested as a priority with all vanguard missions, in particular those relating to the maintenance of order, the guarding of sensitive points of the territory, the fight against Communism...

Pétain's attribution of the Milice to Laval may have reflected concern for the formalities of the structure of the government, but it hardly represents an attempt to distance himself from the organization.

Maurras heralded the creation of the Milice in the aftermath of the SOL and other organizations, particularly in its capacity to act against his habitual list of internal enemies, as well as the Russian hordes who were his new preoccupation:

> A third affair is in sight: the Milice. Oh, joy for it! The legitimate recommendations no longer need to be made. They have been warned. We did what had to be done, said what had to be said, and well... with the help of a reliable and good police force, we can, at home, crush any revolutionary inclination and any attempt to support the hordes from the East... Great good can come of it, no harm will come of it.[4]

Whatever its pretensions towards mass movement status, the Milice numbered only some 29,000 by the end of 1943, over half of them more sympathizers or nominal members than active participants. With a leadership mostly stemming from the higher echelons of various other pre-war nationalist groupings, the Milice drew most of its manpower from a typical far-right cross-section of *petit-bourgeoisie*, unemployed, students, and a smattering of workers, peasants, criminals and adventurers. They soon developed a disproportionate reputation by virtue of their brutality, corruption, and indiscipline, as well as their readiness to work with the Germans, who were increasingly resented as occupiers. Their ambitions to be a 'revolutionary' force, transforming France in the spirit of the National Revolution and beyond, sorted ill with their pretensions to be the upholders of stability and order. Statements in their favour by Pétain had little effect; support from Laval's government discredited them as much as they did it. Darnand, meanwhile, became an S-Frw. Obersturmführer (lieutenant) in the Waffen-SS in August 1943, swearing an oath of allegiance to Hitler, and was duly followed into the SS by a number of his subordinates. His close relations with the Germans disturbed so many that his followers moved to counter suspicions. His subordinate Francis Bout de l'An declared in *Le Petit Parisien* of 27 January 1944 that, 'as soldiers, we do indeed swear an oath to the Führer... But Joseph Darnand also swore his political oath to the head of state: he will not fail the latter any more than the former, both are sacred.'

The Milice was initially unarmed, thanks partly to German reluctance to see an autonomous armed force on French soil, and thanks to Laval's wish to keep the movement relatively impotent and under his thumb. It was the target of Resistance attacks, and scores of Miliciens fell during the year, stoking the organization's resentment against the Maquis and the population in general. In November 1943, Pétain acceded to Darnand's urging and approved the arming of the Milice. Darnand, meanwhile, cultivated his relations with the Germans, using them to put pressure on Laval. The following month, with German approval, Darnand was made Secretary of State for the Maintenance of Order, with control of all French police forces across the entire country, as well as the Milice. This appointment was partly to satisfy Pétain's craving for domestic order, partly to appease German concerns after Pétain's attempted withdrawal from the Axis embrace, and partly because Laval thought he could still control Darnand. His appointment was the occasion for Laval's notorious statement, 'democracy is the antechamber of Bolshevism'.

Why were so many French fascists, supposedly nationalist, so ready to accept Nazi domination and tutelage from Germany, the sworn enemy of France since 1870? Of course, some did so out of self-interest, and because their earlier compromising activities had left them with no alternative but to continue down the same path. Many other former supporters of the Vichy regime, however, ended the war as heroes of the Liberation, with Jean de Lattre de Tassigny as the shining example. Hannah Arendt maintained consistently that extreme fascists, no matter how supposedly nationalist, were ultimately the enemies of their native lands, beholden to foreign powers and internationalist movements. George Orwell's definition of nationalism as power-worship tempered by self-deception also comes to mind. Other French authorities, such as the historian of French fascism, Pierre Milza, contend that the fervid French collaborationist supporters of Nazism grew more extreme in isolation both from the French public and the Vichy National Revolution, and reconciled themselves to a subordinate role for France in some future Nazi-led European order in a final retreat from any dreams of national resurgence and revitalization. It was an ideological vision not far removed from the goals of Laval's actual collaborationist policy, and it was their last stand against the *bourgeois* capitalist ordinary world of Third Republic France that they had railed against since the First World War.

One of the strangest episodes of this period unfolded in July 1943. Faced with reports that the Milice in southwest France were blaming President Laval for denying them weapons, Joseph Darnand raised the issue with Laval and threatened to resign. He then approached Pétain, who reportedly responded, 'since the Milice isn't working, go back to the Legion'. Temporarily disaffected from the Marshal, Darnand contemplated joining the Resistance. He approached Colonel Georges Groussard, a former Cagoule member who had gone over to the Free French in 1942 and ran the Gilbert Resistance networks from Geneva, but apparently refused to sign the declaration of personal obedience to Groussard that the colonel had required. Darnand then tried approaching London directly, but received no response. According to one source, when informed that Darnand was seeking to join the Free French, de Gaulle responded angrily, saying 'So? If Darquier de Pellepoix were circumcised, I would have to accept him too!'[5] Darnand abandoned any idea of attempting to change sides and continued to work and fight for the collaborationist camp until the end of the war.

As the war situation worsened for the Axis and attitudes towards Vichy hardened, the more extremist and unprincipled collaborationists saw their opportunity. On 17 September 1943, Déat, Luchaire, Darnand, and his Milice subordinates Noël de Tissot and Georges Guilbaud, produced a *Plan de redressement français* (French Recovery Plan), castigating Laval's government, and calling for a more extreme and intransigent pro-Axis regime in France. Approved by Fritz Sauckel, the Nazi official overseeing the STO programme, and circulated to all prominent Nazi leaders, but kept from Pétain and Laval, the document warned of Resistance bands 'pullulating in France during the period of decomposition of central power', and the risk of a general uprising of the French people. In response, the signatories urged the Nazis to 'exert immediate and sufficient pressure on Vichy so that the current government gives way without delay, always under the direction of President Laval (he is the only French collaborationist statesman capable of turning back the tide of unpopularity...)' to a new collaborationist government ready and able to assure the security of the occupying forces; to combine all the collaborationist leaders in one body; to unite enough prominent and diverse leaders to act as figureheads for all French citizens outside the Gaullist and Communist camps; and to set in motion 'a truly revolutionary and socialist policy'. This manifesto for the Nazification of France, issued by the would-be leaders of the French New Order, testifies to their extremism, their ambition, and their disloyalty to Pétain and Laval. Nonetheless, Pétain and Laval were eventually forced to accept Déat and Darnand's inclusion in the residual Vichy government.

Maurras, by 1943, was calling for extreme reprisals against Communists and Gaullists. On 1 September he declared, 'If the death penalty is not enough to overcome the Gaullists, we must take hostages among their family members, and execute them.' On 8 September, he turned the same venom on the Communists. 'Those who have attracted reprisals against France should also suffer them from her... it would be better to treat a certain number of Communist prisoners as hostages and execute them without delay'. On 27 April 1944, he added, 'the Gaullists are armed partisans who are not regulars and who a French army would have the right to shoot on capture.' His justification for these and similar statements, advanced later at his trial, was that domestic resistance should be suppressed by the French authorities to avoid further intervention by the Germans.[6]

Pétain's legitimacy, and that of the Vichy state, was also increasingly facing a challenge from the Allied side. The institution in Algiers on 3 November 1943 of the Comité Français de Libération Nationale (CFLN), in a French possession hitherto regarded as a legal constituent of the French metropole, and the removal of General Henri Giraud from co-presidency with de Gaulle on 8 November, consolidated the Free French into a genuine alternative, representative, professedly democratic challenger to Pétain's claims. With the Allied cause increasingly prospering after the Battle of Kursk, the invasion of Italy and the fall of Mussolini, Pétain could easily foresee a time when the contest for legitimacy would be decided on French soil.

In keeping with these developments, in the autumn of 1943, Pétain made a remarkable, albeit abortive, attempt to dismiss Laval and return to the

Third Republic. By the summer of 1943, he was already hatching with his inner circle secret plans for a new governmental structure excluding Laval, less aligned with the Germans, and more able to treat credibly with the Allies while preserving the National Revolution and his own claims as head of state. On 26 October 1943, he informed Laval that he was 'no longer the man of the situation', and instituted complete separation with his own head of government, avoiding all contact between his own floor and Laval's floor in the Hôtel du Parc. On 12 November, he informed Laval of his intention to dismiss him and put forward the long-delayed draft constitution to be voted on by the members of the defunct National Assembly. On 13 November, he attempted to make a radio broadcast announcing this plan, and confirming the right of the National Assembly to elect his successor, but the broadcast was blocked by the Germans. Maurras, ever the doctrinaire authoritarian, contributed his advice in a letter dated 24 November 1943:

> I do not have the naivety, Marshal, to ask of you, according to my well-known ideas, the constitution of a hereditary monarchy... Everything in its time. For the moment, the essential is that you should give France a constitutional statute as far as possible from the democratic type, which plebiscitary or parliamentary, has lost her 150 years from invasion, depopulation, demoralization.[7]

Pétain was promptly put under closer surveillance, and the Germans moved to stop any initiative for a constitutional reform. On 4 December 1943, Pétain received a letter from Ribbentrop dated 29 November, stating that Hitler opposed any transfer of power to the National Assembly, that elections could not take place in wartime, that any modification of French laws should henceforth be submitted to the Reich for approval, that Laval should immediately be tasked with reshuffling the current government, that the Wehrmacht was the only guarantor of order in France, and that the Marshal could either accept the terms or resign. Abetz delivered the letter, accompanied by Brinon; after considering abdication, Pétain capitulated, stating in a letter to Hitler that he wished for Franco-German reconciliation, and asked only that the members of the new government under Laval should be good Frenchman 'who have not shown me hostility in the past'.[8] Significantly, Pétain attempted, at this critical juncture, to revert to democratic sovereignty, and just as significantly, he surrendered to the German diktat, careful ultimately for his personal prestige. On 28 December 1943, Cécil von Renthe-Fink was installed in Vichy as Hitler's special diplomatic delegate to the Vichy government and de facto overseer of the Marshal. Pressured by the Germans, Laval admitted Marcel Déat on 16 March 1944 as Minister of Labour and National Solidarity. However, Laval's opposition prevented Déat from achieving any substantial policy moves during the few months remaining to the rump Vichy government.

As the tempo of Resistance picked up in metropolitan France, and more and more Maquis actions took place, so did the Milice become more prominent and more identified with the entire residual Vichy regime. A few like Maurras hailed it; however, the majority loathed it. And it became a target of choice for the Resistance: at least 250 Milice were killed between April 1943 and May 1944; with at least one notable Resistance atrocity on 20 April 1944, when Ernest Jourdan, local Milice chief in Voiron, was murdered along with his bodyguards and his wife and daughter. Far from being a force for the restoration of order, as Pétain had claimed and Darnand fervently wished, the Milice became an agent of chaos and disruption in town and country alike, overruling local Vichy prefects, throwing its weight around, engaging in brutal tit-for-tat feuds with the Resistance, murdering supposed ideological foes, like Maurice Sarraut, moderate pro-Pétain journalist, Jean Zay, former Popular Front Minister of National Education, Victor Basch, octogenarian former president of the Ligue des droits de l'homme – and so on. In January 1944, Darnand instituted courts martial across France, giving the Milice and other security forces the freedom to condemn and execute suspects without due process. The Milice were too few and too poorly armed, too indisciplined and corrupt, to stabilize the domestic situation, but served very well to destabilize and worsen it. Darnand, if anything, embraced this minority status. In the 1-8 January 1944 issue of *Combats*, he wrote 'Do not be afraid of being only the few. In all of history, it is always handfuls of men who have forced destiny.' Furthermore, he used his new authority to place more and more Milice and sympathizers into the remains of the Vichy political and judicial apparatus.

However, his political manoeuvres and influence on propaganda through the support of Philippe Henriot, a Milice member installed as Vichy Secretary of State for Information and Propaganda from January 1944 against Pétain's wishes, were insufficient to expand the membership of the Milice or to give it the lead in major domestic military offensives against the Resistance, such as the siege of the Glières plateau in March 1944.

Pétain, meanwhile, continued to support the Milice by virtue of his regime's emphasis on domestic order. This staple of Vichy propaganda from 1940 onwards was an essential plank of the Marshal's claims to legitimacy, and therefore to a position of leadership in France when it came to the now-almost-inevitable Allied victory. By 1944, Pétain could no longer count on the domestic police and gendarmerie as reliable defenders against the Resistance. Thus, 'it is undoubtedly because he ultimately relied on the GMR and especially on the Milice that in memory the Milice will symbolize this final Vichy, a Vichy that generated civil war.' And as late as 5 June 1944, Pétain was ready to declare that 'I am glad to know that, thanks to the Milice, I have loyal troops just about everywhere in France'.[9]

Following Allied air raids on 20 and 21 April 1944, Marshal Pétain paid a personal visit to Paris on 26 April, for the first time since the Armistice, to pay his respects to the innocent victims of the raids. After participating in a memorial mass at Notre-Dame, he then went to the Hôtel de Ville to address the gathering crowds. Despite their enthusiastic acclaim for the Marshal, they also spontaneously sang *La Marseillaise*, which was banned under the Occupation, and anathema to Vichy's anti-Republican regime. As the Marshal greeted the notables outside Notre-Dame, two limousines raced up, bearing a German contingent including Renthe-Fink and Carl Oberg, SS chief in France, in contravention of Pétain's wishes, accompanied by Brinon. Louis-Dominique Girard, chief of the Marshal's civil cabinet, asked them to leave, citing Pétain's wishes to have no Germans present; Brinon told him to mind his own business. Girard placed the Germans in the transept; Brinon attempted to have Oberg arrest him for insulting the representatives of the Führer. The next evening, Pétain delivered a message to Parisians that pleased the Germans but further alienated him from the populace at large, stating:

French – Do not commit acts likely to attract terrible reprisals against the population by the occupation troops. Dissidence prepares the way for Communism, indiscipline breeds terrorism; both are two aspects of the same scourge. Germany defends Europe. Addressing parents, peasants, veterans, workers, young people, I ask them to remain deaf to the calls of the Resistance.

Pétain's cabinet was horrified; Darnand and the Germans were delighted.

On D-Day, 6 June 1944, Pétain and Laval made another broadcast, with German approval, urging the French population to 'stay at your posts to maintain the life of the Nation, do not aggravate our misfortunes by acts that risk a call for terrible reprisals. Keep calm, France is not at war!' That morning, Pétain made his final formal public appearance at Saint-Étienne, where he was greeted by enthusiastic crowds. Returning to Vichy that evening, he was ordered by the Germans to withdraw to the Château de Lonzat, where a heavy German military presence awaited him – for fear, supposedly, of kidnap attempts by the Resistance or the Allies.

Chapter 4

Liberation and Relocation

Operation Overlord and the D-Day landings brought an end to the ambivalences of collaboration and faced the collaborationists with the stark choice of siding with the occupier or the liberator. For some, the response was immediate, and all too clear. Following the broadcast on D-Day, Laval reinforced the powers of the Milice and urged Darnand to redouble the struggle against the 'red Maquis' and the Resistance.

Under the new German restrictions, Pétain resided from 7 June until 19 August at the Château de Lonzat, commuting to his offices in the Hôtel du Parc to keep up the increasingly empty facade of official duties. Already, he was practically a prisoner of the Germans, his fuel supply rationed on Abetz's orders to restrict his freedom of movement. Periodically, he received German visitors, such as Generalleutnant Alexander Neubronn von Eisenburg, military liaison with the government at Vichy since 1 February 1943 and General Gerd von Rundstedt's representative, who kept him apprised of the military situation in Normandy, assuring him of the certainty of German victory. Notwithstanding, in a message to SOL members dated 14 June 1944, Pétain called for an end to fratricidal bloodshed, and for France to remain neutral in the evolving struggle.

At this time, Laval was developing fantasies that the Germans were allowing the maximum number of Allied troops to land in order to destroy them all in one go; Pétain, with his greater military experience, already estimated that the Germans, with their growing manpower shortages versus the Allied millions, were lost, and that Laval should stick to political matters. Needless to say, Neubronn was also another channel for the Germans to exercise surveillance over the Marshal. Concurrently, Pierre Taittinger, champagne magnate and President of the Paris Municipal Council since 1943, was urging Pétain to return to Paris, on the basis that his presence would prevent other entities (in practice, the Free French forces) from assuming control of the central government, and that his presence as titular head of state was necessary to welcome the Americans.

Déat, in his collaborationist newspaper *L'Œuvre*, published a statement on 8 June 1944 entitled 'I am not neutral', which made it perfectly clear where he stood on the question of French neutrality – as well as aligning himself against Pétain and others who held that the French should stay out of the Allied-Axis fight. He declared:

> I permit myself to affirm that I do not feel at all neutral in this effective non-belligerence to which I am reduced. After four years of a political combat inseparable from military events, I am as little disposed as can be to reabsorb the French situation in an infinitely flat space of two dimensions. If I had to interpret the legal position of my country, in June 'forty four, as some will try to do, I would seek at once the honour of fighting under the banner of the Waffen SS, and would leave my ministerial responsibilities there. The test has only just begun. It will be harsher than one can imagine. The body of France will be protected and her soul reconstituted if the revolutionaries, an essential minority, remain faithful to their oath.

Needless to say, despite his statements and ample opportunity, and unlike some of his comrades in exile, Déat never actually fought under the banner of the Waffen-SS.

As for Céline, his own actions showed how he expected to be treated by the forces of Liberation, no matter how distant he had been from the inner circle of active collaborators. The BBC and *Les Lettres françaises*, the underground Resistance literary journal, had already numbered him among the collaborationist writers. The recurrent, almost obsessive, references in *Castle to Castle* to Article 75 of the Third Republic penal code, which decreed the death penalty for consorting with the enemy, indicate how fixated he was on his likely fate after the Liberation. By 1944, he was receiving death threats. Fearful for his life, he fled Paris on 17 June 1944 with his wife Lucette and his cat, leaving behind in his apartment in the rue Girardon a huge trove of manuscripts and documents which finally resurfaced in 2021.[1] Among his personal effects was a cache of gold pieces and two phials of cyanide. Finding refuge in Baden-Baden, he attempted to obtain visas to flee to Denmark.

The increasingly poisonous atmosphere of the domestic struggle between Resistance and Milice was typified by the assassination in Paris on 28 June 1944 of Philippe Henriot, shot down by Resistance infiltrators in the Ministry of Information. The Milice reprisals that followed included the summary execution of hostages, the assassination of symbolic targets such as Jean Zay and Georges Mandel, and random shooting of passers-by on French city streets. Henriot's death also put the rest of the Milice on notice as to their fate if they continued active collaboration. After the assassination, Radio-Londres broadcast the warning: 'Murderous Milice: shot tomorrow'.

In the face of such warnings, and of likely Axis defeat, some of the most dedicated collaborationists persisted in their initiatives. Henriot's fate might have helped stiffen their resolve – or close the door to alternatives. A 'Déclaration commune sur la situation politique' dated 5 July 1944, with twenty-eight signatories, including Fernand de Brinon, Marcel Déat, Abel Bonnard and Jean Bichelonne on behalf of the government, as well as Jean Luchaire, Jacques Doriot, Guy Crouzet, Lucien Rebatet, Alphonse de Châteaubriant, Admiral Platon, and other luminaries of the openly fascist circle in Paris, called for the formation of a new government able to fight in France alongside the Germans. As cited by Rousso, this stated that the Allied landings in the West and the Russian offensives, together with the food shortages and other disruptions in France:

> ...have created an atmosphere extremely propitious to the anarchy organized on our soil by the Allies.
>
> A certain delay will no doubt ensue before the Germans can carry a decisive battle to the Anglo-Saxons. Between now and then, opinion will strengthen more and more each day that Germany will lose the war... We are on the eve of the great test of strength between the Government – responsible for order – and the "Resistance", applied to popular masses profoundly indoctrinated by the Allied propaganda. The goal of the "Resistance" is less the seizure of power than the annihilation of what

is left of an organized State [and] the entry in line of Communist forces ... weighs very heavily on the ultimate fate of the French community...

The impotence of the public authorities is known to all... the government is fascinated and paralyzed by the hypothesis of the imminent establishment of Anglo-Americans in France. In such a climate, the disintegration of what remains of the French State can only accelerate. We are heading for chaos...

It is this internal anarchy that we must finish with at once. The evil is a political one.

It is born of the absence of a clear definition of the choice of France in the global conflict... The acts which must be accomplished [are]:

The return of the Government to Paris.

The enlargement of the government by the entry of indisputable elements.

... severe sanctions as far as capital penalties for all those whose actions encourage the civil war or compromise France's European position. It is only through this price that France will regain status. It is only through this price that the Reich will recover at its side a France capable of riding the last stretch of the road which leads to victory in Europe.

Admiral Platon delivered the manifesto to Pétain in Vichy on 9 July. The Marshal rejected it, replying 'My friend, you would have done better to stay home.'

Obviously, this was very much a rehash of the similar document of 17 September 1943, backed by the original signatories plus some additional collaborationists. It is remarkable as much for its selfish ambition as for its indifference to military and political realities. Even if the Germans could spare a moment amid the defensive battles against the Allies for the wholesale restructuring of French politics, they would hardly be likely to suddenly reverse the longstanding policy of degrading and sidelining France in favour of trusted partner status within the fast-collapsing shell of the Axis new European order, or even to trust any French units raised by this new government. On the other hand, after the assassination of Philippe Henriot, the signatories probably had few illusions about their ultimate fate if they fell into Allied hands, and literally had their backs against the wall. Most of them eventually faced death or exile.

With little effect on domestic politics, beyond enraging Laval, the declaration did at least clarify the situation for the Germans and helped set in train the policy that led to the creation of the Sigmaringen enclave. Even if Pétain and Laval refused to support the German occupation to the bitter end, there was clearly a faction – or clutch of factions – on the far right of French politics who were ready to. With Pétain and Laval in their hands, and at least some of the Vichy rump government acting on their behalf, the Germans could maintain a fiction of a legitimate collaborationist government, while using it to obstruct attempts to create an alternative government or platform that might sue for peace with the Allies. With the example of Italy, now a full-blown Allied combatant, before their eyes, the Germans doubtless wanted to prevent a similar situation developing in France; in the process, however, they assisted in confirming the legitimacy of de Gaulle and the CFLN against the collaborationists. Under their control, Pétain and what was left of the Vichy central government apparatus could only appear as even more a tool of the German occupier.

The declaration also, briefly, managed to unite Doriot with the other diehard collaborators, at least in terms of a common front. But it did nothing to bring Pétain and his precious cargo of assumed legitimacy on board. It showed little regard for the interests of the French, and little readiness to fight directly for its stated goals. It certainly chronicled the ambitions of its signatories, and it provided the template for the goals and position of the rump that was eventually installed in Sigmaringen. It should come as no surprise that Brinon, essentially a traitor and an agent for the Nazis since the Munich Crisis, betrayed Pétain for them.

As late as July 1944, the Marshal was apparently still engaged in constitutional projects of his own. A constitutional proposal which he commissioned in May and received on 25 June set forth 'a communitaire, hierarchical, regionalist and social State', with a chief of state elected for ten years by representatives of regional collectives and leading national figures. Only municipal and provincial councils were to be elected directly. Pétain signed and approved the draft on 25 July, although at this point he was apparently thinking of subsequent self-justification rather than actual implementation of the proposal. In a document dated 31 July, he wrote:

> This document will be the supreme witness of the grand idea which I have made of my mission. I wish the French to find there the essential of my thoughts and wishes. I hope it will serve them as a guide in the difficult moments which they still have to pass through.

There were even allusions to the kind of monarchical restoration which would have delighted Maurras, 'so that a regime faithful to our history and adapted to our genius, rallies all hearts and cements unity, saves [the French] both from internal servitude and from the influence of foreigners.'[2]

A less than flattering interpretation of this position is that the Marshal, facing the Allied landings, was casting around for any solution or support that might give him some support against de Gaulle and the CFLN.

Also in July 1944, the French police contributed their advice to Laval on his immediate prospects. They recommended an immediate, discreet departure:

> The Head of Government could safeguard his political future, because he would thus very appropriately dissociate himself from personalities whose devotion to the German cause would risk compromising him irremediably... It is very likely that if Mr Laval were to give up power, the German authorities would certainly not allow him to expatriate himself because he is, without a doubt, the man best informed about the underside of Franco–German politics since the Armistice...[3]

Pétain's own communiques, at least to the Germans, showed no particular wish to split from the Axis or to withdraw from his earlier position of cooperation. At least he did show some regard for the French populace afflicted by German atrocities. On 9 July 1944, Pétain addressed the following letter to Hitler:

Vichy, 9 July 1944.

Head of the Great German State,

The French population, as a whole, has given proof of its calm and dignity in the current tragic circumstances. They have responded to the appeal for wisdom that I addressed to them, and they have followed the disciplinary instructions of the head of the government.

The German military authorities have themselves acknowledged this, especially in the combat zone.

In central France, however, there are a few zones of unrest. This unrest is caused by gangs often made up of foreign terrorists. But the population itself, even if it is sometimes forced, under the influence of threats and terror, to deliver food to these armed gangs, remains most often completely uninvolved in actions against the occupying troops.

On too many occasions, the latter have proceeded to reprisals whose scale and sometimes severity have far exceeded the damage caused.

These reprisals have affected an innocent and irresponsible population, who are all the more moved and outraged by this injustice, because they have been used up until now to seeing the members of the German army conduct themselves with great correctness.

The disorderly elements do not hesitate to take advantage of these ruins and despair which cause so much resentment.

There have been many events of this kind in the past weeks. The most serious have been brought to the attention of the German authorities by the head of government. I have appended an account of some of the most significant.

It is my duty to solemnly bring to your attention these reprisals, which I deplore.

Your Excellency will, I am sure, understand the seriousness of the matter and will agree that it is essential, in the current circumstances, that order should reign in France. The repetition of such events can only aggravate the situation and risk seriously compromising the hopes which we, Your Excellency and myself, have placed in the reconciliation of our two peoples.

Please be assured, Head of the Great German State, of my highest regard,

PHILIPPE PÉTAIN.

The list of reprisals appended to this letter included those at Ascq on 2 April 1944, when 120 civilians were shot; the burning of Rouffignac two days later; the hanging of 99 civilians at Tulle on 7 June; the shooting of 37 civilians, including 6 women and 14 children, at Marsoulas 3 days later; and the massacre of some 800 civilians including many children at Oradour-sur-Glane the same day – the last of these was perpetrated chiefly by troops of French origin from Alsace.

The letter and its appendix was presented to von Renthe-Fink, who refused it. Pétain then presented it to the Apostolic Nuncio, Monsignor Valerio Valeri, as a record. On 6 August 1944, he addressed a letter to Darnand, berating him for the various crimes committed by the Milice, including the extrajudicial murders and 'the atmosphere of police terror unknown until now in our country'. Darnand replied tartly:

> For four years, I have received your compliments and your congratulations, and you have encouraged me. And today, because the Americans are at the gates of Paris, you begin to tell me that I am going to be a stain on the history of France. We could have started earlier.[4]

A few of the more technocratic Vichy functionaries continued their duties with the same sublime indifference to the wider context that had led them into collaboration. According to Henry Rousso, in July, Jean Bichelonne was still working almost alone in the Ministry of Industrial Production, preparing a series of lectures for the following month. His chosen topics included 'Professional Organization', 'The Place of Syndicalism in the Economy', 'The Fiscal Regime of Enterprises'.[5]

At this time, Pétain apparently still entertained ideas of returning to Paris, in an attempt to head off de Gaulle's assumption of power. Some of his supporters evidently agreed. In a letter dated 7 August 1944, General Brécard, Chancellor of the Order of the Légion d'Honneur, urged him to return to the capital. 'You would be dishonoured if you voluntarily stayed away from Paris. You have a large number of faithful behind you, your absence would mean that you have no confidence in the cause that you have been defending for four years! You alone can reunite France.'[6]

According to an Antenna 2 radio interview with Count René Aldebert Pineton de Chambrun, Laval's son-in-law and sometime special emissary to the US government, later published in the *Revue des Deux Mondes* of February 1985, Laval arrived in Paris from Vichy on 9 August, seeking to dissuade the Germans from the destruction of Paris, and to enact the plan of reconvening the National Assembly to recall the powers delegated to Pétain in 1940. On the same day, the ordinance of 9 August 1944, issued by the Provisional Government of the French Republic (GPRF) from Algiers, deemed all constitutional acts of the Vichy regime from 10 July 1940 onwards to be unconstitutional and null and void, short-circuiting any attempt to reconvene the National Assembly to enact a handover of power to the GPRF, and declaring the GPRF the legitimate successor of the Third Republic in an unbroken continuity.

According to Chambrun, Laval received Abetz on Friday, 11 August, and said to him:

> You are defeated. You bear terrible responsibilities for everything that has happened in France. You have done us much harm… Since you are leaving, leave us in peace. The path to salvation for France is the reconvening of the National Assembly… I want to go and find President Herriot in Nancy. Only a reconvening of the Assembly will prevent blood from flowing once more, and will at last allow the French to reunite.

Laval's motives for making this proposal did probably include concern for the fate of France, but also may well have demonstrated a wish to bolster his credentials following the now-inevitable Allied victory. They also once again demonstrated his personal ambitions to attempt to pre-empt de Gaulle as the creator of a post-Liberation French government.

The Liberation of France hence marked the end, *de jure* as well as *de facto*, of the Vichy regime. Legitimacy had been a prize hotly disputed between Vichy and the Free French ever since 1940, with other powers such as Great Britain and the United States taking different positions on the issue. For France at least, the GPRF ordinance of 9 August 1944, regarding 'the reestablishment of republican legitimacy on the continental territory', settled the question, declaring 'anything subsequent to the fall on 16 June 1940 of the last legitimate government of the Republic is clearly null and void'. The Axis therefore had to put forward its own position regarding the residue of the Vichy regime and its successor in France.

On 11 August 1944, Pétain authorized Admiral Auphan to approach the Allied high command, and through them de Gaulle, on his behalf. On 12 August, he authorized Gabriel Louis Jaray, a counsellor of state and head of the Franco-American Committee:

> to make contact in my own name with the American diplomatic authorities accredited in Switzerland, to make them aware of the French political problem and to make my intentions known at the time of the liberation of the territory, with a view to safeguarding the principle of legitimacy that I embody.

On 17 August, he sent a letter to Jules Jeanneney, former President of the Senate and a principled dissident under the Vichy regime, declaring himself 'ready to complete the execution of the mandate which was conferred on me in July 1940 and to discuss the problems posed by the completion of the Constitution.'[7]

Did Pétain still believe in the legitimacy of his own regime, breach-birthed into being in July 1940 with so much forcible manipulation, and unconfirmed by any election or plebiscite? Gaston Bruneton, whose account may have been biased by his own peculiar quasi-theological view of the Marshal's mission, gave his interpretation in a statement dated 2 October 1944:

> The Marshal explained to me that in 1940 he had not taken power, he had not ultimately intended to assume a political power, but rather a moral power, estimating that his role was to remake the unity of the French morally, and that once the war was over, and when France was freed, the French could look among themselves to let the French community decide its fate.[8]

The letter and spirit of constitutional law may diverge where decisions were taken under duress. But legitimacy means what it says, and Pétain's actions clearly contravened the founding laws of the Third Republic from the start, let alone the republican and democratic basis of its own legitimacy. Ironically, in addressing his message to the Americans, he was approaching perhaps the sole Allied power, long reluctant to embrace the Gaullists, that might still have accepted that claim.

Amid the continuing manoeuvres within the collaborationist camp, the Germans made their own moves regarding the continuity of the Vichy regime. On 12 August, with Abetz's approval, Laval tried to reconvene the XVIth National Assembly of the Third Republic. As so often with Laval, his motives appear to have been at least partially selfish, born out of fear that Pétain would treat separately with the Allies and throw the blame for Vichy crimes onto him. With the support of Otto Abetz, he had Édouard Herriot, former President of the Chamber of Deputies, released from his internment in an asylum, and brought to Paris. As Herriot temporized, Laval tried and failed to enlist other former government members. Encouraged by Déat and Fernand de Brinon, the Nazis decided instead to deport Laval and the rest of the Vichy government by force, under the pretext of ensuring their safety.

According to Chambrun, late in the afternoon of 16 August 1944, Bussière, the Prefect of Police, who had Déat, Brinon and Darnand under surveillance, informed Laval that they had just left for Germany, after being received a few hours earlier on Avenue Foch by SS General Oberg, Himmler's representative in France. They had presented the Laval-Herriot plan as a betrayal by Laval and had pressed Oberg to immediately telephone Himmler, who was ready to order the arrest of Herriot, and the deportation of Laval and the government.

Déat left an account in his post-war memoirs of a sober and considered departure to the east, with the continuity of the French government assured, and proper arrangements made for the flight of his RNP subordinates and their families. Georges Albertini, his cabinet chief in the Laval administration and secretary-general of the RNP, painted a very different picture. According to Albertini, as recounted by Cointet, Déat was in a state of panic from 7 August onwards, paralyzed by indecision, making no provisions for the other RNP members, seeking only to save himself and his family. In the event, Déat left early in the morning of 17 August with his family, leading a small convoy of subordinate functionaries and Milice. Those other members of the RNP who decided to follow him had to make their own way east.

Laval was instructed by the Germans on 17 August 1944 to decamp from Paris to Belfort, the provisional domicile of the Vichy government-in-exile. Pétain in Vichy received the same instructions. Abetz had orders to remove them both by force if necessary. The Germans freely used Laval's name with Pétain and vice versa, in order to convince them to move, although both were cognisant of the real situation. Laval and his rump cabinet refused to cooperate, and were removed from the capital under duress. With Laval and his wife went Jean Bichelonne, Vichy Minister of Industrial Production, Maurice Gabolde, Minister of Justice, Paul Marion, Secretary of State, and Pierre Mathé, Commissioner General for Agriculture and Nutrition.

Once at Nancy the next day, Laval composed the following letter to Jean Faure, the Regional Prefect:

Nancy, 18 August 1944.
To Mr Jean Faure,
Regional Prefect.
I have had to leave Paris under German compulsion.

In view of these events, and the fact that I may not be able tomorrow to give you my instructions, I have made it my duty today to tell you what your mission is.

You should refer to my circular of 5 April 1944 and consider yourself the holder, for your region, of all governmental prerogatives, and act accordingly.

I know you, I know your dedication and your passionate love for France. You have been given the opportunity, in this crucial hour, to serve her. You will do so with the dignity of your character and the grandeur that your mission demands.

With you, with all our hearts, for Lorraine and for France.

Pierre Laval.

More or less simultaneously, another more voluntary exodus was taking place in Paris. The Parisian collaborationists grouped around Jacques Doriot and his PPF evacuated the city under Doriot's orders – well before the Liberation of Paris, with the Allies still reducing the Falaise Pocket. On the night of 16-17 August, Victor Barthélemy, acting under Doriot's orders, assembled a convoy of vehicles to evacuate as many as possible of the party elite, including writers and media figures such as Lucien Rebatet and Jean Hérold-Paquis, to Nancy, historic capital of Lorraine and fallback position for the retreating German forces. The drive to Nancy passed without incident, but according to Hérold-Paquis' account, Rebatet's wife Véronique moaned the whole way, 'Lucien! I've had enough of this French Popular Party caravan!'

Temporarily ensconced in Nancy, the collaborationist elite started to play out a kind of dress rehearsal for the political parlour games they would continue in Sigmaringen. Hérold-Paquis recorded the scene in his post-war memoirs, written shortly before his execution:

> As for politics, it was everywhere. It was the sole sovereign of the kingdom of Picrochole [the ludicrous tyrant in Rabelais's *Gargantua and Pantagruel*] and the mistress of all the partisans assembled in Nancy. It gave life to these men – and women – who, upon discovering Lorraine, spoke of the "last square", and drew from this soil of the eastern marches a new patriotism, this time with their eyes turned towards an imaginary blue line to the west. It gave life to this diminished world, while the healthy air of Lorraine vexed their brains as surely as the local grey wines and the mirabelle plums... They recreated the antechambers of ministries. And others, keen on commands and uniforms, gave themselves the illusion of barracks... De Brinon held press conferences for journalists without newspapers. The Ambassador complacently laid out his plans, spoke of convincing the Marshal, threw Laval a last armful of thorns, and ran to the telephone to assemble the pawns of a genuine game... of chess. Darnand was in Belfort, "on operations", according to the popular rumour. Déat was a neighbour. And politics was also in this manor house where he was waiting for news of Madame, who had disappeared between Paris and Nancy. Milice

[from the RNP] stood an austere guard before the steps. The park was pleasant, but narrow. The room where Marcel Déat received had a Moroccan theme. I remembered, in spite of myself, Lyautey's salon. [Hubert Lyautey, former general, colonial governor, and eventually pro-fascist.] I preferred not to make the difference. Déat was still ferociously hunting the heads of "Lavalians". But one could tell that he was disappointed, worried. His very solitude singled him out for comment. The entourage of the leader of the RNP was dreadfully reduced. A few women, a few men: it was all that remained of a party that had had its day. Politics had entered the small convent (behind the cathedral) where the PPF set up its services and housed its militants who arrived every day in greater numbers from Paris, from the west, the centre, even the south. Victor Barthélémy gave orders, "contacted" the Germans, who promised and forgot, received entire families, entire convoys, and found a way to feed everybody and bed them down. I do not wish to sing the praises of the PPF, to which I belonged. But I must say that in those final hours it was the only movement that retained a force, a cohesion, an authority and a leader.[9]

After a few days' delay in Nancy, the PPF refugees received instructions from Abetz that they would be installed in Baden-Baden. They boarded a train for Germany on 28 August. Within a week, the town was under assault by the US Third Army in the opening phases of the Battle of Nancy. Confined in one carriage in a train of a dozen wagons, the PPF elite waited for departure, according to Hérold-Paquis, while the Germans struggled to find an engine for the train. A full moon lit up the station, terrifying Rebatet with the prospect of Allied bombing: 'Oh God! … It's too much to be blown into the fucking air in this damn station!'

The train crawled out of the station at around 1.30 am. Some four hours later, it screeched to a halt. Amid the shower of luggage, Rebatet panicked:

'Look, they're shooting at us! They're mowing us down!'
'Shut the fuck up. It's Algarron lighting a cigarette.'
'Oh! You think so? You think so? Fine… ah… fine…'

The train had stopped barely 15 kilometres from Nancy. It stayed there in the middle of the countryside before resuming its slow crawl around midday. The journey continued in relative tranquillity – barring the incessant complaints of Rebatet's wife:

> 'Lucien, if you hadn't got involved in politics, we wouldn't be here! Lucien, why didn't you stick to literature...?'
> 'Véronique, you're being a pain...'

The train finally pulled into Metz in the early evening, only to be ordered to depart at once: fearful of an imminent Allied advance, the Germans had ordered a full evacuation. The train resumed its slow crawl and by 3.00 pm had reached Bernsdorf. US planes overflew the station an hour later, triggering general panic. The train's passengers scattered into the fields. Rebatet, throwing himself on his stomach in the grass, pulling up stalks and covering his head to camouflage himself from the Allied planes. An hour later, following the all-clear, everyone boarded the train once more – then came one final interruption from Rebatet:

> 'Look out! There's more coming! A whole pack of them!'
> 'Calm down, Rebatet. It's a flock of birds.'
> 'You think so...?'

This was the same Rebatet who had proclaimed exactly one month before, in the 28 July 1944 issue of *Je suis partout*, his undying fidelity to National Socialism, declaring:

> I admire Hitler. We admire Hitler, and we have very serious reasons for doing so. In the struggle against all the outdated drivel of the 19th century, Hitler had countless predecessors, analysts, dialecticians who were far more brilliant and agile than he. But it was he who really put the immense current of anti-democratic ideas into action. It is he who will bear before history the honour of having liquidated democracy.

It hardly needs saying that he did not have the courage of his convictions.

Rebatet's behaviour, like that of Céline, fits Pierre Milza's acid characterization of the intellectuals of collaborationism:

As aggressive as they were in the manipulation of words and threats, the journalists and writers of collaborationism remained, barring a few rare exceptions, paper warriors. They sat on the committee of honour of the Antibolshevik Legion like Luchaire, they demanded like Rebatet to "go to the Russian front", but just to visit the rear (as they had already done in the war in Spain), they could even "play cops and robbers in the night with real guns", as Cousteau had done in Brittany, in the tracks of a group of Milice: the call for heroic service was by and large destined for others.[10]

Two days later, they finally arrived in Baden-Baden, Céline's first port of call after his flight from Paris.

Once installed at Belfort, Laval gave his complete account of events for Pétain. Given the nature of the events, and the consistency of his subsequent actions, he probably did not do too much to exonerate himself in his account.

Department of Belfort. Belfort, 19 August 1944
Office of the Prefect.
Marshal,

I have just had a visit from Counsellor Hoffmann who shared with me a communication from his colleagues Mr Struwe and Mr von Renthe-Fink.

I thus have a chance to let you know the reasons why I am in Belfort with a certain number of ministers.

On Thursday, 17 August, around midday, Ambassador Abetz informed me of his government's desire to see the seat of the French government transferred from Vichy to Belfort. He added that I would have to leave the same evening with all the ministers, and indicated that a similar invitation would be made to you.

That afternoon, Mr Abetz gave me a letter which reads as follows:

'Mr President

In view of the fact that Paris and Vichy may be affected at any moment by internal or external events due to the war, the German government wishes me to inform you that to preserve order in the regions of France not affected by the operations, it considers it necessary that the French government should move its seat from Vichy to Belfort.

I know that, as head of government, you have made the decision to remain, come what may, in the midst of the population of the capital and I have informed my government of your decision.

The German government, which certainly understands the national significance and personal importance of your decision, feels obliged nonetheless, given the reasons set out above, not to reconsider its position.

It goes without saying that it would never be a question of inviting the French government to quit the national territory, and that, as soon as the dangers mentioned in this letter have dissipated, the German government would be completely disinterested in any subsequent decision regarding the seat of the French government.

I have asked the commander-in-chief of German forces in France to give his approval for the First French Regiment to march towards Belfort.

This approval has just been given. If you so wish, I would like to ask you to give the orders.

Please be assured, Mr President, of my best regards,

Signed: ABETZ'

I convened, at 18.30, a Ministerial Council, and following this meeting, I gave the following response:

'Mr Ambassador,

I acknowledge receipt of your letter, which I have conveyed to the Council of Ministers.

The French government does not agree to transfer its seat from Vichy to Belfort, whatever the reasons you cite.

Under these conditions, and after having conferred with them, I believe, along with all the ministers present, that they cannot respond to the invitation that you have extended to them.

Please be assured, Mr Ambassador, of my best regards.

Signed: LAVAL.'

Mr Abetz told me that he could only confirm the decision of the German government. I told him that, if I was not physically forced, I would refuse to leave Paris.

He then sent me this last letter:

'Mr President,

The communication which I had the honour of making to you this afternoon concerning the transfer of the members of the French government to Belfort represents an irrevocable decision of the government of the Reich. I therefore regret to have to respond to the protest of the French government received this evening, that in the case of a refusal, the application of means of coercion will become inevitable.

Most Honoured Mr President, you yourself and the members of your government will see in this German decision not only the expression of concern to maintain peace and order in the rear of the German army, but also the legitimate concern to ensure the personal safety of the French government.

Do accept, Mr President, my sincerest consideration.

Signed: ABETZ.'

And here is my response:

'Mr Ambassador,

In response to your letter, I regret to ascertain that the German government would not hesitate to use coercive measures to ensure the transfer of the French government to Belfort.

You are good enough to tell me of your concern to ensure the personal safety of the French government; but let me tell you that my concern was higher: I wanted to fulfill to the bitter end, whatever the risk, my duty as head of government.

So I must bow out.

But you understand that, under these conditions, I cease to exercise my functions.

Please accept, Mr Ambassador, my sincerest consideration.'

It was under these conditions that I had to leave Paris. I had previously informed the prefects of the Seine and the Police, as well as the presidents of the Municipal Council and the Departmental Council, of the situation. In their presence, Mr Abetz, came to pick me up at the Hôtel Matignon, which I left with my wife, at around 11 pm, bound towards Belfort, accompanied by Councillor Hoffmann.

Mr Abetz will be joining us shortly.

I did not telephone you because the line had been cut and I did not send a messenger, on the understanding that you had been alerted at the same time as me.

Present at Belfort: Messrs Gabolde, Bichelonne, Marion, Bonnard, Darnand and Mathé. Messrs de Brinon and Déat had left Nancy prior to my notification and are now in Nancy. Messrs Cathala, Grasset and Chasseigne have not yet reached Belfort.

Before leaving Paris, I gave Mr Bouffet, Prefect of the Seine, and Mr Bussière, Prefect of Police, the following instructions:

'I have made it clear on many occasions my wish to remain in the midst of the Parisian population, come what may.

The government has been physically compelled by the German government to leave Paris, and the very firm protests I made to the German ambassador had no effect.

I am therefore instructing the Prefect of the Seine and the Prefect of Police, each in what concerns him, to take all necessary measures to ensure public order, supplies, transport and, in general, to deal with all matters concerning the material life and morale of the people of Paris.

I also give you the task of receiving the Allied military authorities and representing the French government to them.

You will be assisted in your task by the President of the Paris Municipal Council, the President of the Departmental Council of the Seine, and their colleagues, whose support, I am convinced, will not fail you in these dark hours.

The loyalty, dedication and patriotism that you have consistently demonstrated since assuming your high offices make me certain that you will carry out these difficult missions with the dignity that the circumstances demand.'

I sent to Mr Taittinger and Mr Victor Constant the following letter:

'I have been forced by the German government to quit Paris and I wish, before terminating my duties, to perform one last act. A few days ago, I expressed to you the comfort I felt, in these dark hours, to be in Paris.

I felt it was my duty to share its perils and join it in its fate.

As head of government, I certainly owed it to all the people of France, but I owed it most of all to the capital.

I cannot forget that I was deputy, and then senator, for the Seine. I am still Mayor of Aubervilliers and President of the Union of Mayors of that department. So I owe a special debt of gratitude to those who, having put their hands in mine, have never withdrawn them.

To those who have placed their trust in me for so long, please be assured that, as history unfolds, my role and my love for France will be better understood.

I ask you, at this tragic moment, to use your authority to support those to whom I have confided the destiny of Paris, Prefects René Bouffet and Amédée Bussière, with whom you have always worked as a team.

Your legitimate influence on the population will allow you, I am sure, to better ensure the continuation of Parisian life.

A day will come when a peaceful France will no longer be plagued by summary judgements and unjust hatred.

In the meantime, work with your Assemblies and all men of goodwill to bring together all the French people, as is so necessary.'

I believe, Marshal, that I have thus informed you of the events that I have just experienced, and I regret not having been able to do so earlier. I am giving this letter to Councillor Hoffmann, who will be sending it to you by air.

Please be assured, Marshal, of my deepest respects.

Pierre Laval

Pétain composed the following letter before his involuntary departure, intended for Laval but destined never to reach its destination.

Vichy, 17 August 1944
20 h 00.

Mr President,

I have just received the visit of Mr de Renthe-Fink who came to inform me orally that the German government has given its assent to a convocation of the National Assembly.

Due to military developments, the National Assembly cannot be convened at Versailles and Mr de Renthe-Fink informed me that it would be convened at Nancy, where President Herriot currently is. Mr de Renthe-Fink calculates that Vichy is not secure and he has asked me to move to a town in the East which could eventually become the seat of government, but he did not specify the name of this town. He told me that you would have left Paris yourself. Your departure under such conditions did not seem to correspond to the arrangements that you told me about before leaving Vichy, and that you confirmed yesterday morning by telephone, arrangements according to which the seat of government could not be in your view anywhere else besides Vichy or Paris.

I answered that I could not make a decision without contacting you.

An officer of my military cabinet will bring you this letter. I would ask you to give him your handwritten reply, which will let me know your position. Only on the return of this officer will I make decisions that seem to me to be in the national interest

Please accept, my dear President, the assurances of my highest consideration.

Philippe Pétain

Renthe-Fink wrote a final written ultimatum to the Marshal, on Hitler's orders:

Marshal,

In the name of my government, I have the honour to inform you of the following:

Due to the military developments of the last few days, there is a risk that Vichy will be cut off from the northern half of France. In addition, the news received by the German authorities gives rise to the gravest fears that Vichy will be encircled by major Resistance forces.

The Head of State himself has stressed, on several occasions over the past few days, this looming threat. The person of the Head of State, in these circumstances, is in great danger in Vichy.

The Government of the Reich has therefore given its consent to the transfer of the residence of the Head of State to the Northern Zone, in accordance with the wish it previously expressed.

President Laval and the members of the government are already in Belfort, the new provisional seat of the government. The Government of the Reich gives its solemn undertaking that the head of the French state will remain, under all circumstances, on French soil. The Government of the Reich further assures that the French Head of State and the French government will be able to return to Vichy as soon as the situation is safe enough to permit this. During the stay of the Head of State and the government in the Northern Zone, the Government of the Reich concedes the same conditions as in Vichy. The Government of the Reich has also agreed to the transfer of the residence of the diplomatic corps to the new provisional headquarters of the French government.

Since the declaration made to the Head of State in the name of the Government of the Reich, the situation has deteriorated still further; it is so much so at present that, from the German side, it is no longer possible to take the responsibility of letting the Head of the French State stay any longer in Vichy.

In consequence, the government of the Reich gives the instruction to execute the transfer of the residence of the French Head of State, even against his will.

Please be assured, Marshal, of my highest regards.

Renthe-Fink

Almost immediately afterwards, Renthe-Fink sent another letter to Pétain:

Vichy, 19 August 1944.
Marshal,

Following my letter of today's date, I have the honour to inform you, on behalf of my government, that, in view of the situation, departure is scheduled for this evening.

I understand that Madam Marshal plans to accompany you.

I would like to propose that the members of the French government who have remained here, notably the Secretary

General of the Ministry of Foreign Affairs, Ambassador Rochat, the Secretary of State for Defence, General Bridoux, and the Secretary of State for the Navy, Admiral Bléhaut, should accompany the French Head of State.

In addition, I would like to express the wish that General Debeney and Dr Ménétrel should also take part in the trip.

The designation of other persons who will accompany or follow the Head of the French State to Belfort will remain subject to agreement between the competent authorities.

The settlement of all other matters will also remain subject to mutual understanding.

Please be assured, Marshal, of my highest regards.

Renthe-Fink

Pétain received this message at about 7.00 pm. At around 7.50, Commander Féat of the Marshal's civil cabinet reported the true circumstances to the Marshal – that Laval and his ministerial colleagues had been transported to Belfort under duress, regardless of any question of reconvening the National Assembly. According to records, the Marshal confronted Renthe-Fink and declared, 'You are a liar!' After this, despite Renthe-Fink's vehement protests, he received the Apostolic Nuncio, Monsignor Valerio Valeri, and the Swiss Minister, Mr Stucki, and presented them with his written statements on the forced relocation.

Vichy, 19 August 1944.

Nuncio,

I have the honour to bring to Your Excellency's attention the following:

On Sunday 6 August 1944, President Laval asked me to come to his house at once. In the presence of Ambassador Rochat, Secretary General of the Ministry of Foreign Affairs, he told me:

I have learned that the Occupying Power intends, given the development of the military situation, to place the head of state as well as the head of government 'in security'.

You know the declaration that the head of state presented to the Dean of the Diplomatic Corps, HE Apostolic Nuncio, regarding a possible departure from Vichy.

As for me, I wish to declare to you, in the most categorical terms, that I will never, under any circumstances, assume the functions of head of government anywhere but in Vichy or Paris. I will not do so in Nancy, nor in any other city in the East, much less outside France.

If one day it is said that Mr Laval is exercising the functions of head of government in another city than Paris or Vichy, you can be sure that this does not correspond to the truth. I will then be nothing more than a private prisoner, without any official function.

On the morning of 18 August 1944, Francis Bout de l'An, Secretary-General of the Milice, arrived in Vichy, fresh from orchestrating a series of massacres of Jews and partisans at Saint-Amand-Montrond in central France. Darnard had ordered him to organize the evacuation of Milice members and their families to Germany. He conveyed Darnand's instructions to each regional Milice commander, to withdraw their units to rendezvous points and proceed eastwards towards Germany. The regional Milice groups were ordered to assemble at Bordeaux, Poitiers, Toulouse, Montpellier, Marseille, Dijon, Lyon, Limoges, Clermont-Ferrand, Vichy, Lille, Paris and Reims, to evacuate France via Nancy and Belfort. The actual evacuations were poorly organized convoys, usually short of fuel, with some unable to find their way or force passage against Resistance opposition. One of the better organized convoys, arranged by Jean de Vaugelas, Milice commander for Marseille and later for Limoges, consisted of some ninety-five vehicles. Under recurrent Maquis attacks for much of their journey, they suffered their worst assault at Saint-Sulpice-Laurière, barely 20km northeast of Limoges, where they lost three men killed and ten wounded, and were only able to extricate themselves after calling for German assistance. In the face of continuing Resistance harassment, the convoy was only able to cover some 80km in seven days. Nationally, some 6,000 Miliciens and 4,000 family members may have been involved. From Belfort they were conveyed to Mulhouse, then Struthof, finally arriving by train at Ulm on 22 September 1944.

En route, the Milice units forced various contributions from banks that collectively formed the legendary 'treasure of the Milice', wartime France's equivalent to Yamashita's Gold, the mythical horde of bullion supposedly looted from South-East Asia by Japanese general Tomoyuki Yamashita during the Pacific campaign. At Guéret in central France, having looted the local wine cellars the day before, a Milice delegation presented itself at the local branch of the Bank of France on 24 August 1944, demanding funds. They presented a requisition order for 10 million francs. The director of the bank branch responded that such a requisition should not be directed to the Bank of France, but to the Treasury. The Milice unit then forced the bank to hand over the funds, as the director recorded afterwards, giving a receipt in return, with an illegible signature. Looting fuel, food and goods at almost every stopping point along their way, the Milice repeated their spoilation of the local office of the Bank of France at Belfort, as they were about to leave French territory. On 6 September, a Milice detachment led by Bout de l'An presented a requisition order for 533 million francs, signed by Darnand, to the Belfort branch: informed that there were not sufficient funds in the bank, and that any requisition should also be signed by the Minister of Finance, they carried off some 300 million francs, as well as some gold coins. They also engaged in various atrocities, executing prisoners in their cells and general terrorizing local populations: at Saint-Michel-de-Maurienne in Savoy, a Resistance ambush of a column of fleeing refugees and German escorts provoked a massacre of twenty-five victims; at Marigny, in Haute-Savoie, Vaugelas' column mutilated and killed six Maquis who had been involved in an ambush.

The Germans duly proceeded with the forcible 'evacuation' of Pétain. The Apostolic Nuncio, Monsignor Valerio Valeri, and the Swiss Ambassador, Walter Stucki, were present when von Renthe-Fink and Generalleutnant Neubronn returned to the Hôtel du Parc at 10.30 pm on 19 August 1944. The Marshal insisted that von Renthe-Fink should repeat his ultimatum in their presence. He did so, adding that the deadline would expire the next morning, Sunday, 20 August, at 7.00 am, hinting that if the Marshal did not comply he risked an artillery and aerial bombardment of the city and the execution of 500 hostages.

Pétain continued to work in his office until the early morning. A crowd had assembled overnight around the Hôtel du Parc. At 6.45 am on Sunday morning, a cordon of German troops took up positions around the hotel. Pétain's guards withdrew into the Hôtel du Parc and closed the door at the arrival of Captain Detering, deputy head of the Gestapo in the Southern Zone. When Detering's request to open the door was refused, SS troops forced an entry with hammers and tongs. Pétain's guards, following the Marshal's orders, offered no resistance. Observed by the Apostolic Nuncio and the ambassador, the SS then broke down two interior grilles and made their way to the second floor and the entrance to Pétain's chambers, where they were confronted by Colonel Barré, head of his personal guard, and three guards. When asked for admission, Colonel Barré replied, 'The Marshal is resting.'

The SS called Generalleutnant Neubronn, who made the same request, and Barré gave the same reply. The SS troops then forced open the door to Pétain's chambers and at around 7.15 am broke into his bedroom. Pétain repeated his formal protest in the presence of the diplomats, then left his chambers, in civilian dress, and went downstairs in the elevator. The assembled crowd cheered him, and his guards presented arms.

Pétain left behind him two documents, inscribed in the hand of his physician, Dr Ménétrel, 'Discourse in case of forced departure'. The Marshal had almost certainly composed these overnight. Both were dated 20 August 1944.

The first, a general address to the French population, read as follows:

Frenchmen,
By the time this message reaches you, I shall no longer be free.

In the extremity to which I am reduced, I have nothing to reveal to you that is not the simple confirmation of all that, up till now, has dictated my conduct.

For more than four years, resolved to stay in your midst, I have, every day, sought what was best suited to serve the permanent interests of France. Fairly, but without compromise, I had only one goal: to protect you from the worst. And everything that was done by me, everything that I did not consent to, suffered, whether willingly or by force, was only for your protection, because if I could no longer be your sword, I wanted to be your shield.

At times, my words and my deeds may have surprised you. Know then that they did me more hurt than you could have felt yourselves. I suffered for you, with you. But I never ceased to stand, with all my strength, against that which threatened you. I kept certain dangers from you; there were some, alas, which I was unable to save you from. My conscience bears witness that no one, no matter what camp he belongs to, would be able to contradict me on this.

What our adversaries wish today is to take me away from you.

I do not have to justify myself to them; I care only for the French.

So, once more, I implore you to unite. It is not difficult to do one's duty, even if it is sometimes hard to know it. Yours is simple: to group yourselves around those who will give you the guarantee to lead you on the path of honour in the ways of order.

Order must reign, because I represent it legitimately; I am and remain your leader. Obey me, and obey those who will bring you words of social peace, without which no order can be established.

Those who will bring you a language fitted to lead you towards reconciliation, the renovation of France, through mutual forgiveness of slights and the love of all our people, those are the leaders of France. They will continue my work and follow my disciplines. Stand with them.

As for myself, I am parted from you, but I do not leave you, and I have everything to hope from you and your devotion to France, which you will, with the help of God, restore to greatness. It is the moment when destiny takes me away. I submit to the greatest constraint that a man can be made to suffer. I accept it with joy if it is the condition of our salvation, if, before the foreigner, even if he is an ally, you know how to be faithful to true patriotism, to those who think only of the interest of France, and if my sacrifice helps you retrieve the way to the Sacred Union for the rebirth of the Fatherland.

Philippe Pétain

Despite its mode of address to the French public at large, the message was never broadcast, and its distribution was very limited. It goes without saying that the Marshal composed this document with an eye to self-justification, even self-exculpation, and it formed part of his defence in his post-war trial. The talk of 'what camp' references the judgments he had already received from the Free French and was expecting from other quarters after the war. His continuing insistence on his incarnation of legitimacy and his role as France's leader begs multiple questions that had been open since 1940, for all his assertions. His role as France's shield, however sincerely assumed, never entitled him to be her dictator, let alone the persecutor of her Jewish, Masonic and other citizens. And his pose of martyrdom sits ill alongside the fate already endured by the various victims of the Milice and the Germans, let alone the relative comfort which he was to endure in Sigmaringen. And talk of 'the path of honour' from the man who had led France down the path of collaboration and dishonour invites contempt.

That said, there are less damning passages of the statement that bear remarking on. The phraseology of the Sacred Union borrows the terminology of the First World War, when France's labour movement and left wing agreed not to disrupt the war effort or call any strikes. Catholic right-wing interests smarting from the Third Republic's anti-clerical policies could also claim to be participants in the Union; Germany had a similar pact during the war, in its so-called *Burgfriedenspolitik*. Such terminology speaks of the longing for reconciliation of the bitter social divisions that had plagued France in the inter-war period – although as demonstrated earlier, much of the bitterness seems to have been on the Right. The talk of peace and order mirrors the concerns of the Free French to restore Republican legitimacy in French territory, for fear of internecine bloodletting, or the kind of full-scale civil war that Greece descended into in 1946.

Pétain also addressed a short message to Hitler:

In concluding the armistice of 1940 with Germany, I manifested my irrevocable decision to join my fate to that of my country and to never leave its territory.

I was therefore able, with faithful adherence to conventions, to defend the interests of France.

On 16 July, in the face of persistent rumours concerning certain German intentions with regard to the French government and myself, I was moved to confirm my position to the Diplomatic Corps in the person of its dean, his Excellency the Apostolic Nuncio, specifying that I would oppose with all the means in my power a forced departure to the east. Your representatives provided me with arguments contrary to the truth to make me decide to leave Vichy.

Today they wish to force me, through violence and in defiance of all engagements, to depart for an unknown destination.

I raise a solemn protest against this act of force which makes it impossible for me to exercise my prerogatives as French Head of State.

Philippe Pétain[11]

On 21 August, Pétain arrived at Belfort in old Alsace, whose gigantic Lion of Belfort statue commemorates its dogged resistance to German forces during the Franco-Prussian War. He was greeted by an enthusiastic crowd outside the town hall and met with Laval at the prefecture. He was then installed in the Château de Morvillars, a nineteenth-century pile built by a local industrialist, about 10km south of Belfort. Both Pétain and Laval declined to cooperate with their supposed rescuers: without their participation, the collaborationist initiative passed to others.

There is little question of how the situation looked to neutral observers. Over the border in Switzerland, the 23 August edition of *Feuille d'avis de Neuchatel* bore the headline 'Marshal Pétain and Mr Laval have been arrested by the Germans', adding 'The Vichy government has now ceased to exist'. Whatever the question marks over the legitimacy of the Marshal's position in the Vichy regime, outsiders had no illusions about the continuity of that state without him. A letter dated 28 August 1944 from the Chief of the Foreign Affairs Division of the Political Department of the Swiss Federal Government, Pierre Bonna, to the Swiss ambassador in Berlin, Hans Frölicher, stated that, in the light of Pétain and Laval's declarations that they could not continue their official functions under duress, 'these documents do not allow us to retain any illusion about the fiction whereby there would still be a French government at Belfort with which diplomatic relations could usefully be conducted'.[12]

From 23 August, Brinon negotiated with Joachim von Ribbentrop, the Third Reich's Foreign Minister, in the village of Steinhort in East Prussia, near Hitler's Wolf's Lair – in an atmosphere of anger, suspicion and surveillance, according to later statements from some of the participants. The Third Reich Foreign Ministry kept complete records of the negotiations between Ribbentrop and Brinon, as well as between Ribbentrop, Abetz and von Renthe-Fink and Brinon, Darnand, Déat and Marion on 31 August, and between Hitler and the five French participants on 1 September. The German position, as stated in the records and articulated between Ribbentrop and Brinon on 31 August, was that it was absolutely essential to give Doriot a chance to participate in any continuing French government, while retaining the legality represented by Pétain – even though that legality was now far more tenuous following the Marshal's own public statements and the non-participation of his subordinates. As an interim solution, Brinon could continue to manage the ordinary details of government with the help of any willing members of Laval's cabinet, while supporting and facilitating the eventual formation of a government led by Doriot. The German Foreign Ministry estimated that Doriot was the only figure able to lead a French national political and military effort against the Resistance and de Gaulle. Their evaluation was that only he was able to develop suitably revolutionary tactics against the Free French while also heading an effective nationwide propaganda campaign. Doriot had a public profile, a position at the head of a party of faithful followers, oratorical gifts, and the courage and persistence needed to lead a campaign of French 'national' resistance on territory still occupied by the Germans, and ideally in liberated territories as well, against de Gaulle and his Communist allies. Brinon, Darnand and the others would be given positions in a Doriot government, so long as the Marshal's cooperation could be secured. Abetz's negative assessment of Doriot was dismissed, and in any event, the Ministry advocated pursuing this strategy for want of a better.

Brinon countered the German plan by pointing out that it would be impossible to persuade Pétain to endorse a Doriot government, in view of the current military situation and the anti-German hostility across France. Ribbentrop observed that, in that case, it might be necessary to eliminate the Marshal. Brinon, however, maintained that Pétain might be brought round to endorsing a Doriot government if it was presented to him in the most reasonable terms, given a more favourable military situation and greater resentment by the Marshal against de Gaulle. Laval, meanwhile, should be kept from interfering, and had no more effective authority. In any event, there was no way to circumvent the Marshal as a totem of legality while his personal prestige in France remained so strong. Only a few hundred of Doriot's faithful remained on French territory still occupied by the Germans, and he had never managed to attract many elsewhere in France. Whatever the Reich's hopes and dreams, Doriot would never be able to attain power without the Marshal.

Ribbentrop persisted in supporting Doriot, warning that if the Marshal could not be brought onside, then he and Laval would be completely isolated in Germany, while France would be put under a purely military German administration, with Doriot left to form a regime according to his own preferences. Brinon's final proposal was that he would manage an interim administration with a delegation of French officials, while attempting to obtain, within a given deadline, the Marshal's endorsement of a Doriot government. He also confirmed that he and other figures in the Vichy administration would take part in a government under Doriot. Brinon also undertook to obtain from the Marshal authorization for his new duties within forty-eight hours.

How realistic was the German position? Whatever Pétain's known antipathy for Doriot, the real problem remained the strength of French popular hostility to the German occupiers, and the military and political success of de Gaulle and the Allies. Events on the battlefield were reducing the scope for any kind of collaborationist government by the day. The atrocities perpetrated by retreating German forces and the Milice had already managed to blacken the whole thesis of collaboration even further. Doriot's movement lacked anything like a basis of true popular support, no matter how congenial he was personally to the Nazis. And any attempt to eliminate the Marshal would have been a disaster for the Axis – which did not prevent the Germans from considering it.

Brinon, meanwhile, found it necessary to demand that Doriot extend his support for the delegation and abstain from any activity or attack against it – a measure of the level of conflict and mutual suspicion within the collaborationist camp. Ribbentrop assured him that with the help of his own liaison officers, he would assure a 'loyal collaboration' between the delegation and Doriot.The Germans wanted a government of a 'national France' to set up against de Gaulle's supposed 'Bolshevik France'. Brinon appeared to be next in line of succession to Pétain and Laval in the Vichy structure, but other leading ultras – Déat in Nancy and Jacques Doriot in Neustadt an der Weinstraße – were already trying to position themselves as heads of new regimes more closely aligned with Nazi Germany. Ribbentrop maintained the position that events on the battlefield might eventually lead the Marshal to collaborate, insisting that the mobilization of men, women and materiel in Germany, combined with new weapons, could stabilize the military situation and eventually reconquer France; while the presence of Communists within de Gaulle's administration might also eventually drive the Marshal closer to Doriot.

On 25 August, Brinon refused an invitation from Hitler to attend him in the Wolf's Lair, sending Paul Marion, Pétain's former secretary of state, instead. The German garrison in Paris formally surrendered the same day, and Charles de Gaulle made his famous speech from the Hôtel de Ville.

Ribbentrop declared on 28 August, before Déat and Marion, that 'the legality of Petain or Laval, for Franco-German collaboration, can only be a sham legality and not a true legality'. His French collaborators exhibited few signs of dissent:

Déat: Petain is an old man, he suffers from loss of memory, so one can take advantage of him by making him sign the necessary documents and deliver the speeches that we have need of.

Marion: Any government placing itself beyond legality will perforce be considered as a clique of traitors, only living by the money of the Germans and sustained by their bayonets. That is why it is necessary to wrench legality from the Marshal, by whatever means.

The Nazi agenda, as defined by Hitler and Ribbentrop, was to replace Laval's government with a new 'national-revolutionary' entity, ideally led by Doriot, but with Pétain's sanction. Brinon was required to secure this by obtaining Pétain's agreement and overseeing the transition process. This was on the understanding that, if Pétain refused to comply, the Reich would seek other measures.

On 1 September, the five French negotiators, together with Doriot, were received by Hitler in his bunker. As recorded by the German interpreter, Hitler spoke of the Bolshevik advance as a wave which, 'in conformity with the laws of nature', would weaken as it covered more ground. He spoke of the Generals' Plot of 20 July as the opportunity for 'a process of purification'. Maintaining that a conflict between the peoples of France and Germany was 'pure folly', he insisted that the current war had been provoked by 'the Anglo-Saxon plotters and global Jewry'. Regarding the government of France, he professed that a 'truly national' government would accede to power. 'This government, despite a revolutionary programme imposed by the moment, would take into account the points of view of nationality, population and race, without which one cannot conceive of Europe and her culture.'

Brinon declared in response:

It was a great satisfaction for me, and for those French who accompany me, to salute the Führer and assure him that many of our compatriots approve and understand his work, as they follow with great admiration his efforts for the defence of Europe. In order to implement the plan worked out with von Ribbentrop, he emphasized the necessity of securing that Marshal Pétain retract the declarations which others inspired him to make, profiting from his age and his temperament, then to make all possible efforts for the Marshal to accept and name a new government of a national and revolutionary government, of such a kind that legality remains attached to it.

If this cannot succeed, the resulting situation must be reexamined and the French personalities around me would do their all to save what is dear to France's national and social character and the collaboration with Germany.

Brinon attempted to see Pétain on 4 September 1944. The Germans pressed Brinon to obtain Pétain's official sanction for the formation of the new government, but Pétain refused, conceding only Brinon's authority to continue 'to deal with the matters for which he has hitherto been responsible' – in this context, the interests of POWs and other French citizens and institutions in the Reich. Pétain's private physician conveyed this message to Brinon on 6 September, who wilfully interpreted it as authority to form a new government. He proclaimed the formation of a new Governmental Commission, in the following terms:

> French! The Marshal of France remains the sole repository of legal power. In consequence, the protection of French interests provided over four years under his authority will continue. From today, I am assuming the responsibility of defending those interests, particularly in Germany, where they are so strongly represented.

This declaration became practically the founding document for the *Délégation gouvernementale française pour la défense des intérêts français en Allemagne* (French governmental delegation for the defence of French interests in Germany), the collaborationist government-in-exile in Sigmaringen, despite its lack of any legitimate foundation, even the endorsement of the Marshal. The next day, at 5.00 am, Pétain was removed from Morvillars by the Germans.

As a result of the note of 6 September 1944, sustaining his previous responsibilities, with a head of state and a head of government who both declared themselves unable to fulfil their functions, Brinon was now the only French political figure formally entitled to exercise power over the only French citizens who he had any practical power over – the POWs, deportees, refugees, and forced labourers in German hands. In due course, when the Sigmaringen enclave was created, this rationale could also extend to the refugees there. Brinon could present this to the Germans as aligning with their demand for a government-in-exile formally sanctioned by the Marshal. He could also count on the support of Otto Abetz, a longtime ally, who continued his former role of ambassador to the Vichy government, and who shared his antipathy towards Doriot. Meanwhile, on 27 August, Admiral Auphan presented his 'plenipotentiary letter' to General Alphonse Juin, but de Gaulle refused to receive him, and had him arrested.

Chapter 5

The Sigmaringen Statelet

O n the same day as Brinon's declaration, Cécil von Renthe-Fink, Hitler's ambassador to Vichy France, recommended that Pétain and the other active or inactive members of the Vichy government should be transferred to a safe location inside Germany, although the final decision was apparently Hitler's. The plan to remove the French government and head of state to a location within Germany was first hatched by Abetz in 1943, over fears that Vichy was increasingly being encircled by Resistance forces, and as a contingency in case of Allied landings. After 6 June, the plan suddenly became far more pertinent. At the beginning of September, Ribbentrop had presented Hitler with a list of potential venues: Sigmaringen, Baden-Baden and Freudenstadt were all considered as candidates. Sigmaringen was finally chosen primarily because of its isolated position, surrounded by relatively empty farmland and mountains, leaving the whole site easier to watch over and control. The small town lies to the south of the Swabian Jura, a limestone mountain range that forms an effective barrier against any assault from the west, with many small winding valleys hemmed in by karst outcrops so formidable that in places they recall the spires of the famous Stone Forest in southern China. Another rationale, aired by André Brissaud and other historians, was that Hitler sought to punish the house of Hohenzollern-Sigmaringen for possible complicity – or simple guilt by association – with their relative King Michael of Romania's anti-Axis coup on 23 August 1944. The Gestapo forced them out of their princely home and moved them to the nearby Castle Wilflingen. To add one more sour twist to an already rich cocktail of ironies, the house of Hohenzollern-Sigmaringen had provided Otto von Bismarck with the pretext for the Franco-Prussian War of 1870-71 and the unification of Germany. Leopold, Prince of Hohenzollern, born into the dynasty's Sigmaringen branch, was offered the Spanish crown in 1870; Bismarck manipulated perception of French pressure against the plan so adroitly via the Ems Dispatch that he soon had public opinion on both sides clamouring for war.

Anti-French resentment certainly survived among the natives of Sigmaringen, although this was likely thanks to local loyalty to the evicted Hohenzollern-Sigmaringens. Lucien Rebatet described them thus: 'The indigenes, firm reactionaries, descendants of the castle servants, understood nothing of this invasion of shabby, penniless French.'[1]

Sigmaringen Castle itself dates back to the eleventh century, but was substantially rebuilt and refashioned at the turn of the twentieth, after a disastrous fire. The resulting eclectic confection 'irresistibly recalls Disneyland', as Rousso remarked. Pétain was installed on the seventh floor, reached by a private elevator, the summit of the building, styled 'Olympus' by the collaborationist rank and file. On the floor below was Pierre Laval and his wife, and the other 'passive' ministers in the Vichy regime who declined to participate in the new arrangements; Jean Bichelonne, Maurice Gabolde, Pierre Mathé, Paul Marion, Charles Rochat. Rousso dubbed this the floor of Sleeping Beauties. The 'active' ministers and power-players – Fernand de Brinon, Joseph Darnand, Marcel Déat, Jean Luchaire and Eugène Bridoux – were installed in a separate wing. Karl Bömelburg, former head of the Gestapo in occupied France, was appointed head of security for the enclave.

The German press distributed the following message to the French:

CALL TO ALL FRENCH

The French head of state, Marshal Pétain, has removed from Belfort to Germany to defend the true interests of the French people against the Gaullist usurpers and the English and American exploiters of the French people.

Availing himself of the position of general delegate of the French government, conferred on him by the head of state, Ambassador de Brinon has undertaken the creation of a "French Governmental Delegation for the Defence of National Interests":

To this French delegation belong

- The Minister of Labour, Déat, delegated for national solidarity and the protection of French workers in Germany
- The Secretary of State for the Interior and maintenance of order, Joseph Darnand, delegated for the organization of the national forces of the Milice, the Legion of Volunteers against Bolshevism, and the French Waffen SS
- The Secretary of State for Defence, General Bridoux, delegated for the protection of prisoners of war and their means of assistance.
- The President of the Press Corporation, Jean Luchaire, delegated for Information and Propaganda.

Ambassador de Brinon, in taking on his functions, has addressed an appeal to all French; in that appeal, he insists on the fact that the French Head of State, Marshal Pétain, remains the sole holder of French legal power. French interests, defended for four years by the Authority of the Marshal, still continue to be under his protection.

Ambassador Brinon affirms in conclusion that it will be his task and that of his collaborators to maintain the interests of his country. His appeal finishes with the words: "Vive la France, Vive le Maréchal!"

While the de Gaulle committee is recognized neither by the French people nor the so-called Allies, and while France is engaged in civil war and Bolshevik chaos, Marshal Pétain and the French governmental Delegation remain the sole defenders of the legal and national interests of France.

Under German pressure, the delegation changed its name to the French Governmental Commission for the Defence of National Interests. Deprived of Pétain's cooperation, Brinon also faced the challenge of marshalling and enlisting the other functionaries within the Vichy government. Gabolde, Bichelonne, Bonnard and Paul Marion all followed the Marshal in declining to participate in the workings of the Governmental Commission. Déat and

Luchaire formed an internal opposition to Brinon within the Commission, and full meetings of the Commission took place only rarely.

Following the German decision to grant the Sigmaringen enclave extraterritorial status, Brinon formally requested Pétain to officiate at the inaugural ceremonies – and was refused. Pétain did, however, receive Gaston Bruneton on 29 September – a meeting which was to have significant consequences.

On Sunday, 1 October 1944, at around 11.15 am, a detachment of Milice in uniform lined the principal access to Sigmaringen Castle, aping the parade of the Republican Guard at the Elysée Palace. Facing them was a detachment of Wehrmacht. With a roll of drums, the French flag was raised over the castle. Fernand de Brinon appeared at the castle's first floor, accompanied by Joseph Darnand, Marcel Déat, Jean Luchaire, Lucien Rebatet, Lucienne Delforge, Bridoux, even Gabolde, Bonnard, and Mathé. The staff of the German 'embassy' – Abetz, Renthe-Fink, Hoffmann – were also out in force.

Brinon then delivered his first address from the castle balustrade:

French compatriots,

We have just experienced one of the deepest, rarest feelings. In this beautiful, noble city, we saw a French guard relieve a German guard and our tricolour rise to the sky atop this monument steeped in history that the Reich government has kindly made available to the French Commission for the Defence of National Interests.

My first words will express our gratitude to the Führer who himself noted that, on the land of the great German Reich, entirely focused on the war effort, the French who work for their country remain in France. It is with joy that we find in this gesture the justification of our hopes. The confirmation of our political faith and a serene confidence in the future.

What is the task we claim to fulfil?

We are here, at the side of the Marshal, the only legitimate head of the French State.

We fully endorse the instructions that he himself gave on the morning of Friday 29 September to Mr Bruneton, and that he authorized to be transmitted from him to the French workers in Germany. The Marshal said: "Repeat to them that they are soldiers, that it is to me and not to others that they owe obedience, because I remain incontestably and legally the leader of the French." This is the conviction that drives us; our only goal is to continue to serve the policy that the Marshal embodies for all those who have served him since the collapse of the warmongering democracy. And through this, we serve the French interest.

French prisoners and workers in Germany, we think of your fate and your concerns. We would like to be able to improve the one and alleviate the others. It is this that we will work towards as far as possible, with the assurance of finding support from the German authorities. Help us to do this. Ground yourself on your reason and your patriotism, on your French common sense, and not on the excitations of foreigners who have dragged our country into the greatest trials it has suffered. Simply do your daily duty and put your trust in those who do not intend to throw you into delusions or into grave faults with serious consequences. French of France who will shortly learn, alas! how justified were the warnings that the Marshal gave to you, and that many of you refused to heed, were justified, reflect now on the past and the present and judge in your hearts.

Soon those French who have not given up hope in a national renovation which, in 1940, represented the wish of the immense majority, will address you through the airwaves. They aim simply to tell you the truth. Listen to them. The future will teach you who best defended your interests.

Here we persevere. We keep the same faith in the destiny of the Fatherland. the same assurance of better times through the reconciliation of France and Germany, the same certainty that so many sacrifices will find their reward.

This is why, in the neighbouring church, a French priest will shortly invoke divine benediction on our dead and on our hopes.

This is why finally, on this German land, in contact with the German population, so magnificent in its prodigious effort and in its confidence, I cry out to you: Long live France, long live the Marshal!

As articulated by Dr Ménétrel at the time, and reiterated by Louis Noguères and many other commentators on the situation ever since, Pétain now faced the choice of doing nothing, and at least preserving his honour by not becoming an active collaborator; or doing something, where any positive action towards the Commission and the Germans would be taken as a sign that he was no longer their prisoner under duress, but their accomplice. Even receiving Bruneton, who was actually opposed by Déat and the rest of the Commission, could be seen as breaching this status, as Bruneton was practically guaranteed to make approaches and requests to him which he could not act on, but which still effectively presumed an active role in the machinery of Sigmaringen government. As it happened, his private statement to Bruneton, reported to Brinon, gave Brinon enough cover to claim endorsement by the Marshal of his own and the Commission's authority – as well as allowing an unfortunate misinterpretation. 'It is hard to understand today the importance given to Petain's phrase, cited by Bruneton and falsely reported by Brinon, if we disregard the sense given to it in Germany, as well as in Switzerland and France, where it was believed that the Marshal imagined, in pronouncing it, of one day mobilizing the French workers in Germany to engage them alongside the Germans in a fratricidal struggle.'[2] The raising of the tricolour over the castle and the Axis recognition of extraterritoriality also served to give some purely legal colour to the German commitment to allow the Marshal to remain on French soil.

Brinon expanded on these themes in an editorial dated 26 October 1944 in the first edition of *La France*, the collaborationist Sigmaringen newspaper created by Luchaire,

A few men, men dedicated to History and a French Governmental Commission, that is what the walls of the Castle of Sigmaringen shelter under the Tricolour. But these walls also enclose a common good for all French, an incorruptible good: the principle by which the power of the Marshal alone is legitimate, in the midst of the ills that we see our unhappy country plunged into.

Pétain, however, addressed the following message to Brinon on 2 October:

You sent me on 30 September, at the end of the afternoon, a letter to inform me that a colour ceremony would take place the next morning, 1 October, at Sigmaringen Castle. In the course of this ceremony, you delivered a discourse in which you implicated me. You did not think it necessary to communicate to me the text of this speech in advance. I regret even more this infringement of the universal rules of courtesy, as it was impossible for me to note at the time such material errors as the words that you attributed to me in the audience that I granted to Mr Bruneton. On this subject, I have sent a *Note verbale* to Minister von Renthe-Fink, which I have copied to you. I have learned, via press and radio bulletins, that you have assumed direction of a "French Delegation for the Defence of National Interests", which the German press have entitled a "French Governmental Delegation for the Defence of National Interests". This "Delegation" affects to place itself under my authority.

I must note however that I have never confided such a mission to you, nor to General Bridoux, nor to Déat, Darnand or Luchaire, since I ceased on 20 August to exercise my functions, and I am deprived of any possibility of delegating such authority.

I wish to point out to you that, in the current situation, you cannot plead your old title of General Delegate of "the French government for occupied territories", as it must be evident that the function which I entrusted to you in 1940 has lost its reasons for being: the government has suspended its functions and your activity can no longer be exercised in occupied French territories. I cannot accept that such an ambiguity should arise; if it is not possible, for the moment, to act with authority, I can at least, I think, make an appeal to your sense of honour and to the discipline that you have shown towards me, and pray to you to reestablish the truth. I also reserve the right to contact the German authorities who have authorized such broadcasts or press insertions.

Pétain also prepared a second *note verbale* to Minister von Renthe-Fink, which read as follows:

Sigmaringen, 3 October 1944

Marshal Pétain is aware of the official DNB note inserted in the German press of Monday 2 October titled "Appeal to all French". The first line of this communique declares that the Marshal has decided to move to Belfort in Germany for the protection of the true interests of the French people.

This declaration is contrary to the truth: the Marshal left France under constraint, he addressed a complaint on this subject to the Greater German head of state, given to Minister von Renthe-Fink on the morning of 7 September.

The rest of this communique announces the constitution of a "French Governmental Committee for the Defence of National Interests", under the patronage of the Marshal. This declaration is equally erroneous. The Marshal can only repeat that he has, on two occasions, solemnly declared that he has been obliged to suspend the exercise of his functions. It therefore is not possible for him to confer his patronage or to delegate his authority.

The Marshal appeals to the loyalty of the German High Authorities to make the necessary denials and rectifications appear without delay; he asks finally that the question of his residence is regularized in a way that avoids any equivocation and any cohabitation with the aforesaid Committee.

Predictably, the Germans finessed their responses regarding the actual receipt of these *Notes verbale*, which do have a formal diplomatic status, and did nothing to alter or correct the announcements.

Brinon wrote his own reply to Pétain, as follows:

French Delegation for the Defence of National Interests.
Sigmaringen, October 4, 1944.

President.

Marshal,

I have taken note of the Note dated 2 October, which was given to me yesterday morning. Please permit me to tell you, at once, with respectful candour, that reading it caused me as much surprise as it did pain. This note states, in fact, that I did not feel it necessary to communicate to you the text of the speech which I delivered on 1 October, at the end of the colour ceremony, which did not allow you to point out in time material errors such as those words which I attribute to you in the audience that you granted to Mr Bruneton.

I shall therefore repeat, first of all, what I said to General Debeney who came to see me on your behalf, namely that the details of the ceremony of 1 October were fixed on 30 September around 2 pm, and that it was materially impossible for me to communicate this to you other than by letter, since, despite all the efforts made by me since our arrival in Sigmaringen, silences or refusals, based on the attitude that you have decided to take, were opposed to my requests for an audience.

I add that I do not accept being forced to go through an intermediary to report to you or to explain myself.

For four years, Marshal, you have given me, either at Vichy or during your stay in the region of Paris, expressions of esteem and sympathy which I was proud of. I do not believe that I would come to Vichy without you doing me the honour of receiving me, of inviting me to your table, of asking my advice on government affairs and on those of the occupied French territories. I have always spoken to you freely and with the total frankness also established in the written communications that I made to you. My conscience therefore does not make any reproach to me. I served you faithfully because I had the honour of approaching you in 1916 and because I was convinced that your person embodied the hope of the recovery of France. That is what made it possible to speak to you directly. That is what, even today, obliges me to express the truth to you.

The Note that you signed on 2 October states that you did not confide either to myself, or to General Bridoux, nor to Darnand, Déat and Luchaire, a mission for the defence of French national interests, since you ceased to exercise your functions on 20 August and have deprived yourself of any possibility of delegating any authority whatsoever. However, I explained to you, in Belfort, the interest that there would be for France to continue to protect, thanks to the agreement of the Reich government, certain key national interests in Germany.

On the evening of 4 September, you first summoned me to Morvillars, for 5 September at noon, by Mr Rochat, a meeting which was cancelled the same day by Lieutenant-Colonel de Longueau Saint-Michel. It was under these conditions that General Debeney, accompanied by Dr Ménétrel, came to give me a Note whose preamble was so clearly contrary to the facts that I requested its rectification, a rectification which was promised by General Debeney, but of which I was never made aware.

However, in the evening, once I found myself at the Belfort prefecture, Doctor Ménétrel communicated to me a new Note from you, noting that you fully recognized the interest of what I proposed to accomplish, that you would help me in all possible measures, but that you could not take an official position, given the general attitude that you had decided to maintain. Doctor Ménétrel, naturally, put the text of this document back in his pocket.

Would you please ask me to re-establish the truth by appealing to my sense of honour and discipline? It is precisely this truth that I establish here. As for the sense of honour and discipline, you know too well, Marshal, that men who are not afraid to say what they think serve better than courtiers.

General Debeney told me the other day that the interests which concerned you most in Germany were those of the political internees and that, precisely, our commission could not defend them. This is a strange reasoning to which I must reply that:

1. The political internees are, for the most part, the most bitter adversaries to the ideas and doctrines that you have publicly defended as head of the French State and, on the other hand (notably that of civil servants), the misguided ones that a firmer conduct of government would have defended from themselves.

2. I am precisely the only one to have obtained valid results regarding the fate of political internees. Thanks to the accord that I obtained in Paris from the competent German authorities, news was given,

releases granted, important improvements conceded. This accord would certainly have produced other results if the aftermath of the Anglo-American landing and the spread of armed resistance movements, solemnly condemned by you, had not led to the suspension of the measures taken.

Perhaps it is not necessary to add, seeing as it is so obvious, that in order to ask the German government to examine the condition and regime of political detainees, there needs to be, on their part, a minimum of confidence in the representatives of the French government.

However, the main difficulty lies in this lack of confidence, the justification for which is, unfortunately, clear. It is painful to hear about the breaches of the sworn word that have occurred around you. As for the prisoners released thanks to the special benevolence of the Führer, the examples of Generals Juin and Laure are incontestable, as far as senior military figures are concerned.

You yourself condemned General Giraud's perjury.

Need we conceal the fact that Dr Ménétrel is formally committed to having no political activity? However, he wrote and distributed documents which carry condemnation of your labour of four years, under the pretext that it was imposed by constraint, but, in reality, to try to please the dissidents who responded with manifestations of insulting contempt. Finally, it has been established that in Sigmaringen itself, Dr Ménétrel, taking advantage of the freedom he possesses, searches for French workers and prisoners to let them know that the men of the Maquis had all your approbation.

Who serves you most usefully, Marshal, the one who spreads such remarks or the one who asserts that there is an absolute contradiction between the words that you said personally to Mr Bruneton and that he repeated himself, and the self-interested and cynical exploitation of a position held by your favour?

I have a duty to say such things in response to your Note of 2 October. I also said them to Morvillars, to General Debeney and to Doctor Ménétrel. By continuing to serve you in this way, they will destroy for posterity everything that you have been and everything that you are. You will no longer be the leader who, by asking for the painful armistice of June 1940, preserved his country from a worse defeat, the one who made it possible to live relatively peacefully and prosper from 1940 to 1944, the one who represented the hopes of revival; you will be the man whom some have treated as a usurper, while others said that, after having stifled the Parliamentary Republic, he believed himself to have powers more extensive than those of King Louis XIV.

A great number of French people cannot accept this interpretation and even fewer would uphold it. They have heard from you so many severe and just judgments on institutions and on men, on the unacceptable power of the economic trusts which have done so much harm to the country, and on the certainty that if Germany were defeated, Communism would settle in Europe, that they refuse to believe that we can, with you, create equivocation and contradiction. They clearly observed that the so-called National Revolution of Vichy was no more than a revolution of panic soon transformed into an atmosphere of hypocrisy in pursuit of prebends and old combinations, but for all that, they did not give up the hopes that they had placed in your person and in your deeds.

Marshal, I am one of them. This is why I want to think that you will excuse my frankness. In April 1942, when you decided to recall President Laval to the government, Admiral Darlan declared to you, in my presence: "What I want you to know, Marshal, is that in this whole affair, Brinon was loyalty itself." You replied: "I know that well", and you asked me to accompany the Admiral to Châteldon in order to resolve the outstanding questions.

I preserve this memory with gratitude. I also remain convinced of serving you faithfully because you are, for me, the Leader that I knew in 1916, the one who in 1917 held the French Army to its duty, who thereby enabled the victory of 1918; the man which, in June 1940, stopped an even greater debacle by opening the way to essential reforms.

By maintaining the political line that I have always followed, that of complete reconciliation between Germany and France, necessary for the prosperity of our country, I claim to remain in accord with your aspirations. I also intend to protect French prisoners and workers in Germany, for whom you have often appealed against foreign excitations and for whom I cannot believe that you now intend to give them the sole guarantee of legal texts.

That is the entire explanation of my words and my actions and this is how I ask you to accept, Marshal, the assurance of my deepest respect.

Fernand de Brinon.

The exchange of notes continued between the two of them in more or less the same tone, without much alteration of position – and with one important consideration. Pétain made no public or overt protest about the situation. So long as he did not do so, Brinon could keep up the facade of continuing to act under his authority. Despite his insistence that he was being held under duress, Pétain could have made some effort to either break out of the situation or at least communicate to the outside world, given the relatively lax conditions of his confinement. He could have at least tried to convey a communique to the outside world denouncing the puppet government of the Commission. He could have formally resigned from his self-appointed role as head of the French State. For whatever reason, whether fear of reprisal or reluctance to cede his title, he did none of these things. Brinon was effectively free to exercise all the authority he could, without having to confirm his decisions with the Marshal.

Few outsiders, though, even in the restricted conditions of the prisoner-of-war camps, appeared to have any illusions about the true state of affairs. Schillemans' testimony, from his own experiences in the camps, prior to his appointment as Pétain's doctor-designate, indicates how ineffective Brinon's attempts to identify the Sigmaringen regime with the Marshal were: 'For most French prisoners, indeed, the Marshal remained the living symbol of their suffering and the man who, notwithstanding the difficulties, had tried to oppose the actions of certain members of his entourage, who were trying, under pressure from the Germans, to drag our country into adventures with no way out. So, now, he appeared to us as a victim, and his forced exile seemed to us a final act of violence by the Nazi enemy, exasperated by his obstructions.'

Sustaining the facade of a legitimate extraterritorial entity and a government-in-exile, the enclave had its diplomatic representatives from the Axis powers: Otto Abetz as German ambassador, flanked by Renthe-Fink and Hoffmann; Longhini, the Consul-General for the rump Italian Republic of Salò; and Takanobu Mitani, the Japanese ambassador. Jacques Guérard, the former secretary-general of Laval's collaborationist cabinet, arrived in Sigmaringen in mid-November 1944. He had fled separately to Switzerland in August, but the Swiss authorities had him arrested and duly deported him to Germany. In Sigmaringen, he joined the circle of inactive former ministers around Laval. He was briefly under suspicion by the Gestapo supervisors of the enclave, who suspected him of being an emissary of the Allied high command.

Other lesser figures in exile in Sigmaringen included Marcel Bucard, founder in 1933 of the Mouvement franciste, a Gallic imitation of the Italian Fascists, financed by Mussolini. As a co-founder in July 1941 of the LVF, he had urged his followers to join the Germans fighting the Allies after D-Day, but fled to Germany in August 1944 with a few of his followers, after a period of imprisonment for theft from a Jewish jeweller. Another even more marginal figure from the pre-war far-right fringes of French politics was the journalist and activist Pierre Clémenti, founder in April 1934 of the Parti français national-communiste, later the Parti français national-collectiviste. Yet another journalist, Jean Fontenoy, had followed Jacques Doriot from the political left to the PPF, but fled to Sigmaringen rather than follow Doriot into his rival fiefdom.

The enclave naturally needed funding as well as supplies to keep going, and the German government, naturally enough, paid to keep its client government afloat. The funding took the form of a 5 million reichsmark credit per month to the enclave – formalized as an interest-bearing loan to be repaid by France to Germany after the cessation of hostilities. The Sigmaringen administration had to provide a monthly statement of accounts to the Germans, detailing the use of funds. Much of the funding went to support the Sigmaringen rump government's involvement in the administration of French prisoners of war and forced labour in Germany. Some 50,000 reichsmarks per month went on the running expenses of the castle, with a 'civil list' to provide the Marshal and Laval with some income. Laval's little nest egg of French francs was not valid currency in Sigmaringen.

According to Henry Rousso, Pétain and Laval, even though they occupied different floors in the castle, never had a face to face conversation throughout the entire duration of the enclave. Given the Marshal's personal detestation of Laval, it is not hard to imagine.

Pétain was served by a small entourage in his de facto confinement. His personal physician, Dr Bernard Ménétrel, had already played a disproportionate role in the Marshal's personal court in the latter days in Vichy, and his importance only increased at Sigmaringen. Laval remarked of him, 'I was ready for anything, except that France would be governed by a doctor.'[3] The Marshal's small entourage also included Henri Bléhaut, rear admiral and former Vichy Secretary of State for the Navy and the Colonies, later credited with providing intelligence to the Allies and preserving France's naval infrastructure during his tenure. Victor Debeney, general and former head of Vichy's armistice services, assumed the role of Pétain's head of secretariat in August 1944, and kept it until the end of the war. A half dozen or so aides and servants attended to the personal needs of the Marshal and his court.

Pétain lived in reasonable comfort at Sigmaringen, more or less unmolested. He benefited from sixteen ration cards, four times the basic allocation for the refugees in the enclave, enjoying an exclusive menu. Clearly, the Marshal's famous declaration on 17 June 1940 that 'I give the gift of my person to France to alleviate her misfortune' did not extend to sharing the privations of the other inmates of Sigmaringen, or the malnourished millions in metropolitan France. He took regular walks, driving out of the castle with two Gestapo cars as escort, for perambulations in the countryside. He led a sedentary life in his apartments. Rousso reports one incident when his wife sought to take shelter in the castle cellars from Allied bombing – the Marshal went on sleeping and refused to stir. He made notes on his own version of the events of the Fall of France and the Armistice. Occasionally he appeared in public, but otherwise remained in retirement while the Commission continued to invoke his presence as a talisman of legitimacy.

Speculation about Pétain's state of mind during this period, and his possible senility, seems little borne out by actual eye-witness accounts. Céline provided his own assessment, laced with the usual doses of self-exculpation:

Above: Sigmaringen Castle seen from the river. (*Author*)

Below: First government of the Vichy regime, July 1940. Pierre Laval and Philippe Pétain stand side by side at centre. (*Szukaj w Archiwach, Poland / Wikimedia Commons*)

Page from a collaborationist tract, 'Paroles françaises, paroles d'espoir', featuring prominent collaborationists (l-r): Marcel Déat, Jean Luchaire, Eugène Deloncle, Jean Goy, Jacques Doriot, Pierre Costantini, Pierre Clémenti, Jean Boissel. (*Archives nationales / Wikimedia Commons*)

Above left: Joseph Darnand in 1940. (*Keystone France / Wikimedia Commons*)

Above right: Pencil portrait of Louis-Ferdinand Céline. (*Public Domain*)

Above: Fernand de Brinon (right) and Edgar Puaud (centre) inspect French volunteers on the Eastern Front in 1943. (*Szukaj w Archiwach, Poland / Wikimedia Commons*)

Right: Pierre Laval, Joseph Darnand and Francis Bout de l'An leaving the Milice headquarters in Paris, April 1944. (*Musée Carnavalet, Histoire de Paris*)

VICHY. LE PRÉSIDENT LAVAL, CHEF DU
GOUVERNEMENT PRÉSIDE UNE RÉUNION
DES CHEFS DÉPARTEMENTAUX DE LA
MILICE FRANÇAISE.

LE PRÉSIDENT LAVAL, ACCOMPAGNÉ DE
M. DARNAND, SECRÉTAIRE GÉNÉRAL AU
MAINTIEN DE L'ORDRE ET DE M. BOUT DE
L'AN, SECRÉTAIRE GÉNÉRAL ADJOINT DE
LA MILICE FRANÇAISE QUITTE LE SECRÉ-
TARIAT GÉNÉRAL DE LA MILICE.

V. 96.663

Fernand de Brinon, Joseph Darnand and Edgar Puaud at an LVF reunion in the Vélodrome d'Hiver, Paris, April 1944. (*Musée de la Libération de Paris – musée du Général Leclerc – musée Jean Moulin*)

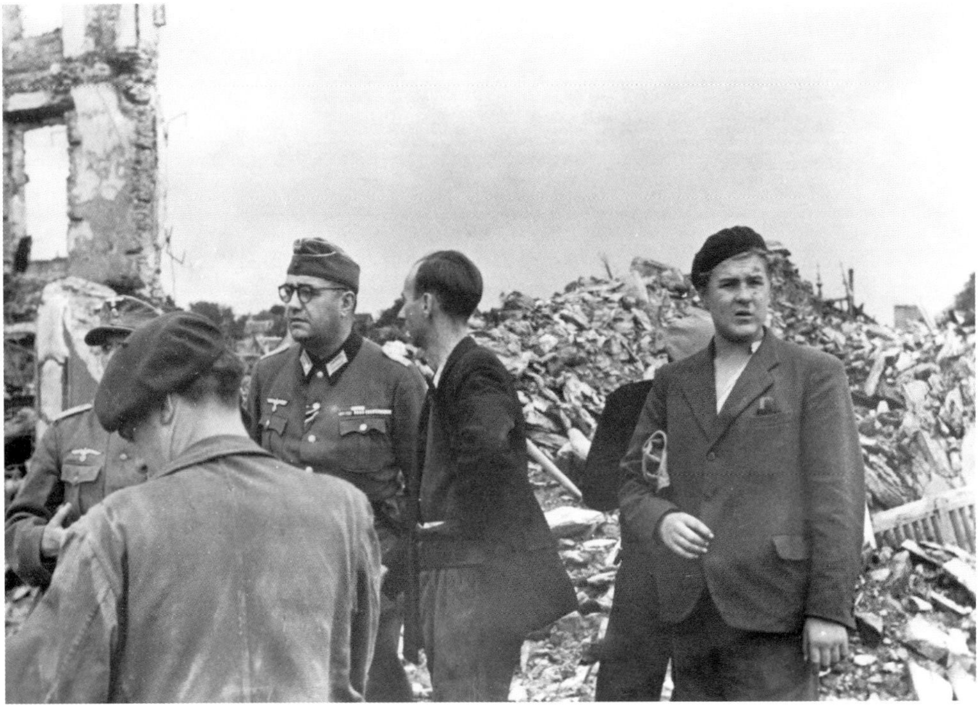

Le numéro : 3 fr. 50 — En page 3 : NUIT BLANCHE, nouvelle inédite de O. G. GUIGNARD

Le prochain numéro de Je Suis Partout portera la date du VENDREDI 25 AOUT

JE SUIS PARTOUT

Le Grand Hebdomadaire Politique et Littéraire

L'UNION DES RÉVOLUTIONNAIRES

Il y a en France des forces révolutionnaires dont l'Europe pour vaincre ne peut plus se passer nous dit :

DÉAT

par Lucien Rebatet

espoir de LA FRANCE

L'expérience montre qu'à notre époque c'est l'action qui est le seul facteur d'ordre nous dit :

DORIOT

par P.-A. Cousteau

« JE SUIS PARTOUT » EST LA

« ROYAL SECRET » (the rigth man...)

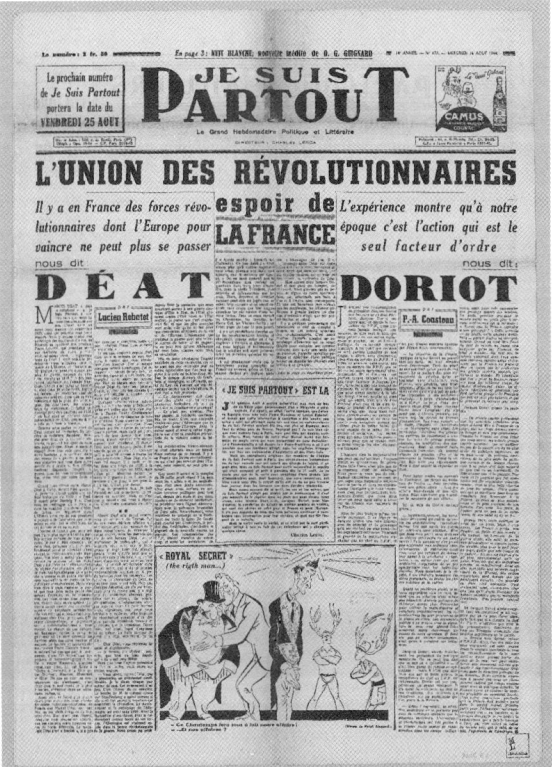

Above: Jacques Doriot at the front in Normandy, July 1944. (*Szukaj w Archiwach, Poland / Wikimedia Commons*)

Left: Last number of Je Suis Partout, from 16 August 1944, celebrating Déat and Doriot. (*Musée de la Libération de Paris – musée du Général Leclerc – musée Jean Moulin / Wikimedia Commons*)

Above: The main gate of Sigmaringen Castle. (*Author*)

Below left: Sigmaringen Castle staircase. (*Alf van Beem / Wikimedia Commons*)

Below right: Sigmaringen Castle gallery, from a period picture. (*Wikimedia Commons*)

Interior of
Sigmaringen Castle.
(*Alf van Beem /
Wikimedia Commons*)

Sigmaringen station,
the haunt of pimps and
prostitutes in wartime,
according to Céline.
(*Author*)

The period signal
box at Sigmaringen
station. (*Author*)

Above: The Schön cafe in Sigmaringen, former haunt of many of the collaborationist elite in the wartime enclave. (*Author*)

Right: The former Hotel Zum Löwen in Sigmaringen, onetime residence of many elite collaborationists in the enclave. (*Author*)

Left: Philippe Pétain during his trial. (*Getty Images / Wikimedia Commons*)

Below: Charles Maurras at his trial in Lyon in 1945. (*Keystone France / Wikimedia Commons*)

When it comes to Pétain, it's been said that he had become so senile that he couldn't hear the bombs or the sirens anymore, that he took the Fritz soldiers for his own Vichy guards…that he mistook Brinon for the Nuncio… I can reestablish the truth, I who he detested can say it, I speak in perfect independence.

Pétain's sustained policy of non-cooperation with the Commission invites questions as to his motives. The tone and the issues under dispute do not suggest that this was some last-ditch defence of French sovereignty and French interests. Nor do they suggest an overriding concern for the fig-leaf of constitutional legitimacy that the rump Third Republic government conferred on him in 1940. Rather, they look very consistent with a continuing concentration on his own supposed personal authority as the incarnation of French sovereignty, and resentment at Brinon and the others for usurping this. Nazi Germany's role in forcing the creation of this puppet government looks a very much lesser concern.

Pétain's non-cooperation certainly does not look like a protest against the policies of the Nazis, to who, after all, he had been allied since 1940. That is at least one possible reading of Pétain's mindset at the time. He certainly never abdicated or openly denounced the puppet regime in Sigmaringen, which would have stripped it of its last shred of legitimacy. Rousso declared in his 2011 introduction to the revised edition of his history that 'it was thanks to the analysis of Pétain's attitude in the castle of the Hohenzollerns that I perceived at what point the old Marshal became attached to a certain idea of legitimacy – his own legitimacy.'

Another, more objective, view of Pétain's legitimacy was articulated by Ribbentrop while talking to Déat: 'The legality of Pétain and Laval, regarding Franco-German cooperation, can only be a sham legality and not a true legality.' In one bizarre sense, the Germans remained Pétain's allies even during his imprisonment. By continuing to pay some kind of backhanded tribute to his self-proclaimed status as head of the French state, they reinforced his own self-image as embodiment of the nation, which would have been punctured far sooner if he had remained in France, as he requested, to face Gaullist judges.

On the floor below Pétain, Pierre Laval pursued his own version of non-cooperation. According to his secretary Gérard Rey, he complained about the luxurious apartments and sumptuous bed – so ill-suited to his peasant roots – and averred that he had asked the Germans time and again to lodge him in a simple farm; but he made no apparent attempt to quit his quarters. Unlike Pétain, he was only granted six ration cards, but among his personal effects were 20 million francs, jealously guarded. Like the Marshal, he spent much time reviewing and justifying his actions in office, declaiming his defences and self-justifications to Rey and others, or just to the walls of his apartments. At least, while he and the Marshal held onto their positions and refused to step down, they could not be replaced by the more openly pro-German collaborationists eager to supplant them; and that shred of legitimacy remained in their hands.

Called as a witness post-war in the trial of Marshal Pétain, Laval described the conditions at Sigmaringen as follows:

I was naturally conducted, like the others, to Sigmaringen, but the Marshal was upstairs, and downstairs, in a neighbouring building, were all the delegates of that organization that called itself the Governmental Commision of Sigmaringen... I was the only one who could not move about outside Sigmaringen. The Marshal had a car which allowed him to go for walks in the surrounding area; the ministers could go into the other towns they preferred. I was not able to leave Sigmaringen.

As for the formation of the new 'government', he added:

It was the delegation that the Marshal had given him [in December 1940] that allowed de Brinon, he said, to continue his functions... he had put "Delegated by the Head of State and the Government." I had asked him, at Belfort, to modify the formula and put the date: "By the Marshal, Chief of State, then head of government", because I did not wish, in any way, even indirectly, that anyone could believe that I had given my approval and my assent to such an organization.

One illuminating exchange of letters between Laval and Pétain did take place in October 1944. Laval wrote:

8 October 1944

Marshal,

I have read an article which appeared in the *Tribune de Genève*, which I believe I have to bring to your attention.

According to this article, I would have considered, as compensation for the loss of Alsace and Lorraine, the annexation of Wallonia. This would have been, according to the author of this article, the reason for my disgrace of 13 December 1940.

At other times, I would have dismissed such a fantastical allegation, but in the current conditions, I cannot let it pass.

I never received such a proposal from the German government and I was therefore never able to submit it for your examination and approval.

I would be glad if you took note of this.

If such a proposal had been made to me, I would naturally and spontaneously have rejected it, judging it contrary to the traditions of France and her interests.

I ask you to accept, Marshal, the assurance of my respect.

Pétain responded immediately:

Sigmaringen, 8 October 1944

Mr President

I have just read the article which appeared in the *Tribune de Genève* that you sent to me.

I will readily confirm that you have never informed me of any proposal from the German government concerning the eventuality of an annexation of Wallonia or any other portion of French-speaking foreign territory.

If such a proposal had been made, like you, I would have rejected it.

I would in fact have considered that the proposal, contrary to all the principles of French politics, constituted an offence in regard to a country which we are bound to by a traditional amity.

Please accept, Mister President, the expression of my distinguished sentiments.

Philippe Pétain

Laval clearly had more than his good name in mind; he acted immediately to counter a potential accusation that could resurface in any post-war accounting of his actions in office. Whatever their past differences, Pétain was obviously quite ready to countenance him in this.

The only refusenik not quartered in the castle itself with the rest of Laval's dormant cabinet was Abel Bonnard, the former Vichy Minister of Public Instruction. He lived in the town, with his aged mother and his brother.

On the third floor of the castle, in another wing, resided the ministers and officials who still played out the role of an active government-in-exile. Their offices were approached through the castle's long and impressive armoury, hung about with suits of armour, halberds and muskets. Fernand de Brinon headed the ensemble, supported by Joseph Darnand, Jean Luchaire, General Bridout, and Maurice Déat. This arrangement was not a practical hierarchy so much as a loose collaboration-within-a-collaboration among figures with their own separate agendas and ambitions. Fernand de Brinon, despite his position as head of the Governmental Commission, had little in the way of a personal power base, no party or militia of his own. Darnand had brought some 10,000 Milice members and their families with him, but spent much of his time outside the enclave, most often at Ulm, organizing his collaborationist units serving with the German military. He did very little with his formal portfolio as Commissioner for the Interior. Luchaire was Commissioner for Information, but his practical power was also limited by his want of followers, and his many enemies among the fugitives. Bridoux, at the instigation of Brinon and the Nazis, spent much of his time outside the enclave, attempting to rally French POWs and internees in Germany to the Axis cause. Déat, retaining his labour portfolio from the last days of the Vichy government in

Paris, devoted much of his time to the remnants of his RNP power base, often in rivalry with Darnand and his followers.

Among the cabinet of this supposed government, only Déat had held any kind of position in a pre-war government, his six months as Minister of the Air in 1936. Brinon and Luchaire were both former journalists and media figures. General Bridout never had any political role under the Third Republic. Darnand was a former terrorist. This was the calibre of collaborationist that the Reich had to work with at this stage of the war. Jean-Paul Cointet has pointed out the 'quasi-vacuity of collective debate at the heart of the Commission' where every one of its members 'sought only to play their own card'. Given the type of figures who remained aligned with the Axis at this stage in the war, it is hardly surprising.

At least the new situation gave the Sigmaringen 'cabinet' a chance to exercise their vanities and dreams of importance. Brinon occupied a 'superb, well-lit and sumptuously furnished office', according to Schillemans, equipped with 'a vast, ornate black wood table, with copper carvings, cluttered with files and various papers'. This also served as the meeting place of the Commission, allowing Brinon to assert his authority. In person, he was 'pretty elegant, with a receding hairline, heavy batrachian eyelids, slightly dull eyes, a fixed gaze, lips sketching a disgusted but very aristocratic pout that perhaps wanted to resemble a smile'. Despite the presence of his wife at Sigmaringen, he was served constantly by his secretary and mistress, Simone Mittre, who served as custodian of his memoirs and his memory after the war.

Déat, as described by Schillemans, was clearly:

very proud of his title of 'President of the Provisional Government', a title that might allow him to go down in history, or at least to appear in future editions of *Larousse*, he was dressed most of the time in a black jacket and striped trousers, giving him the appearance of a 'Herr Professor' in his Sunday best. Flat, cosmetic hair, an impeccable middle parting, sly eyes and a false smile, such was the outward aspect of this wily-looking politician, who gave, to my mind, an impression of being very vindictive. For the rest, it was really very difficult to guess what he was thinking because he gave little away, almost never speaking to you directly, and very rarely looking at his interlocutor, except perhaps when it came to Brinon. He listened to the conversations with his eyes downcast, an enigmatic smile fixed on his thin lips, which made him seem sibylline. He was, in my opinion, terribly proud, infatuated with himself and very secretive. For one thing, I never saw him get carried away during a discussion; he was content only to approve or disapprove, but in a completely impersonal way.

Looking to consolidate his own position both within and outside the Commission, Déat paid numerous visits across the Reich after his arrival in Sigmaringen – to Germany and particularly Berlin from 18 to 27 October 1944, to Dresden and Berlin from 25 to 28 November, to Vienna and Berlin from 11 to 20 December, and to Weimar and Berlin from 11 to 27 January 1945. On each visit, he sought to position himself as the key representative of French collaborationist circles, while also making contact with residual RNP cells among French POWs in Germany and reaching out to other fascist groups under the Nazi umbrella. Ultimately, he achieved little, especially in terms of building his and the Commission's credibility in German eyes versus Doriot. All the same, Déat's hyperactivity did at least help to confirm – in his eyes – the authority and legitimacy of the Commission versus Doriot and his German backers.

Jean Bichelonne, former secretary-general at the Vichy Ministry of Industrial Production and Communications, was one of the most intellectually qualified of any of the refugees, and a bureaucrat in several pre-war Third Republic ministries. He was a graduate of the elite École Polytechnique and the Corps of Mines, a point which seems to have obsessed Céline.

Bichelonne had the biggest head, not only because he was champion of the Polytechnic and Mines... History! Geotechnics! Excuse me! A real cybertechnic all by himself! If he had to explain to us the what and the wherefore! The peculiarities of the castle! All of them! That it leaned south rather than north? ... if he knew? why the chimneys, battlements, drawbridge, worm-eaten, leaned rather more towards the west?

Céline was writing in the post-war period, when the technocrats, some of them former Vichy collaborators, had become a conspicuous force in politics and policy, so he may have projected the post-war situation back upon Bichelonne. However, Bichelonne himself might well have ended up as a technocratic official or even minister in some post-war government if post-operative complications had not killed him following surgery on his knee in December 1944. Politically naive is a charge often levelled against him and his ilk – he may simply have been cynical and narrow-minded enough to focus on his goal of economic and industrial modernization, whatever the cost elsewhere.

Jean Luchaire, who had been angling for political office throughout his career as a collaborationist journalist and bribe-taker, finally received a government appointment of sorts, as Commissioner for Propaganda and Information. He owed the appointment primarily to Abetz, his friend and effective handler since his days in Paris under the German occupation. From the enclave's Ministry of Information building at 3 Karlstrasse in Sigmaringen, some 220 functionaries operated the enclave's propaganda machine, many of them superfluous staff simply there to honour the fiction that all the enclave's refugees should perform some useful work. Luchaire's seven immediate subordinates, nominally directors, managed operations, all of them former staffers at *Nouveaux Temps* in Paris.

The French Office of Information, the official collaborationist press agency since 1942, was located on the first floor, and acted in practice as an arm of the German press agency. *La France*, Luchaire's personal project as a collaborationist newspaper, was run from the second floor; the first issue appeared on 26 October 1944. The paper's editorial line was that Sigmaringen was the 'fortress' of the Marshal's legitimacy, and its inhabitants were 'French patriots' sustaining the reconciliation between France and Germany. Its target readership was primarily the French forced labourers still working in Germany, as well as the refugees in the enclave itself. Financed by German money via Otto Abetz, which enabled Luchaire to support his large staff in Sigmaringen's straitened conditions, the paper also served as the journal of record for the decisions of the Commission, which in practice mostly amounted to the activities and decisions of Marcel Déat's Ministry of Labour. Luchaire also had a radio station at his disposal, Radio-Sigmaringen or Ici la France, broadcasting on 278m 60 with a 120kw transmitter, and staffed by some ninety personnel under Jacques Bouly de Lesdain, an aristocratic sometime travel writer, stalwart of Action Française, and anti-Freemasonry activist. A typical evening broadcast consisted of a series of musical programmes, interspersed with 'informational' bulletins on such topics as the devastating effects of the German V-weapons, the corruption and anarchy in liberated France, etc., often read by Luchaire himself. The German money enabled Luchaire to pay himself and his staff very generously: he received 160,000 francs per month, according to Cointet, while a radio announcer received 24,000 francs and a typist 15,000 francs.

Schillemans painted an acid word portrait of Luchaire after his first meeting with Sigmaringen's press baron and his wife:

> The two newcomers did not, at first glance, form a very homogeneous couple. He was tall, thin and blond, with a very refined elegance. He looked barely forty-three or forty-four years old, even though he was in fact much older; he must have dyed his hair, because this blond mien seemed very suspect. She, on the contrary, despite her peroxide blonde coiffeur, looked much older in comparison with him. This physical contrast was reinforced by the mischievous childish attitude of Luchaire, always very infatuated with himself, loving to discourse in front of an admiring audience, juggling paradoxes to make himself interesting, ingeniously finding puns and amusing expressions.
>
> He exhibited the syndrome of the journalist with the gift of the gab, a great raconteur, always ready to tell stories, anecdotes, in which, moreover, he knew how to show off very agreeably. Not letting a single opportunity pass by to put himself in the spotlight, he was witty all day long; intelligent, very careerist, he succeeded well enough in this character who wished to be amusing; from the first moment, however, I found him deeply unpleasant. All his antics were so artificial, so insincere, that one felt a kind of unease seeing this backward child, strutting and showing off for the gallery.

General Bridoux was tasked with responsibility for French POWs in Germany, a duty which kept him out of the enclave for much of the time, although with little visible effect on the POWs. Schillemans reported his ambitions in this area, as they stood in late 1944:

> Bridoux had found one of his propaganda themes and, encouraged by his colleagues, continued in a seductive tone: "We are actively dealing with them and trying to get them set free. We have never been so well placed for this, and it is within the realms of the possible, provided we put a little goodwill into it on both sides." After a while, he added: "Naturally, it is not possible, nor even desirable, especially with what is going on right now, that these prisoners return to France. Certainly, we would like, with all our heart, that they can soon return to see their loved ones." Brandishing a prophetic index finger, he added: "That will come, and sooner than we think. Meanwhile, we are going to arrive at a result that one might have thought unachievable just a few months ago. The Government of the Reich, which until now had been very reluctant to extend this degree of liberation to so great a number of individuals, is now considering, far more widely, the transformation of prisoners of war into civilian workers." We were there: Bridoux had passed the stage of declaration of principle and was now approaching the so-called constructive proposals. He was in the process of summarizing the lecture he intended to give in the Stalags. In a charming tone, he continued: "These men would therefore lead, in Germany, a free, paid life: the nightmare of captivity would be over for them."

Joseph Darnand spent more time with the Milice units that had been sent to Ulm by the German authorities, just under 2,000 of whom ended up serving in various SS infantry regiments under the 33rd SS Grenadier Division Charlemagne. He at least appeared to genuinely believe in the struggle he was fighting, unlike the rest of the Commission. He told Schillemans:

> Germany alone is capable of blocking Russian Communism and annihilating it. It is this revolutionary ideology that is the main

adversary, the beast to be destroyed. America is too far away and does not realize the danger, England is too weak; as for us, we no longer count as a preponderant power. The war that Germany supports is a final battle on which the fate of Humanity will depend.

Marcel Déat, preserving his portfolio of Minister of Labour from his position in Laval's government, had theoretical responsibility for the French forced labourers in the Reich. In practice, he had most actual power over the work assignments in the Sigmaringen enclave, trying to find useful employment for the refugees. An education department was created by decree on 7 November 1944 to educate the children of refugees; a hygiene department was created on 1 December and did nothing to alleviate the miserable living conditions of the refugees. Déat's paper ministry in the Commission's impotent government mostly served to give the appearance of some kind of governmental activity to this unreal shadow.

Much of Déat's time and effort was in fact consumed in a futile struggle for control of the Délégation officielle française (DOF) under Gaston Bruneton, which had hitherto been responsible for the forced labourers in Germany. In a message of 17 November 1944, Pétain reiterated his charge to Bruneton to take responsibility of the forced labourers 'in my name'. Déat, meanwhile, attempted to gain control of the forced labourers' youth group, the Chantiers de la Jeunesse en Allemagne.

One document from a 'neutral source' quoted by Louis Noguères gives a fairly blunt evaluation of the actual scope of political activity in Sigmaringen:

It has to be borne in mind that within the French Delegation, whose numerous personnel seethed in the chambers of Sigmaringen Castle, only one active cog functioned: Information-Propaganda, directed by Jean Luchaire.

Darnand's "Interior" corresponds to nothing, and the "Labour" of Déat, apart from the threat of sending everyone under the age of 35 to factories, has no practical application. The services of the Chantiers de Jeunesse and de Bruneton continue to function as in the past, which does not prevent Déat from publishing some decrees and glimpsing some achievements.

The Head of the RNP [Déat] takes his role of "future head of state" very seriously.

He seeks to broaden his narrow assignments: he does not look to go beyond Sigmaringen like the others; he inflates himself in Sigmaringen. Between Doriot and Déat, there is no difference in ambition, but only a difference in perspective ...

He [Doriot] has a protector whose star is in the ascendant, Sauckel, who supports him more and more with Hitler and Himmler. Plus, Doriot, who knows perfectly well that Brinon is, at best, the manager of an empty store on the way to becoming the trustee in a bankruptcy, looks to go immediately beyond the Governmental Commission to something bigger. He has as adversaries Brinon, timid and used to sitting down in a distinguished manner when the Germans tell him to sit; Déat, who simmers in isolation between three old utopian socialists and a handful of young fanatics of doubtful morals, who confines his universe to legislative papers and the textual interpretations of an École Normale Supérieure graduate; Darnand, who misses his command of the SS Charlemagne Brigade; Luchaire, increasingly disillusioned and following the spirit of Briand, who hopes for some compromise on the French side, a Gaullist without stating it too plainly...

Doriot's idea is as follows: To govern.

But France is not confined to the few refugees in Sigmaringen, it comprises, after all, the French in France, many of whom must have been shocked by the Allied occupation, by the abuses of the Liberation, by the return of the triumphant Israelites, by the Communist menace brutally unveiled. All of these are retrievable for the cause of collaboration.

We must reach out to them, establish liaisons with them, give them posts in what we create – in a word, we must govern them and associate them with our government. Now, the Commission of de Brinon appears as a little group of people of the lowest value, who try to form a government all ready to return to France. This is a mistake. Doriot's plan is vaster, but before revealing it, he needs formal promises from Hitler which will cost nothing to the latter: the independence of the French government, the retention of the colonies and the restitution of Alsace-Lorraine. These are the key assets in Doriot's game.

Unfortunately, as Pétain and Laval had found, those promises were exactly the ones that Hitler was least likely to honour. Doriot's game might have extended and deepened collaboration among the few exiles and fascist zealots still left in Germany, if he had lived, but he would never have been allowed to achieve his goals. Nonetheless, by late 1944, Hitler and the rest of the German political elite were convinced that Doriot was the heir-apparent for the government of France, with Brinon, Darnand, Déat and his other rivals at best temporary caretakers.

Efforts to pressure Pétain and push him into open endorsement of the Commission continued. On 22 November 1944, Bernard Ménétrel, Pétain's doctor and supposed *eminence grise*, was arrested by the Gestapo, ostensibly on suspicion of clandestine contacts with the Allies. He had accompanied the Marshal on his regular promenade, returning to the castle in the escort car, but on the way back, his car was diverted and he was arrested – possibly at the instigation of Fernand de Brinon. The exact motives for the arrest are unclear but it appears that Brinon and the Germans thought that the removal of his trusted doctor would render the Marshal more tractable. Predictably, it had the opposite effect. Furious, Pétain refused the services of another doctor. During his interrogation by the High Court of Justice on 8 June 1945, he made the following statement regarding the doctor's confinement and the subsequent events:

He annoyed the Germans, because he observed them. So, firstly, they separated him from me. He left the house where I lived and was installed in secret in a house about a dozen kilometres away. I asked to see him for an hour per week as a doctor. The Germans did not authorize this. They refused energetically to admit me to his presence, as they were extraordinarily suspicious of them. He played tricks on them that I knew nothing of… He was in contact with the French, prisoners, workers… Finally, the Germans took him further away and all communication between us ceased. He never came to see me. From that moment on, I did not know where he was interned and knew nothing more of him.

Louis Noguères quoted a letter from the doctor to Brinon as follows:

Doctor B. Ménétrel
Sigmaringen, 28 October 1944

Dear Minister,
I have always considered myself responsible for the health of the Marshal.

But at Belfort, Mr Bohland let me know that Minister von Ribbentrop had decided that I was responsible "on my own account".

With that warning in mind, I have the duty to bring to your attention the anxieties that I have regarding the Marshal's health.

Everyone, French or foreign, who came near the Marshal in France, before his departure from Vichy, admired his excellent health, sustained by a harmonious physical and moral equilibrium. He is not the same now!

Certainly the transfer of the Marshal from Vichy to Belfort, then to Morvillars and Germany, were accomplished with very correct conditions as regards comfort.

Since his arrival in Sigmaringen, the Marshal has been the object, from the German authorities and yourself, Minister, of particular attentions which make his stay perfectly supportable. Nothing is spared to ensure, as far as possible, the material comfort indispensable to a man of his age.

But the situation in which the Marshal finds himself in Sigmaringen in relation to certain personalities engenders cares and preoccupations in him which keep him in a state of nervous irritation and agitation, especially causing insomnia which is likely to gravely impair his health.

All doctors can testify that, at no matter what age, and especially at that of the Marshal, morale impacts the physique; it is this which never ceases to worry me – ironically, because it is not up to me to furnish a remedy, and that is why I wanted to inform you of the worrying and dangerous situation for the health of the Marshal.

I think that you will be good enough to see no ulterior motive, no tendentious intention, in my communication.

My role beside the Marshal, however debated it is, is only one of disinterested devotion, and it is for me a duty of conscience, in this grave situation, to ask you to believe me when I alert you to a danger that I see increasing every day!

Only the transfer of the Marshal to another residence, far from the political climate of Sigmaringen, could allow a relaxation of his nervous state and a calming of his thoughts. This state worries him himself, as is witnessed by his fear, often expressed to those who approach him, of dying in a foreign land.

I permit myself to suggest this solution, but attach no political significance to it.

It is not up to me to judge the problem from any other aspect than a purely medical one.

I only wish to strictly fulfill my duties as a doctor, whatever the consequences for me. I fear only one thing: to not have done my duty.

Now, today it is imperative: I must warn you in time of the dangers that can be brought to the Marshal by creating around him an atmosphere which can have serious repercussions for his health.

It is according to my conscience that I make this declaration to you and I am sure that you will wish to take it into consideration.

Be assured, Minister, of my highest consideration.

B. Ménétrel

In the light of the doctor's comments, there is little doubt as to the context of his position and his arrest. Brinon and the Nazis clearly saw Ménétrel as an obstacle to bending the Marshal to their will, and impeding the objectives of securing his general participation in the Sigmaringen government-in-exile, and in endorsing the elevation of Doriot as its head. Ménétrel's subsequent detention a short distance from the Marshal has been cited as an additional tactic to put pressure on Pétain.

General Debeney wrote to Abetz on 12 December, warning of the possible consequences for the Marshal's health.

Sigmaringen, 12 December 1944

Dear Ambassador,

Since 22 November, the Marshal has been deprived of the care of his doctor and the sanitary assistance so necessary for a person of his age. He has courageously borne this ordeal, but, today, symptoms have appeared which cannot be ignored and which I believe make it my duty to bring them to your esteemed attention.

In excusing myself for such a confidence, I must inform you that these symptoms are of two kinds.

First are intestinal troubles which the present medication has not succeeded in calming.

Secondly are upsets (vertigo, hot flushes, etc.) inherent to his circulation which normally would be remedied by periodic bloodletting. Normally, the Marshal would have submitted to such a precaution at the beginning of December.

The removal of Dr Ménétrel has not allowed this to proceed. It seems to Madame Marshal, like myself, that there will be danger in letting the current state of things drag on, regarding which Madame Marshal is ready to give you whatever details you deem useful.

The Marshal has requested, by a *Note Verbale* sent on 2 December to Minister von Renthe-Fink (which you will permit me to refer you to in the attached copy), where practical measures are envisaged for allowing him to continue to receive the treatment of Dr Ménétrel, who alone knows the precise temperament of the Marshal and the remedies appropriate to his age. No response to this Note has been communicated to us so far.

I permit myself to respectfully insist that a decision be made and that Dr Ménétrel be put in a position, according to the appropriate modalities, to continue the work of sanitary support for the Marshal which circumstances render particularly necessary.

I ask you to accept, Mr Ambassador, the expression of my highest consideration.

General V. Debeney

Brinon suggested Céline as a replacement: the suggestion did not go down well. 'The Laval floor... Laval I looked after a little... Pétain I never got close to... Brinon had suggested it, Ménétrel had just been arrested... "I'd rather die, right now!..." that was the effect I had on Pétain'.

Eventually, the Germans arranged for a French doctor in a nearby prisoner-of-war camp, to attend to the Marshal. His memoirs of his time as the Marshal's physician-designate, published in 1964 under the name Gérard-Trinité Schillemans with a preface by the noted right-wing lawyer Jacques Isorni, are suspect as an objective account of the Marshal himself – a topic which they cover very sparingly – but give some of the more piquant personal accounts of the environs and atmosphere at Sigmaringen. 'I was in fact summoned to the infirmary one day by Doctor Gross who unexpectedly offered me a mysterious mission,' Schillemans recounted. Explaining the assignment, General Bridoux represented Dr Ménétrel's removal as voluntary. 'At present, the situation is very tense between Ménétrel and the Reich authorities. Also, fearing for his very existence, and wishing to be forgotten for a bit, he would like to temporarily relinquish his functions.' Bridoux also emphasized the need to abstain from any political activity, whatever the circumstances.

From the nearby town of Scheer, some 6km east of Sigmaringen itself, Ménétrel wrote a letter of protest to Renthe-Fink on 8 January 1945. Full of protests and justifications, the letter objected in particular to the lack of any subsequent decision or conclusion following his interrogation. 'What have I done to justify such a morally painful fate, which is already starting to affect my health?' Ménétrel protested:

I left my family and my country despite the Marshal's insistence on advising me to stay with my people. The only consolation in this harsh abandonment was to share the fate of he who I wished to follow out of duty and personal attachment. Far from him, these sacrifices have become as unsupportable to me as they are in vain ... I have the duty to remind you, Minister, that continuance of the current situation cannot fail, sooner or later, to have grave repercussions for the health of the Marshal. The professional confidentiality by which I am bound, as well as the trust that I have been honoured with, prevent me from making any further comment. I do not need to report the reasons, internal, medical, or otherwise which make my presence with the Marshal necessary. I can however affirm that those reasons are and remain entirely foreign to politics, but relate to my profession … It is no longer, in my eyes, a question of politics, of suspicions, of misunderstandings; it concerns the health of Marshal Pétain, for which I am responsible before all France. I note that I have been placed in a position where it is impossible to exercise the duties entrusted to me. If I am not guilty, I demand to be set free! If I am believed to be guilty, let someone tell me of what, so that I may defend myself, as every accused has the sacred right to do! I fear no man's judgment, my conscience reproaches me with nothing and my honour has not been stained by the perfidious and ridiculous insinuations which certain vile compatriots, I fear, have undoubtedly used with the objective of reaching, through me, the legal head of France.

Needless to say, his protests had no effect, and on 16 March 1945, Ménétrel was transferred to confinement in Czechoslovakia. As late as 20 April 1945, Pétain was still sending *Notes Verbales* to protest Ménétrel's removal, but they were never to see each other again.

Brinon presented Ménétrel's arrest to Schillemans as inevitable, and furthermore, blamed him for much of the difficulties in getting the Marshal to collaborate:

Given the harmful ascendancy that Dr Ménétrel had over the French Head of State, who he had been treating for a long time, who his father had already treated in the past, he used this influence to advance a policy of collaboration so grudging that it became practically non-existent. This did the greatest harm to Germany, which wished for a more cordial understanding with France. The Marshal only followed this policy of collaboration as little as possible, when he really could not do otherwise, and always reluctantly. This was largely due to his immediate entourage, which thus prevented all the achievements that should have borne fruit.

Brinon may have actually believed what he told Schillemans: more likely, it was cover for the successive ploys to put psychological pressure on the Marshal. There is certainly little to suggest in all Pétain's statements, recorded comments or reported actions to suggest that he deferred to his doctor or anyone else in making such crucial decisions. He had certainly attempted to achieve a more cordial understanding with the Reich – but on terms that the Reich was unwilling to grant, including greater respect and consideration for France's sovereign status. The German decision to abduct him across the border and confine him in Sigmaringen had done nothing to soften his attitudes, and he was fully cognisant of the complicity of Brinon and the others in facilitating that abduction. On 29 October 1944, Pétain wrote to Brinon, asking him to produce a single line or document to prove that he had confirmed the personal delegation conferred on him in December 1940. He also wrote that, 'to avoid any equivocation, I ask you to stop wearing henceforth the insignia of the Francisque'.

Schillemans recounted a fairly typical dinner of the Commission in the great dining hall of the castle in late November 1944, soon after the French 2nd Armoured Division under General Philippe Leclerc de Hauteclocque had liberated Strasbourg. Seated at an immense table laid with white linen and glittering silver were Jean Luchaire and his wife, Déat and his wife, Brinon with two of his secretaries, and Darnand and his wife. Despite all the privations of wartime rationing, the Germans provided a small bottle of white wine for each diner, to wash down their cabbage soup. Everyone's mind was on the news from Strasbourg. Rousso gave his own version of the conversation:

'It's a tactic,' Luchaire proclaimed. 'Subtle, yes, very subtle. The Germans certainly are canny fighters… You see, by letting Leclerc penetrate to Strasbourg, they're narrowing their front. Yes, it's a great idea! They draw closer to their supply bases and catch Leclerc in a trap…'

Seeing no reaction from his audience, Luchaire went further.

'Besides, this Leclerc is a small-time soldier, a poor adventurer, who made his way in Eisenhower's baggage!'

At this, Brinon burst out:

'No, Luchaire, General de Hauteclocque is no adventurer or small-time soldier as you say. I knew that officer before, and consider him a magnificent soldier and even an excellent Frenchman, even though, I grant you, he has been abused by a band of thugs and was mistaken about events. Your paper is inept... You have no right to smear the name of General de Hauteclocque, least of all *you*, Luchaire.'

Such was the atmosphere and the level of mutual respect among the active collaborationists at Sigmaringen.

Soon after the liberation of Strasbourg, Schillemans was finally invited into the inner circle of Pétain's most faithful acolytes. Admiral Henri Bléhaut sent an invitation, slipped under his door, to see him on the third floor of the castle – with an added exhortation to burn the letter after. Going up by a little spiral service staircase, Schillemans made his way to the admiral's apartment and, after an exchange of pleasantries, was invited to join him the next morning, in the castle's little courtyard beside the main gate, for the promenade that he usually took daily with the Marshal and General Debeney. 'We will leave on foot, so that we can talk at leisure about everything that concerns us,' he said. Admiral Bléhaut duly met Schillemans the next day and led him across the town on foot to meet the Marshal on his usual promenade. On the way, the admiral explained that the Marshal wished to know from him the current atmosphere and state of opinion in the prisoner of war camps, and whether a visit from him would bring some comfort to the prisoners. By his own account, Schillemans counselled that any such visit would be misrepresented by the Nazis and the Governmental Commission, and that Pétain should dissociate himself completely from the French and German interests at Sigmaringen. He also claimed to have suggested escape via Switzerland to the admiral, who objected that such an escape would almost certainly fail. Soon after, they met the Marshal, walking with General Debeney, and exchanged glances, but no words. According to Schillemans, at this point Pétain still appeared relatively active and fully in control of his faculties, with a direct, searching gaze:

They were eyes that seemed to question, the eyes of an intelligent chief, seeming to await the answer to a question already posed. That gaze fixed on me for a brief moment, long enough for him to take three or perhaps four steps, but it had a limpidity, a flame, such a beautiful luminosity, that it seemed to me that I could still feel it resting on me, while he had already passed by, and his tall silhouette was melting into the shreds of mist drifting across the road.

Again, it is important to remember that Schillemans, whatever the real identity concealed by his pseudonym, was writing very much from the post-war right-wing camp of apologists for Pétain.

In December 1944, Otto Abetz was dismissed from his formal position as 'ambassador' to the Sigmaringen enclave, ostensibly due to his antipathy to the clique around Doriot under the patronage of Ribbentrop, and his failure to create a functioning government-in-exile. Louis Noguères described the result of Abetz's attempts to form a functioning regime as follows:

Instead of this result, life in isolation in Sigmaringen had created an unbreathable atmosphere. The resentments, grudges, jealousies, hopes and disappointments, direct and indirect contacts, rumours peddled by one or another about each other, the suffocation of defeat as well as the disgust of treason, all agitated in a perpetual ambience of police surveillance – of all the police and all the denunciations! – had led to the collapse of the policy advocated by Abetz.

Céline reported his constant encounters:

Every time I get out of the Löwen [to see patients, with the current of rumour and forced optimism in Sigmaringent] the blabbermouths who grab you and won't let go!... to see this one [patient]... that one... I can't avoid it!... you run into some nutcase who stops you dead in your tracks!... every doorway... every street corner... so you can tell him what you think about what's going on?... and not just a bit! and not later! straight away! and very frankly! squarely! the slap on the shoulder! enough to knock it out of joint and dislocate it! the handshake forceful enough to rock and stagger you, you know!... "Ah, our dear Doctor, here he is!"... what a surprise!... what joy!... oh!... but you there, be careful! super-careful! with great care! It's the moment to reply very spontaneously! Dynamic!

Optimist! Terrific conviction! the man who's asking your opinion isn't any everyday little snitch! Don't stutter! Don't quibble! Go for it! "German victory is in the bag... the new Europe is set to go!... the secret army has destroyed London!... razed flat! Von Paulus is in Moscow but they won't announce it until after winter!... Rommel is in Cairo!... everything will be announced at once!... the Americans are suing for peace... and here we are, on the pavement, at home, as it were! Marching down the Champs-Élysées!... just a matter of trains, of transport... not enough trains!... a matter of weeks! Back home via Rethondes and Saint-Denis!"

One bizarre rumour, reported by Schillemans, was that there were small light planes with very long range hidden on the terraces of the castle, ready for its occupants to flee at a moment's notice – and that this was the only explanation for their bizarre optimism in the face of events. Other fantasies of wonder-weapons that would magically turn round the progress of the war persisted right up until the bitter end. As late as 6 April 1945, Déat recorded in his journal a rumour that 'six hundred English planes have been destroyed by an ochre cloud which persisted for twenty-four hours over certain parts of England', though adding 'will see tonight if it's true'.

Some of the refugees' actual plans were just as bizarre. Céline reported an effusion by Alphonse de Châteaubriant:

"Understand! Understand, Céline! As I have written: victory will go to the most tempered soul!... the spirituality of steel!... we have this quality of soul, don't we, Abetz?"

"Oh! certainly, Chateaubriant!"

Abetz isn't about to contradict him!

"The soul!... the soul, our weapon, the bomb... I have it! I will have it!"

Damn! I want him to tell me everything!...

"What bomb, Alphonse?"

"Understand me my dear Céline! With a few 'shock' companions, we have chosen our position!... Oh! I have known other tests!"

He collects himself... three enormous deep sighs!... and he continues...

"A place, an absolutely inaccessible valley, very narrow, a cirque, we should say, between three peaks... in the depths of the Tyrol!... and there! there Céline!... we will isolate ourselves!... you understand me?... we concentrate!... we will develop our bomb!"

Hoffmann does not quite understand...

"Your bomb with what?"

"Oh! dear Hoffmann!... not a steel bomb! nor dynamite!... a thousand times no!... a bomb of concentration! of faith! Hoffmann!"

"So?"

"A message!... a terrible moral bomb!... isn't that right, Abetz?... has the Christian religion triumphed in any other way? a terrible moral bomb!... isn't that right, Céline?"

Abetz was replaced by Otto Reinebeck, a career diplomat from the Weimar era who had continued his activities under the Nazi regime. On 13 December, Laval, now superfluous to German plans, almost got his wish for removal to a rural retreat – but not in the way he wanted. He was informed that he was to be relocated to Silesia, far closer to the Eastern Front. The Germans, Ribbentrop above all, felt that his refusal to cooperate with the Commission was setting a bad example to other refuseniks who might otherwise join the puppet government. Furthermore, the Nazis suspected that he had attempted to contact the Allied high command after the Normandy landings. Clearly frightened by the risk of falling into the hands of the Russians, Laval applied repeatedly to the German Foreign Ministry, and finally reached Hitler's ear via Arno Breker, the leading sculptor of national-socialist realism. Hitler ordered Ribbentrop to leave Laval where he was.

Henry Rousso published a very interesting letter from Ribbentrop to Laval, dated 6 January 1945, which he found in the unpublished manuscript of the memoirs of Maurice Gabolde (Chapter XXI). It reads as follows:

Dear Mr Laval,

It is with great interest that I have acquainted myself with the declarations which you sent to me on 15 and 27 December 1944. We are not at all unaware that you have served the cause of Franco-German understanding with a courage that has gone so far as to put your own life at risk; on the German side, we have always had the greatest confidence in you.

Unhappily, I must say that your attitude during and after the Anglo-American disembarkation in France gave rise to grave doubts among us, to say the least, to your perseverance – so important in these times of historic conflict – in maintaining a political line whose pursuit over the years has levied so much pain and hard work on us both.

However useful it might be to discuss the questions you have raised, as well as the possible misunderstandings which might require clarification, one thing appears to me to be of the greatest importance: that you were saved – despite yourself – from certain death at the hands of your enemies in Paris, a fact which I note with profound satisfaction and joy. It seems to me that the cause of Franco-German understanding, which concerns you to the same degree as us, was better served thus than if we had *condoned* that you should be delivered in Paris to the Gaullist executioner.

As for the rest, I have gladly followed your wish to take up another domicile than the one that was prepared for you by us in Silesia.

It is with deep regret that I learned of the illness that struck you recently. I would like to believe that you will soon be sufficiently recovered that nothing would stand in the way of your transfer of domicile.

I will take great pleasure in speaking with you again personally in due course, and express my best wishes for your health.

Yours,

H. von Ribbentrop

Laval was eventually installed in Wilflingen, just 12 kilometres from Sigmaringen.

As the lists of collaborationists executed in liberated France grew, the climate of fear and anxiety in Sigmaringen worsened. Brinon eulogized Georges Suarez, sometime collaborationist journalist and biographer of Pétain, who was executed on 9 November 1944. Robert Brasillach, collaborationist journalist, protege of Charles Maurras, and man of letters, executed on 6 February 1945, was one of the most significant writers to die. After his execution, Rebatet proclaimed in the pages of *La France* that 'Germany is the last refuge of individual liberty'.

Years later, in 1963, de Gaulle gave his verdict on the execution:

So many poor fools were being summarily shot during the Liberation, for having allowed themselves to be drawn into collaboration! Why should those who drew them in – the Darnands, the Déats, the Pucheus, the Henriots, the Brasillaches – have slipped through the cracks? An intellectual is not less, but more responsible than the others. He is an instigator. He is a leader in the strongest sense. François Mauriac wrote to me that a thinking head must not fall. And why this privilege? A big head is more responsible than the head of a nobody! Brasillach was intelligent. He had talent. What he did is all the more serious. His commitment to collaboration strengthened the Nazis. An intellectual has no more right to indulgence; he has less, because he is more informed, more capable of critical thinking, therefore more guilty. The words of an intellectual are arrows, his formulations are bullets! He has the power to transform the public mind. He cannot enjoy the advantages of this power and refuse its inconveniences! When the time comes for justice, he must pay.[4]

Obviously, the remaining collaborators in Sigmaringen could expect little mercy in these circumstances.

Collaborators from further afield occasionally visited the enclave, to court Pétain or for other reasons. One such was Léon Degrelle, the leading Belgian collaborator and commander of the Walloon Legion, a sometime protégé of Abetz, who had briefly indulged his dreams of partitioning France. Degrelle also attempted occasionally to recruit for his Legion in Sigmaringen, and on 13 November 1944, addressed the following letter to Pétain:

Sigmaringen, 13 November 1944

Marshal,

Passing through Sigmaringen, I observe with emotion those walls behind which you, the great solitary victor, await the resurrection of France.

Soldier, I would have the honour and joy of saluting you briefly.

Far from politics, I wage a hard struggle on the Front. I would have been happy to see, in his exile, that the great soldier who you are remains for all those who believe in the honour of arms and the joy of duty.

In 1937, Marshal, you showed the kindness to write to me when I published a book entitled: *Revolution of Souls.*

It is through the memory of the sympathy that you demonstrated towards me before, that I permit myself to ask you for a brief moment of audience.

It is not a journalist who asks you this, Marshal, nor a politician; it is a soldier at the front who would see the most glorious soldier of the Front of the Great War.

I hope, Marshal, that you would make this exception in your solitude. And I ask you to accept the profound respect of

DEGRELLE

Commander of the Walloon Division

Sigmaringen Castle

General Debeney replied for the Marshal:

General Debeney

Sigmaringen,

My Dear Major,

Marshal Pétain has asked me to acknowledge receipt of your letter and to let you know that he regrets not being able to give a response to your request for an audience contained therein. Since being forced to leave France, the Marshal has made it a rule to receive no visit.

Please accept, my dear Major, the assurance of my distinguished sentiments.

V. Debeney

Cabinet of the Marshal

Brinon may have encouraged Degrelle's visit as yet another bid to open up the Marshal's rigid stance; needless to say, this initiative failed like so many others.

Meanwhile, Henry Charbonneau and other Milice higher-ups were still looking for new recruits among the French POWs in Germany, to augment the Milice units in Sigmaringen, and to furnish manpower for the planned infiltration activities in France. A passage from the 16 November 1944 edition of *La France* gives some more details:

> Henry Charbonneau expressed the goals of the French Milice in Germany: to unearth, among the French workers, an elite amenable to take the responsibilities and assume the tasks that would be entrusted to them, and form groups of sincere and committed militants ready to bring about the triumph of the ideal of a true National Revolution.

Darnand still entertained hopes of turning the Milice into some kind of paramilitary political force for the reconquest of France, even without the more capable personnel he had lost to the Charlemagne Division. As late as 18 February 1945, as recorded by Giolitto, he was still proclaiming that 'it is only in France and in the breast of the French people that the movement will spring which, struggling against Bolshevism and plutocracy, will build the basis of the French renaissance.' His plans for such initiatives involved as much emphasis on politics and ideology as on subversion. During his presentation in the cinema at Ulm on 23 October, he declared that 'we must return to France with a doctrine and a force. You must be ready for the political tasks that await us. I need to be able to find among you political figures necessary for the national recovery.'

Darnand and other Milice leaders claimed that they had their own fifth column of 'white maquis' behind the lines in France, ready to spring into action at the appropriate time to carry out their own partisan warfare against the Allies and the new Gaullist regime. Around 100 recruits did enter the specialist Milice partisan training schools, the Organisations Techniques O.T.1 and O.T.2, at Krauchenwies, near Sigmaringen, where they were instructed by Jean Filiol, a veteran of the Cagoule assassination campaigns of the 1930s, and a participant in many of the most notorious Milice massacres during the Liberation of France. The few 'white maquis' who were parachuted into France – eleven on 15 December 1944 and three on 7 January 1945, both times into Corrèze to the east of Bordeaux – were rounded up promptly by Free French forces and local peasants. This could be confirmation that there was a spy in Sigmaringen alerting the Allies to their destination. As late as 18 April 1945, in a diplomatic document entitled '*Note sur l'activité des émigrés français à Sigmaringen*', the post-Liberation French government demonstrated detailed understanding of the entire situation in the enclave. On the other hand, there is no need to look much further than the incompetence and amateurishness of the Milice for an explanation.

Ideas and preparations for suicide periodically surfaced among the Sigmaringen elite, as they oscillated between febrile hope and bleak despair. In *Castle to Castle*, Céline records one bizarre, hallucinatory, and quite probably fabricated conversation with Laval and Bichelonne, where the titular President appoints him Governor of Saint-Pierre and Miquelon, the French North American territories, which Céline had visited briefly in the 1930s, in exchange for a phial of cyanide:

"You personally, do you have a little something you want?"

Then another idea comes to me! Still I can say I refused everything! Everything! ... but where we are, no ... nothing matters anymore! ...

"Mr President, perhaps you could have me appointed Governor of the Saint-Pierre and Miquelon Islands?"

I don't need to hold back!

"Promised! ... Agreed! Understood! You'll take a note of that, won't you, Bichelonne?"

"Certainly, Mr President!"

Still, Laval had a little question:

"But what gave you the idea, Doctor?"

"Just, Mr President! the beauties of Saint-Pierre and Miquelon!..."

I tell him... I don't speak from hearsay... I've been there!... it took twenty-five days from Bordeaux to Saint-Pierre... on the very fragile *Celtique*... there's still fishing in Saint-Pierre... I know Langlade and Miquelon well... I know the road well... the only road from end to end of the island... the road and the marker of "Memory", the road dug into the rock by the sailors of the *Iphigénie*... I'm not making this up... a real memory, a real road!... not just the sailors of the *Iphigénie*!... the convicts too... they had a penal colony in Saint-Pierre... which also left a marker!...

"You should see that, Mr President! In the middle of the Atlantic Ocean!"

The important thing: I was appointed Governor... I still am!...

Even if the conversation ever did take place, it is unlikely that Laval took it seriously, given his stance of exercising no official functions, least of all the appointment of governors. But it was very like Céline to repeat it and insist on it.

According to Louis Noguères, Francis Bout de l'An, the Milice secretary-general, attempted an abortive political volte-face during the December days when the Sigmaringen enclave dreamed of a return to France in the wake of the Ardennes Offensive. He anticipated dropping the discredited name Milice in favour of a more political formulation, like the National Revolutionary Party, and discarding the organization's twenty-one points in favour of something like a reversion to pre-war Republican formulae, with parliamentary sovereignty and recognition of the Declaration of the League of the Rights of Man, aiming at the creation of a Fourth Republic. Diehards within what remained of the Milice immediately accused him of treason.

Exactly how genuine and serious this effort was is unclear, and in any event, Bout de l'An immediately rejoined Doriot in support of his push to create a Nazi-backed emigre united front. But Noguères also reports discussions within the Sigmaringen camp around the anticipated German victory, with the possibility of reconciliation with the more moderate and acceptable factions among the Gaullists. Of course, any such reconciliation was fantastical while it was based on the chimera of a German victory and a return to France. But this may have signalled the grudging and qualified recognition among the refugees that their old dogma had been exploded, and the time had come for some sort of adjustment to the new realities.

Others were not so flexible. General Debeney wrote a letter to Bruneton dated 18 December 1944, in which he said: 'Myself, I too believe, that in the present difficult circumstances, we must, above all, keep holding on.' The Commission's difficulties were worsened by the growing domestic power struggle within the Reich, which mirrored their own petty squabbles on a far larger scale. The establishment of the Volkssturm on 25 September 1944, formally mobilizing the entire male German population for a war of popular resistance, threw far more power into the hands of Heinrich Himmler and Martin Bormann. Himmler patronized Doriot and his separate power base against Ribbentrop and Abetz, who still mostly favoured the Commission and the residue of legitimate authority from Pétain – on both sides, the French collaborationists were just pawns in the wider internal power struggle. Hitler had always favoured such internecine rivalries to protect his own pre-eminent position; this late in the war, they contributed to a disastrous division of effort. Abetz's demotion from his post in December 1944 signified the haemorrhage of authority and credibility from the Commission to Doriot and his grouping.

Bichelonne, suffering complications from a fractured knee he sustained in April 1944, was moved to the SS hospital at Hohenlychen, where he was operated on and died on 22 December 1944. The recorded cause of death was a pulmonary embolism, but speculation persisted that he had been assassinated. The Nazis laid on a grand funeral for him, with Vichy dignitaries from Sigmaringen – brought by train to Hohenlychen – treated to post-funerary entertainments including a film show of the autopsy of Bichelonne. Laval did not attend the funeral, apparently due to his continuing anxiety over his own position with the Nazis.

The customary Sigmaringen rumours followed Bichelonne's death. Had the great technocrat and savant been killed because he knew too much? Subsequent speculation broadened this into some knowledge of atomic bomb secrets, perhaps inside knowledge about the manufacture of heavy water? Who better than Bichelonne to be custodian of French secrets regarding heavy water production? Needless to say, there was no apparent substance for these speculations, but that did not stop the rumour mills from turning.

On Christmas Eve 1944, the pianist Lucienne Delforge, virtuoso, athlete, mountaineer, anti-Semite, sometime mistress of Céline, gave a grand recital in the Portuguese Gallery of the castle. Pétain, formerly her patron and commissioner of a report from her on the place of music in the new Europe, declined her invitation to attend.

In his Christmas radio broadcast from Sigmaringen, Brinon said:

I assure you that, so long as she does not reject those responsible for her woes, France will go from trial to trial until annihilation. Those who are responsible for your illusions, for your weaknesses, are those in command, who dispose of you, who make you suffer today and will get you killed tomorrow... You have not finished serving. Now, you must triumph or die for Soviet Russia. This, according to de Gaulle and Bidault, is the supreme national interest... We say that the cause of Germany is a sacred cause. We believe in her victory because we see, and because we know...

To the French who suffer under de Gaulle we cry: "Know in order to see, understand, and act. The power that is imposed on you is an usurped power. The mobilization that it decrees is dictated by foreigners. The alliances which it has concluded are against French interests. The policies of pretended liberation are policies of destruction and death. French, resist, disobey, aid us. It is only with our victory that you will see the end to your ills".

The first issue of *La France* for 1945, published on 2 January and proclaiming its second year, bore as its lead headline, 'Germany Invincible!' and quoted Adolf Hitler's proclamation 'At this hour, I am the spokesman of the Great German Reich before Providence, and I can affirm to her that the German people will hold out until She grants victory to the one most worthy of it.'

Christian de la Mazière, a survivor of the SS Division Charlemagne and a journalist in his post-war career, recounted a very curious incident in February 1945. Two soldiers in German uniforms bearing a tricolour shoulder badge got off the train and headed straight to the castle, where they demanded an audience with the Marshal. They claimed to have arrived from Czechoslovakia, en route to the Eastern Front, and insisted that they had a right to a brief conversation with the Marshal or Laval. Refused an audience, the two soldiers decided to take a meal at one of the local restaurants before catching their train. There, they were greeted with uniform hostility as traitors, on account of their German uniforms, despite the status of the enclave's inhabitants.

All this time, Jacques Doriot had remained aloof from the Sigmaringen enclave and the puppet government of Brinon. He refused German attempts to unite his followers with the Milice, claiming that this was simply a manoeuvre by Darnand to reinforce his own position. He had also refused Ribbentrop's blandishments to join a government with Brinon and the other collaborationists, insisting that he would only enter such an administration as its head. He fled to Germany soon after the Normandy landings and attempted to establish an alternative centre of power on the island of Mainau in Lake Constance, in his own equivalent to Sigmaringen Castle. Jean Hérold-Paquis described it as a:

Montmartre hill planted on the water. At the top, a red and white castle with the Baden coat of arms shining on the facade, with tall 17th-century windows, balconies in the form of loggias, and in front of the wide staircases, awful dirty 1900s streetlamps. But the terrace in front is beautiful, and the lawns, the flower beds... lend nobility to what would be, without the frame, without the immensity of the lake, without the skyline of the Alps, without the decor sought by men, a vast tenement house perched on a wooded hill...

Behind the chapel, a surprise garden in imitation of Le Nôtre, peopled with gods and Cupids, with laughing basins, and roses, roses, roses everywhere... We contemplate the park that a strange collector has stocked with all the conifers in the world. The gigantic sequoias of North America, the powerful cedars of Lebanon shelter a crowd of bizarre trees born in Chile, Japan, Tibet, Africa, Australia... From the windows of the castle opening on the lake, we see only the water and the mountains. Three borders can be guessed: Germany with Lindau, Austria with Bregenz, and Switzerland. Far off, in their blue light, loom the Dolomites.

Seen from within, this folly of a Swedish prince is an extraordinary museum, where centuries and masters have piled, higgledy-piggledy, works of art and fake bronzes, amateur paintings and great tableaux. The vast ballroom, on the second floor, affirms the taste of the 17th century. But the cinema and the theatre confirm that the last owner is a man of the 20th century.[5]

Another memorialist, the writer Marie Chaix, daughter of the PPF militant Albert Beugras, wrote her own impressions of life on the island in her 1972 book *Les lauriers du lac de Constance*:

On Mainau, the PPF survivors lead a grand life. Those ladies hold salons under the crystal chandeliers of the King of Sweden, those gentlemen court them, get drunk, play, chat, and forget, deep in the brocade sofas, their rough lives as militants. Candlelit dinners are served on small tables covered in Ukrainian-style lace in the huge reception rooms on the ground floor, in the atmosphere of a *fin-de-siècle* palace. Dinners end in costume balls performed under the glass roofs of the terrace or as a comedy in the castle's theatre.

Doriot's court in exile was supported by his own radio station, Radio-Patrie, and his newspaper, *Le Petit Parisien*. Amply funded by his German backers, both of these easily outperformed their Sigmaringen equivalents, with *Le Petit Parisien* reaching a print run of 80,000 copies at its peak, versus 45,000 at best for *La France*, plus far better layout and content, and Radio-Patrie broadcasting for six hours per day versus ninety minutes for Ici la France. All this establishment, of course, was supported by German resources and money.

From September 1944, Doriot began training a unit of pro-Nazi agents and saboteurs to be inserted into liberated France, under the name of 'Pâquerette'. At most 300 were installed at the castle of Hohenbuchau around 10 kilometres from Wiesbaden, and drilled in a curriculum that emphasized political organization and ideology as much as practical infiltration techniques. The Germans remained suspicious of the enterprise and its recruits and kept it under close observation. Four of Doriot's trainees were parachuted into France on 10 January 1945 in the forest of Montargis, but were soon rounded up by the police. On 6 January 1945, with Ribbentrop's backing, Doriot announced at Mainau the formation of a Comité de libération française, a supposed rival both to de Gaulle's CFLN and the Commission in Sigmaringen. To make this into a true rallying point for collaborationists and French fascists, however, he had to win the endorsement and cooperation of Déat, Darland, Luchaire, and the other most influential participants in the Sigmaringen enclave.

André Masson, Commissioner-General for Prisoners of War under the Vichy regime, gave his reasons for adhering to Doriot as follows:

> In adhering to the Comité de libération française, I also adhere to certain declarations of Jacques Doriot.
>
> In particular, he has declared: by our struggle, we reestablish France in her territorial and imperial unity which National-Socialist Germany has never threatened in the past and will not threaten in the future... A German victory will end in the salvation of a Europe in which France will keep a place worthy of her history...

According to the collaborationist journalist and writer Maurice-Yvan Sicard, otherwise known as Saint-Paulien, Doriot had obtained personal commitments from Hitler including the return of Lorraine and the occupied territories of northern France to French control, a joint Franco-German administration of Alsace for a decade, guarantees of the integrity of the French colonial empire, and promises of non-reprisal against French territories. This source is highly untrustworthy, and even if Hitler had made such promises, he would be unlikely to give them much attention in the last stages of the war. They do, however, indicate just how many issues would have to be settled in any genuine Franco-German Axis alliance, and how vain were any collaborationist hopes placed in Doriot. Furthermore, Doriot's sponsors, who had been so determined to secure his supremacy in the autumn of 1944, had far more immediate and selfish priorities by early 1945, despite all the fantastic plans hatched while some military return to France still was a faint possibility.

Maurice-Yvan Sicard reported fantastical, delusional statements by Doriot, quoted by Rousso, regarding the significance of his Comité: 'Against them [the enemies of France], for the first time in French history, they see joined together all the healthy forces of the Nation. The creation of the Comité de libération française is none other than their death blow.'

The Commission was poorly positioned at this point to present a united front against Doriot's power grab. Tensions between its members had almost reached breaking point. They only rarely met together, even dining in their quarters rather than collectively. From mid-November 1944, Brinon had attempted to gain power over Luchaire's propaganda operations, by controlling their finances, acting unilaterally without reference to Luchaire or the rest of the Commission. In the end, Luchaire, supported by Déat, had to threaten his resignation to force Brinon to stop undermining him. The Ardennes Offensive, however much it fuelled vague hopes and fantasies of return in the enclave, had also exacerbated the divisions among its membership, as they disputed or took different lines on how to position themselves for a potential return to France, whether to make common cause with de Gaulle against the Communists, to seek some position within a new German occupation, or simply to engage in an orgy of massacre and retribution.

Brinon, aware of Ribbentrop's preferences and his own isolation within the Commission, yielded to the pressure and declared himself ready to align with Doriot. Déat, Darnand and the others, who had their own power bases of sorts, were less ready to fall under Doriot's yoke, and sought negotiations. Déat in particular was ready to extract as many concessions as he could. Cointet records his statement on the issue: 'Doriot is ready to personally give me all sorts of concessions so long as he stays head of the store.'

Some curious rumours and speculations around the combination were already circulating, if some sources are to be believed. According to Henry Lalouel, onetime professor of international law at the University of Nancy and confidante of Laval, who he had followed into exile, one day in February 1945 he met with Laval on the stairs in Sigmaringen Castle, who said to him:

I was just at your place. I must see Brinon in a moment, and I would like to have a witness to that interview. You know that I have held myself rigorously aloof and have never mingled with what they do at the Commission, but I had confirmation of something very serious this morning and I have a duty to intervene. It's like this: The Germans, who realize that they are lost, are very embarrassed by Blum, Daladier, Gamelin, Reynaud, Herriot... They don't dare shoot them, but they are thinking of giving them to Brinon, whose accord with Doriot is imminent, and the both of them will soon be overwhelmed by the most fanatical elements of the Milice who will put them on notice to execute these hostages... I have to open his eyes and prevent this.

Exactly how much truth there is in this report is unclear; Lalouel might well have been trying to whitewash the reputation of his former friend. In the circumstances, though, the fear itself was not unreasonable: the Milice had already murdered prominent politicians in France. In any case, Brinon might have taken the initiative to try to secure the elite POWs as a bargaining chip to trade with the Allies in his own exit plans.

Simultaneously, Darnand's Milice followers who had been inducted into the SS Division Charlemagne, shorn of their leader, were suffering grievously on the Eastern Front. Posted to Pomerania, equipped with nothing better than trucks and Panzerfaust anti-tank weapons, the division's two infantry regiments and anti-tank unit arrived at Hammerstein (modern Czarne in Polish Pomerania) on 22 February 1945. Two days later, the Russians began their offensive. For the next three days, the French SS fought off attacks from the Russian 19th Army, losing some 1,500 men out of the 4,500 total complement. After this debacle, the Germans withdrew and reorganized the remaining forces.

Doriot was on his way to a meeting with Déat on 22 February 1945 when his official car was machine-gunned by fighters at Meßkirch, barely 10km from Sigmaringen. Doriot and his driver were both hit; a woman passenger in the car somehow escaped unscathed. That weekend, *La France* ran a tribute from Luchaire under the headline 'Jacques Doriot, Chief of the Parti Populaire Français, Founder of the Comité de libération française, Assassinated by Terrorist Aviators'. Contemporary photographs of his funeral at Mengen three days later show him laid to rest in a coffin draped with the French flag, but with his Nazi uniform on top of it. All of his rivals were present, Brinon, Déat, Darnand, Luchaire, as well as Reinebeck and many other Axis sympathisers.

Even Céline put in an appearance, although Pétain and Laval were both absent. According to Hérold-Paquis, Lucien Rebatet said to him after the funeral: 'Everything's fucked, old friend... I don't believe in anything any more, neither an idea, nor a man, nor a war.'

Immediately, rumours began to circulate around the true circumstances of Doriot's death, and conspiracy theories have persisted ever since. Some alleged that the fighters responsible were not Allied but German. Maurice-Yvan Sicard, PPF director, advanced the theory that Himmler and the SD had had him killed, for refusing to countenance the transfer of French SS units to the Western Front. Others speculated that Martin Bormann, resentful of Doriot for using his close relations with Goebbels to gain access to Hitler, had had him assassinated. Jacques Bouly de Lesdain, Luchaire's director-general of radio in Sigmaringen and sometime *La France* columnist, entertained the absurd idea that Doriot, conscious of the Allied approach, was seeking to reforge his old ties with the Communists, and that the Germans had him killed before he could defect, claiming that the bullet holes in the car showed that Doriot had been shot, not from the air, but from the ground. An even more bizarre wrinkle on this theory is that Doriot was seeking to ally with the anti-Communist Resistance to sow dissent within the Allied ranks.[6] Still another theory was that the Abwehr, long an independent player in the fragmented Nazi intelligence apparat, had him killed. Some even speculated that he had opened contacts with the Gaullist Resistance and was a double agent. Any rival faction could have leaked his itinerary to Allied intelligence, facilitating an ambush. These and other speculations pullulated in the febrile, paranoid atmosphere of residual French collaborationism.

Doriot's death left many more unanswered questions than just the ultimate perpetrators. Could he have reunited the disparate forces of French fascism and collaborationism? Could he have provided any kind of real counterweight to de Gaulle and the CFLN? Despite his dramatic removal from the scene, he had far less of a real power base than even Darnand with his Milice loyalists. Like the other aspirants to Pétain's tarnished crown, he lacked even the shadow of legitimacy, although he probably was one of the few collaborationist leaders fanatical and self-delusive enough not to trouble himself over that. Despite his personal charisma, he had never been conspicuously intellectual, and he produced nothing like the exhaustive plans of the Free French to remake France institutionally and politically. His attempt to revive the PPF under German occupation had never attracted many adherents, and his efforts to build a clandestine sabotage and subversion organization were feeble and comical. His Comité de libération française was a pitiful copycat exercise. When Brinon and Ribbentrop discussed the possibility of installing him in an administration without Pétain, Brinon pointed out that he had no more than some 300 militants in the zones still held by the Germans. His choice of approach and even the name for his organization suggest envy of de Gaulle and a desperate urge towards emulation, rather than serious political goals.

Furthermore, as Cointet has pointed out, 'the Hitlerian project for Doriot was inseparable from the construction of an "Alpine redoubt" (*Alpenfestung*)'. For so long as all was quiet on the Western Front, the Third Reich had no real interest in a leader with revolutionary pretensions like Doriot, preferring a more conservative, less assertive regime like that of the Marshal. Only when the Axis was on the verge of defeat did Doriot's potential to mobilize more dynamic forces alongside Germany become attractive. Yet metropolitan France, exhausted after four years of war, privation, and social and political trauma, was an unpromising territory for raising a fresh revolutionary insurrection, let alone in favour of its hated oppressors and against its liberators, and by that stage, the Third Reich had other priorities. Doriot and his followers at least kept the fascist penchant for megalomaniac self-delusion going until the bitter end.

Insisting that the only real way to create a new regime in France was for the Axis to win the war, Darnand gave his verdict on the situation afterwards:

There are now, in France, high functionaries, magistrates, personalities, who did not approve of our policies under the Occupation, but who, now, would understand them and are ready to come to an agreement with us if we return. We must give the leading positions to these people, and not give the impression of a camarilla which organizes itself before returning to take over all the levers of command and entrust them to people who are loyal, but more or less capable.

That is why the organization created by Doriot corresponds to nothing. The head of a future French government, if we return, will be in a maquis with our men. Because he is in France and we are in Germany – in that, we were mistaken. We should have managed to stay in France.

As one commentator remarked:

At the moment of the Allied advance towards Paris, these men clung to their illusions which allowed them still to nourish their immense ambitions. They never doubted, never wanted to doubt, the German victory, a victory, besides, which was their only means of salvation. After mocking the isolation of de Gaulle and the first Gaullists, after having pursued the Resistants, they tried to imitate them, imagining that the same methods would have the same results, the same words, the same influence. So we see them parachuting, towards non-existent Milice maquis, men lost in advance, creating in their turn a Committee of Liberation, and announcing the birth of *Ici la France*, a caricature of *Ici London*.[7]

Doriot's death triggered a succession struggle within the PPF no more edifying than the personal rivalries within the Commission. Victor Barthélemy, PPF secretary-general, raced back from his duties in Milan as PPF representative to the German puppet Salò Republic to preside over the party conclave. The final solution was a triumvirate of Simon Sabiani, Christian Lesueur – Barthélemy's PPF opposite number in Berlin – and Marcel Marshall, faithful lieutenant to Doriot. The PPF turned out to be even more brittle than the despised Commission. Without its head, it soon disintegrated, with Sabiani and Barthélemy seeking refuge in Italy.

Barthélemy later claimed in his memoirs, as quoted by Cointet, to have dined with Laval on the evening of his return to Milan, where Laval told him:

I ask you to believe me if I tell you that I also felt much grief. I could not assist at his obsequies. You know that I am no longer at Sigmaringen. They have installed me in a manor at Wilflingen... You know, I liked Doriot very much. I always had the greatest respect for his talent, his courage, his character, which was not always good. We were not always in agreement, we sometimes fought violently… Yet at least Doriot and the PPF always acted bare-faced, unlike all the others. What divided us, Doriot and me, was always a way of acting more than a way of thinking. He was for a strong way, and I was for a peaceful way… I never wanted to make blood flow. I never wanted blood on my hands.

With their last hopes extinguished, the Commission members periodically discussed their escape plans – or rather, brought up the subject to sound out each other's intentions. As described by Schillemans:

What they said about the subject was always very vague, often childish; usually they stuck to brief allusions which had to be caught on the fly. Most of the time, they were content to add to the project put forward by their neighbour, appearing to want to strengthen them in their resolution, which seemed perfectly inept to me, in light of the pending events.

From time to time, De Brinon spoke of Bavarian friends and when he mentioned the great departure, one had the impression, listening to him, that for him it was a question of going to spend a weekend in the countryside. Darnand was considering sending his wife and son to Italy, but he did not breathe a word of his private plans. As I believed I knew at the time that he had decided to seek a liberating death on the Russian front, or whatever was left of it, I felt for him the consideration one can feel for all those friends or enemies who say to you, while looking you in the eye, "Morituri te Salutant". All the same … what was he really thinking about at that moment?

Luchaire was rambling, as was his wont. Either he had decided once and for all to show fierce optimism, no matter what might come, and so was gifted with a sort of smiling fatalism, or he was hiding his game and, having made his preparations, or believing he had made them, he was telling stories, like Radio-Sigmaringen. When one listened to him speak, there was no doubt of the German victory, and for him there was no question of a Bavarian or Italian "redoubt".

As for Déat, in these moments of effusions, he kept a silence full of innuendos; all these stories did not seem to interest him directly. A vague smile hovered on his thin lips; he kept his eyes stubbornly downcast, and one really did not know at all what could be stirring under that forehead with its calamitous hair. His wife, ordinarily so talkative, was also silent, while a big question mark hovered over this household. All the same, I was convinced that Déat had not wasted his time uselessly drinking tea at receptions, but already had a pretty precise idea of how he would try to pull his weight when the time came; the future seems to have shown that I was not mistaken. Did he have accomplices in France, thanks to politicians who had played other cards and whom he had the opportunity to protect during the Occupation? Did he manage by his own means? The fact is, that at the end, all these people were found very quickly, except for Déat and his charming wife.

There was one last postscript to the political shadow play at Sigmaringen. Without Doriot, the Commission members at Sigmaringen, reinforced by Marcel Bucard, founder of the Mouvement franciste, made common cause against Brinon, who still held his presidency but was now also a member of the CLF, aspiring to replace Doriot as its head. Still hopeful of using Doriot's legacy, the Germans cut back the resources allocated to the Commission; in early March, *La France* became a weekly, and radio broadcasts from Sigmaringen were cut by half. Déat, Darnand and Luchaire protested to Reinebeck:

> We have the right to make known to the government of the Reich our most formal and vigorous protest against such proceedings, which are not those that we expected to await us when we left France to continue the political struggle alongside the German people... [The Commission] cannot take it as useful or admissible [to be] totally gagged while French political groups, practically devoid of any legality, deploy instruments of propaganda which you have withdrawn from or refused to us.[8]

Déat, meanwhile, came up with another idea: a consultative 'National Council' to be headed by himself and Luchaire, which he publicized through his remaining RNP faithful. The idea foundered on the opposition of the residue of the PPF. He also reached out to his old patron Abetz, long demoted but still resident nearby in the Black Forest – without result. As late as 17 March 1945, he recorded in his diary, cited by Cointet: 'the Germans are said to have made official offers to the Anglo-Saxons. There will be a final formal warning before the new weapons come into service.'

The Germans never bothered to settle the remaining scores between Brinon and his opponents. The 13 March 1945 issue of *La France* eagerly reported the comments of the Basel *Nazional Zeitung* on the political situation in France itself. 'On every side, the government of de Gaulle is attacked, beaten, breached by the Communists, the Socialists, the members of the Consultative Assembly, the CNR.' Another headline, this time quoting a report from Berne, declares 'Mr Lacoste exposes the distress of France.' Another article, titled 'Resistance to the Resistance' details the supposed resistance to the new government in France by diehard Vichy loyalists.

The PPF lingered on for a few more weeks into March, then made its plans to evacuate Mainau. The organization's militants formed a truck convoy to escape to northern Italy, to join the remaining French collaborationists fighting Italian partisans in the Republic of Salò. Most of the media and propaganda personalities in Doriot's entourage were left behind to await the arrival of the Allies.

Chapter 6

Sojourning and Suffering in Sigmaringen

D aily life in the Sigmaringen enclave resembled the cliche about soldiering: boredom punctuated by terror. As with many refugee camps, there was very little for the occupants to do beyond futile internecine struggles. Unlike most refugee camps, there was the contrast of the almost idyllic fairytale surroundings to emphasize the misery and privation of actual daily life there.

Corinne Luchaire, taking refuge in the enclave with her father, described the place:

> It is an astonishing town, a completely intact medieval town, as if escaped from a period historical film. The Hohenzollern castle was naturally the principal ornament of this town, with its turrets and machicolations. Around it were clustered the houses and three little hotels doubtless for receiving the entourages of the personalities invited to the castle.[1]

Schillemans described his first impressions of Sigmaringen on arriving at the station:

> Sigmaringen was a clean and cheery little town, with the light playing on old walls, ivy on grey facades, fresh streams, little noise, no trams, many trees; all adorned with a pretty layer of snow glistening in the sun. Coming from the station, you didn't immediately notice the castle. You arrived there by a sort of ramp split up by ivy-crowned vaults. It led to the main door of this stately home, while tracing meanders between mossy rocks and rather elegant buildings that were its outbuildings. You crossed small shady gardens where streams flowed.

His impressions of the locals were less positive:

Among the people walking in the streets, I soon detected a great many compatriots. Compatriots? ... yes ... well ... I wasn't really sure. Although they were of the same race as me, they eyed my red cap without any sympathy, and on my part these people didn't inspire me with any confidence; they were on the other side. They were clearly separate from the way the locals behaved, speaking loudly, calling out to each other from one sidewalk to the other, seeming absolutely at home. They struck me as bad-mannered tourists on holiday in some Black Forest resort, and usually moved around in groups of five or six. Although they didn't need it to get noticed, they were dressed in a sort of uniform. Basque beret, blue jacket and iron-shod cane, riding breeches, big mountain boots and woollen stockings reaching up to mid-leg... Up until now, whenever I met French people on my travels, they would at least give me a vague greeting, or a sign of friendly recognition. Sometimes they would even cross the street to say a few words; in any event, there was a sort of trustful racial exchange. Here, on the other hand, I felt assessed, dissected and placed in the category of compatriots who should be distrusted. It is true that it was not the same thing; those who I saw before were STO, people displaced against their will. These ones as well, perhaps, but what had prompted them to cross the Rhine was completely different. And I realized later that these people, who sometimes seemed to have known each other for a long time, felt no real trust for each other. They felt transplanted, isolated in this foreign land, having left so much behind.

Georges Scapini, Pétain's ambassador to French prisoners in Germany, left an unambiguously negative portrayal of Sigmaringen on his arrival there on 6 October 1944. Notwithstanding his blindness, he described his impressions in his memoirs as follows:

The main street is crisscrossed in all directions by noisy militiamen. Inside a brewery, a man sits alone, melancholy, before a glass of bad beer, a cat perched on his shoulder, sad... The strange crowd of aimless emigrants trails miserably towards a public park. Men, women of all ages leading children by the hand, who seem to have not yet awoken from an anguished dream. The population of Sigmaringen, without indulgence, considers them troublesome invaders, most of them impoverished. All this is heartbreaking, it is miserable... to cap it all, there is sunshine and the despair of this vision is exacerbated... over that silent castle, as if frozen, hangs I don't know what sepulchral atmosphere. Those who inhabit it must only come out at night, like ghosts. They have already dissolved in the ether. Their shadows will haunt Sigmaringen long after; their woes cling to the suits of the armour and nestle in the ceiling vaults. They encrust the palace walls.[2]

Even the highest suffered some privations in Sigmaringen – at least, to a level appropriate to their status. On 17 October 1944, Dr Ménétrel addressed the following letter to the Swiss ambassador in Berlin:

Excellency,

I apologize for taking the liberty to address myself to you regarding personal matters touching Marshal Pétain and the people immediately around him.

Leaving Vichy, neither Marshal Pétain nor ourselves brought away sufficient warm clothes and I permit myself to contact you at the suggestion of Mr von Renthe-Fink, to ask you if it would be possible to make purchases in Switzerland.

I know very well that this is an exceptional demand, but, having the heavy responsibility of the Marshal's health, I seek above all to ensure for him the minimum of comfort that his age and situation requires.

Perhaps there is a Frenchman in Switzerland (Mr Jardin or Mr du Moulin de Labarthète who were with the Marshal for a long time), who would agree to make these purchases, as I would not dare to suggest to make a demand via Ambassador Stucki, who we have already had to recourse to so much.

In a list attached to this letter, I have noted the objects which the Marshal, Madame Marshal, and myself have need of this winter.

If the purchase of certain items on this list is regulated, perhaps the Swiss government would agree to give the necessary authorizations once it is aware that they concern the person of Marshal Pétain.

For payment, I place at your disposition the necessary amounts, but in French francs.

The special situation in which Marshal Pétain finds himself, I hope, will excuse my request in your eyes.

I ask you to accept, Excellency, the expression of my highest consideration,

B. Ménétrel

The attached list mentioned in the letter included a warm coat for the Marshal, a black felt hat for his wife, six pullovers, two bathrobes, six heavy Canadian-style coats, two pairs of fur-lined shoes, as well as two Franco-German dictionaries, three pipes, a lighter, chocolate, soap, shaving cream and toothpaste.

Otherwise, the highest residents enjoyed some of the most comfortable surroundings available to anyone at this point in the war. Schillemans described the opulent dining hall provided for the elite occupants of the castle.

It was the dining room, where the Hohenzollerns used to take their meals. A magnificent room divided in two parts; a sort of vast living room, and in the background, the dining room, where an immense table was enthroned.

In the foreground, a sitting room with deep armchairs and several small low tables for taking coffee. Along one stretch of wall, huge windows, fitted with coloured glass and decorated with pastoral designs. Tall carved woodwork, beautiful tapestries attached to the partitions, magnificent curtains, sumptuous carpets, Old Master paintings, the inevitable hunting trophies, heavy hangings and a few finely carved old weapons. Despite all this profusion of beautiful things, the room remained harmonious and welcoming.

In these gorgeous surroundings, the Sigmaringen elite were waited on by:

> the faithful Oelker, very paternally efficient. The old majordomo of
> the Hohenzollerns was really a very sympathetic character. He came
> and went, taking care of his duties in a remarkable way, but he had his
> own preferences, and already at noon I had noticed how certain guests
> seemed to displease him. He was a servant of a Great House who only
> understood the Great Lords or simple people; he seemed, on the other
> hand, to feel only disdain for all these little *parvenu bourgeois*, who
> formed the majority of the clientele of the castle.

According to Corinne Luchaire, 'at first, in the Castle, meals were taken
communally in the immense Gothic dining hall, but this soon became
impossible, because the disputes between rival services continued during the
meal so often that everyone ended up taking their meals in their rooms.'

The fate of the rank and file Milice who had followed Darnand into exile
was far grimmer. On 23 October, assembled in a cinema hall at their interim
refuge at Ulm, Darnand, dressed in full Milice uniform, announced to them
that, after long consideration, he had decided that it was 'useful to decide
the enrolment in the Waffen SS, in a French unit, with French leaders, of all
Milice able to bear arms'. This was the Charlemagne Brigade, which became
the Charlemagne Division in November 1944. Darnand reassured the Milice
recruits that they would not have to serve on the Western Front and would
not have to face Allied French units, and that the unit would be under French
command. His declaration, as recorded by Giolitto, was:

> We cannot be idle in a Germany at war against Communism and
> plutocracy. Our duty is to fight or to work. We have fought in France.
> We will fight on, beside German armies, against the same enemies. I will
> not abandon you. At the cost of many difficulties, I have reassembled
> you here. Today, we must fight on for our ideal. I will fight at your head,
> and if need be, we will die together.

The whole initiative helped to affirm the Commission's relevance versus
Doriot and his supporters, and Brinon reinforced this by dubbing Darnand

Commissioner for the Organization of French Military Forces. In the event, only around one third of the Milice refugees, some 2,500 in all, volunteered to serve in the unit, and Darnand cast further afield for new recruits, chiefly among the French POWs still in German camps, and those already serving in other Axis units. The surviving members of Déat's LVF, under the command of Edgar Puaud, an LVF veteran promoted from colonel to general by Brinon, were incorporated into the new unit. The real commander of the Charlemagne Brigade/Division was its 'inspector', SS Brigadeführer Gustav Krukenberg, officially appointed to command in February 1945.

Out of the residual Milice, some 500 were assigned to Sigmaringen as part of the Franc-Garde unit, under Darnand's direct command. A further couple of thousand were distributed among the French work camps in Germany. Seven or eight hundred judged unfit for service were installed in a camp at Heuberg, near Sigmaringen. The families of Milice members were spread among various camps at Siessen and elsewhere.

Henry Rousso quotes the account of a Milicien's wife, who had followed her husband into exile in Germany:

My son was killed on the Eastern Front. My two school-age daughters and myself were made to go to the factories at Kassel. It was Darnand's order: those who cannot fight must work, except for women with at least two children of a young age. Not staying at Siessen, with the oldsters, the cripples, the mothers with young children. Even such people have to do their corvees. No one has the right to complain. If anyone complains, the Germans say to them: "You came here voluntarily; you must have also volunteered to work".

There were no beds, only straw mattresses. The barracks were not heated, at minus 10° or minus 20°. In the factory, the Germans showed us less consideration than the French in the STO and to the prisoners who had become free workers. In January I contracted pneumonia. I was hospitalized. The German doctors were on the hunt for fake patients. I had to go back to work. I had a relapse. I almost died.

I will never forgive the leaders of the Milice for leading us where they led us and for having abandoned us as soon as they were in Germany.

In the winter of 1944-45, around fifty children died at Siessen. Sent to investigate the situation, Céline reported that they had died primarily from hunger.

All the same, the Milice mostly had little choice. As Céline succinctly put it, they had 'Article 75 on their arses' – the article of the French penal code that specified penalties including death in case of treason. The dependents and families of the Milice and other collaborators may have simply trailed along to Sigmaringen; but those who chose to come there almost always did so out of fear, or out of loyalty to the collaborationist regime.

Schillemans reported on their mood – as remarked on over dinner by their supposed masters on the Commission:

> There was an allusion to a certain anxiety that reigned among the troops of the Governmental Commission, the Milice and their relatives. In this curious assemblage of little people, whose life was not exactly free from worries of all kinds, strange rumours were indeed circulating. Hopes for a better life were diminishing by the day. The initial confidence and the hope of an early return to the fold were no more than a distant memory for these poor people. In any case, this return proved to be full of perils, hence a nagging fear of everything that the next day might bring. Only attitudes remained on the other hand that had to be maintained, so as not to be ill spoken of and suspected of lukewarmness towards the regime.
>
> These people had been transplanted: they were bored far from home and probably thought with nostalgia of that small plot of land where they had seen the light of day; how far away it all was, now... Many of them must have regretted having left and had perhaps even forgotten the reasons for this need to flee, in the face of the threat that hung over them.

The typical French collaborationist refugee seeking refuge in Sigmaringen would usually arrive at the station from other parts of Germany. There, they would be processed by Milice security personnel, who passed for a police force in the enclave, and would be granted their right to reside in Sigmaringen. Then they would be directed to the Commission's administrative headquarters in Prinzenbau, to be confronted very often by a Kafkaesque vicious circle, where work and ration coupons could only be secured if you had a room; but a room could only be secured if you had work. If they were able to get through this bureaucratic obstacle course, the new arrivals would usually be installed in one of the town's inns or other temporary hostels. Shortage of space and the growing numbers of refugees often required the enclave's lesser residents to sleep up to six to a room. There was apparently no question of throwing open the rooms in the castle itself to these lesser beings.

Céline described the situation: 'We were there in the attics, cellars, under stairs, starving, I assure you, no Operetta... a platter of the condemned!... 1,142!... I knew the exact number...' Céline's total seems all too exact, especially in view of the death rates he reported; as with other suddenly precise details in his often hallucinatory account, one suspects he included it to emphasize that his was the true and definitive version of events. Other estimates of the total number of inhabitants in the enclave contradict Céline's figure, some as high as 5,000, although many were doubtless attached to the camps nearby.

Frustrated in his attempt to secure visas for Denmark, Céline moved from Berlin to the small refugee community at Kränzlin, about 50 kilometres outside the capital. Hearing of the creation of the Sigmaringen enclave, he offered his services as a doctor to Brinon, and arrived by train at the end of October, installing himself in the hotel Zum Löwen, one of the better quality residences in the enclave.

As described by Schillemans, the ambiance of the Zum Löwen was:

> in the purest German style: great beer mugs, porcelain pipes hanging on the walls, not to mention the multiple hunting trophies, antelope horns, stuffed birds of prey, etc., etc. Pretty little red and white curtains adorned the small-paned windows that gleamed in the sunshine, sturdy oak tables and well-waxed woodwork smelling of polish. All this gave the atmosphere of rustic comfort that one often finds in German gasthauses.

He found the clientele less appealing: 'The appearance of these people was always vaguely military, semi-soldierly in some way or other. That gave this band of people of all ages and complexions, greying, blond, brown-haired, a martial-touristic air... There emanated from this assembly a sad and disillusioned spite.'

Céline was still something of a literary celebrity at the time, and a small crowd assembled to witness his arrival. As recorded by Lucien Rebatet in a post-war article, he arrived:

> wearing a blue cloth cap, like engine drivers wore around 1905, two or three heavy overcoats overlaying their dirt and holes, a shabby pair of mittens hanging round his neck, and underneath the mittens, on his stomach, in a kitbag, Bébert the cat. One member of the Milice remarked, "That's the great Fascist writer, the brilliant prophet?"

Schillemans recorded his first meeting with Céline:

> Müller and I were heading towards the castle, crossing a small garden at the foot of the ramp that ran along the most rustic façade, when we were accosted by a rather strange individual. He was tall, thin, and his clear, bright eyes, set deep in their sockets, surmounted by huge bristling eyebrows, cast a disturbing gleam. When he looked at you, his pupils had a curious fixity, and his eyes seemed to be constantly asking you questions. He was wearing a faded Canadian-style coat that must have been brown once, and dark blue trousers, wound round his thin legs. Two enormous fur-lined leather mittens hung from his neck by a string, and he held in his left hand the handle of a bulky travelling bag in which he had made a few air holes. In this bag, I found out soon after, he was carrying an enormous cat. That was the attire of this curious character; as for the cat, it was a magnificent beast, which I only caught a glimpse of. It was almost as big as a lamb and seemed, by God, very happy to be walking in this outfit; curious beast...
>
> These two phenomena had names, one Louis Ferdinand Céline, the other Bébert; Bébert was the cat.

Céline, the former celebrity author and habitué of luxury cruises, now perforce became doctor to the poor underserved rank-and-file refugee population of Sigmaringen, a role which did his post-war reputation no harm. The Sigmaringen enclave had only one other serving physician, a Dr Jacquot, a follower of Déat. (Dr Ménétrel, Pétain's personal physician, occupied himself only with his master.) The patients ranged from newborn children to the aged. Céline's past medical training and experience had been more concerned with pharmacology than general medicine, and he had long been occupied with writing and other concerns. Nonetheless, he devoted himself assiduously to the treatment of patients from all ranks of the little society of Sigmaringen, often relying on black market medicines obtained from nearby Switzerland. Thanks to the rampant promiscuity in the enclave, he was often confronted with scabies and venereal disease; tuberculosis, gastroenteritis, and various other diseases of privation and malnutrition were also prevalent. He worked without radiography or most of the other more advanced contemporary medical techniques, through ignorance and through lack of resources.

In his book, Céline recounts a conversation with Brinon regarding other supposed doctors seeking refuge in the enclave – although, as with the rest of Céline's account, it should probably be taken with a grain of salt. He had discovered a mad self-styled 'surgeon' in his room, attempting to operate on a garage mechanic from Strasbourg:

Oh, you know, a mad doctor!... he's not the only one!... not the only one, Doctor!... we know that ten out of our twelve supposed French doctors are mad... really mad, escaped from asylums... and listen to me, Doctor! Berlin has sent us, and you're about to receive, "Privat-Professor" Vernier, "Director of the French Sanitary Services".

As for the promiscuity, here is Céline's take on the situation:

I guessed where she was, Hilda von Raumnitz, and two... three girlfriends... Sigmaringen's young girls in bloom... well, the very well-groomed, very well-fed girls from very good military and diplomatic families... who never wanted for anything!... obviously their age, the very salubrious air, and this invigorating cold, the pimples bugging them!.. the ardent age, 14... 17... and not just the little girls de luxe, closeted, cared for... the tatty ones too!... other excuses, the distance, the constant danger, the insomnia, the men on the hunt!... tatty too! in rags! and freewheeling! and so fervent! all the groves! all the crossroads, the ardent age 14... 17... especially the girls!...

Many of the rank-and-file Miliciens and their families, confined in the camp at Siessen near the castle itself, were living on starvation rations, so indigestible that some young children literally starved to death. Quoting Brinon's figures of some six deaths per week at Siessen, Céline described the situation at the food distribution:

> As they waited for the brioches, they swapped fleas, lice, crabs, scabies... you should have seen how convulsive! a little crowd of epileptics... but still, hunger!... hunger above all!... what they were going to be able to stuff themselves with! Oh, là là!... from one foot to the other... scratching, ploughing, tearing each other's furrows of scabies... they were in a sort of semicircle in front of the drawbridge... rolling their caps! fascinated... by what was coming!... not just bread!... ham with it! sandwiches... and lard!

The Milice combatants judged fit for service was conveyed to a camp at Wildflecken, where a further 200 were weeded out as unfit in the course of induction. Rapidly shorn of their motley Milice and other French uniforms, the newcomers were rigidly incorporated into the SS command structure and put into SS uniforms. Darnand himself, when he came to Wildflecken on 11 November 1944, was refused entry, on the grounds that he was not carrying the correct German unit certifications. Krukenberg duly explained to Darnand that he would have to admit Doriot if he allowed him entry to the camp as a Commission official, and that both could not be present before the same unit. Meanwhile, Doriot was also informed that he should not present himself at the camp, either as a civilian or as a German officer.

Krukenberg delivered the following address, in French, at Wildflecken on 1 January 1945:

> Volunteers!
> For a soldier, the New Year is the time to look to the future. For we, whose hearths are menaced or attacked by the enemy, the future is clear:

We form a common front! No one can stand aside from it. Europe is lost, or we triumph together. There is no wait-and-see with Bolshevism. Anyone who has fought in the East knows this. Those who have defended themselves against the terrorists and maquis in France know this too. Everything that has happened in the West since the autumn proves that neither de Gaulle, nor the Americans, nor the English, are free in the face of Moscow. With de Gaulle, they are responsible for executions and for the lot that now befalls the people of France. Since the last war, some 25 years, only the Führer has understood the danger that the Asiatic and Jewish methods of Moscow and Anglo-American hegemony present for Europe. These are the same powers that in 1939 pushed the French government to declare war on Germany. Today we know the intrigues that led to that outcome. We see that the same people make France a new battlefield. They mobilize the youth of France for the war that they have escaped since the Armistice. Because the Führer wanted peace, and because National Socialism needed peace to accomplish its programme, they attacked on all sides. Now today, our adversaries are forced to adopt similar ideas for their programme. Only, they have no intention of fulfilling them. We, in the Waffen SS, we have the privilege of being among those who are fighting on the front line for Europe. This demands exceptional efforts from every one of us. With fanaticism and hardness we will ready ourselves. Victory will come to those who believe in it. We must never doubt that our struggle is necessary and just. We must set an example for others. Our goal for 1945 is the liberation of French territory after which we and our families will forget our time of suffering as soon as possible. To succeed in this, it is necessary that everyone and especially those at the front must have an attitude conforming to the tradition of a French soldier and the Waffen SS. Those who do not have such a conviction, who entertain other thoughts, who diminish our good reputation, do not belong to us. They must be cut off. Those who remain will form a community joined by faith in the Führer.

Germans and French, we shall renew the oath that we have sworn to him! We think of the motto of the SS, "Our honour is faith", as we cry out together, Sieg Heil! Sieg Heil!

The Charlemagne Division left camp on 17 February 1945, bound for Pomerania.

The higher echelons in the castle, amply provided for, lauded and propagandized for such engagements, while remaining aloof from such privations. Schillemans noted that Herr Oelker, the old Hohenzollern major domo, showed him special favour as a genuine ex-combatant by serving him treats when he was breakfasting alone: white bread, croissants, honey and jam, partly to spite the other occupants, who already received four times the usual ration for the enclave. According to eye-witnesses, the French and other foreign officials and diplomats resident in Sigmaringen received around seven times the normal ration for a German citizen at that point in the war. The Schön pâtisserie, amply furnished with delicacies, became a favourite retreat for the collaborationist *beau monde*. For the lower ranks and their families, as attested by Céline and Rebatet, the staple was often a mash of red cabbage, swedes and beetroots, with occasional potatoes, or a potato and cabbage soup, often washed down with weak German beer. Occasional sausages, sides of ham, and other delicacies arrived from neighbouring farms, courtesy of the black market. At this stage of the war, coffee, by Schillemans' testimony, was horribly ersatz.

Schillemans enjoyed top-class accommodation by Sigmaringen standards on his arrival in the castle. 'The room was quite large, in a rotunda, with three windows overlooking the Hohenzollern Chapel and the main gate of the castle, in front of which an armed Milice trooper stood guard in the shelter of a sentry box, painted in French colours. One of the most beautiful ornaments of this room was a superb earthenware stove, in the Germanic style, which must have been very valuable.' He also received regular room service, with wine. 'The only drawback of this room was perhaps its location in the same corridor as Brinon's.' According to the testimony of the cooks in the castle, around eighty people were dining within its walls every day. The Milice troops ate in the servants' hall.[3]

The lower ranks, in contrast, were often reduced to sharing a single straw mattress, and grew infested with scabies and other complaints. Admittedly, civilians in liberated France and in Germany were faring little better at this point in the war. It is worth recalling that back in metropolitan France after the Liberation, infant mortality approached nearly 10 per cent in the brutal winter of 1944-45.

Schillemans noted that:

For most of the members of the Government Commission, the two thousand or so Milice and their families who were there had only one importance, only one reason for being, in their eyes; that of justifying, as far as possible, their so-called Government; as for the rest...

But two or three thousand people were not many, apart from the inevitable trouble they gave them and the Germans, cunning, knew well at times how to make them feel it, when it was a question of them obtaining something. Plus, all these Ministers and their administered ones naturally had a poor relation complex. This was why Bridoux and his clique could not have asked for anything better than to see the prisoners of war transformed into civilian workers and at the same time, into "loyal subjects" of the Provisional Government.

Sigmaringen station, as well as the portal to the little world of the enclave, was also the refuge for some of the most marginalized and abandoned even among the refugees. Pimps and prostitutes drawn from the emigre community or elsewhere gathered there to service the passing traffic of troops – Germans or Axis allies and volunteers from the Reich's subject territories. Céline recorded the 'waiting rooms of prostitution', and the 'Montenegrins, Czechoslovenes, Vlasov army, Balto-Finns, troops of Europe's Macedonias!.. the twenty-seven armies!' who formed their customers.

Mass was typically held in the castle chapel at 11.00 pm on Sundays. As Schillemans related:

This was a beautiful church, with a bulbous bell tower, adjoined the castle; I saw it from my window, which overlooked the small square in front of the postern ... There was a bit of everything in this Chapel, all the kinds of people that one can see all over the world at a late Mass on Sunday; families altogether or almost, with grandparents and very young children, sowing confusion during the service; women in their Sunday best, especially attentive to their surroundings, a few very young people, isolated old men and even, here and there, a few handsome faces of murderers.

Active members of the Milice, under the command of Jean de Vaugelas, performed police and ceremonial duties in the enclave. As confirmed by Schillemans, their uniform consisted of a blouson jacket, trousers crimped at the ankles by white gaiters, and a beret or a black French helmet. They carried antiquated rifles with bayonets, while the officers wore huge revolvers in their holsters. Most were either very young or too old for military duties, which added to the impression of a mixed bag of amateurs playing soldiers as part of some village fete. In Schillemans' eyes, it at least gave them one way of keeping themselves busy, since they had nothing better to do. Pétain declined a Milice honour guard, saying 'One does not present honours to a prisoner; I do not wish to see these lunatics', but Darnand and the Milice went ahead and did so anyway.

Observed by Schillemans, the changing of the Milice guard at the castle was especially ludicrous:

A bugle call sounded under my windows, a sort of sour little tune whose acid notes resounded in the fresh air of this November morning. I looked at what was happening and so witnessed the changing of the guard conducted by the Milice. They grouped in a row for the salute to the colours, the flag being above the postern, then I saw them disappear under the trees of the avenue, in single file. There were about ten of them parading to the sound of this music, seeming to skip over the snowy carpet that covered the ground. They applied themselves and did their best to look like real soldiers, but this troop composed of individuals of such disparate ages and builds reeked of "reservists". Even for a spectator free from any bias, this ceremony was of a fatuity bordering on the ridiculous, a sort of Laurel and Hardy skit. Alongside this column, where cheerful old men followed in the footsteps of big-bellied men and very boy-scout young ephebes, an officer waddled, seeming very convinced that he had an elite corps under his command. At each step, an enormous revolver bounced on his behind, seeming to kick him in the butt. Either these people were ineffable jokers who liked to have fun, or else, and I believe this to be the case, they had to justify their presence in Sigmaringen.

Conflicts between the different collaborationist factions presented in organizational rivalries among their different units. According to Céline, Doriot's PPF opened its own store in Sigmaringen, manned by PPF veteran Simon Sabiani:

> This shop had two windows... and at each window invalids absolutely on their last legs... from hunger, old age and tuberculosis, and cold... and cancers too... all the while, scratching themselves hard!... of course!... one window was folding chairs, the other reclining deckchairs... I saw in the course of two months a PPF grandfather dying with his grandson on his knees... like that without moving, in a deckchair, coughing up his lungs... the shop itself was full of the dead... the benches... full of benches... along the walls... or on the floor, lying down, or in mounds... Sabiani himself stood in the back room... he took memberships, issued cards, signed, stamped... he had "full powers". France came within an inch of turning PPF... Hitler was less stupid! He had everyone, Sabiani... everyone "joined", everyone who looked at the windows, it was easy to stay there, enter and sit down... surely the PPF was the party that recruited the most, the effect of the windows and the benches... if they had only given food as well, the least billy full, they could have recruited the whole nest, including the Germans...

Other literary and cultural collaborationist celebrities, habitues of the Schön pâtisserie, included the actor Robert Le Vigan, formerly celebrated for his portrayal of Jesus Christ in Julien Duvivier's *Golgotha* (1935), now employed as a speaker for Luchaire's collaborationist radio 'Ici la France', Jean Luchaire's daughter Corinne, Guy Crouzet, collaborationist journalist, Alphonse de Châteaubriant, regionalist writer and pro-Nazi, Jacques Ménard, editor-in-chief of the enclave's official daily newspaper, *Le Matin*. The 7 November 1944 issue of *Le Matin* announced the formation by the intellectuals of Sigmaringen of a Committee for the Defence of the French Spirit, dedicated to 'protecting the true traditions of the national spirit'.

Louis Aragon, at the opposite end of the ideological spectrum from the scribes of Sigmaringen, was inspired to write a couple of poems about the enclave. One, entitled 'Distiques pour une carmagnole de la honte', was written in the winter of 1944-45, and remained unpublished and in manuscript for many years.

> Indeed it must look pretty fine
> The castle of Siegmaringen
> There we meet among felons
> under the lights of the grand salon
> Pétain each evening plays cards
> with the traitor of Stuttgart
> Never says Fernand de Brinon
> Has a fine nose spoiled a good name
> The State is me and I look fine
> pass me my mantle of ermine
> My dear Mr Hérold-Paquis
> Tell us about the Maquis
> Doriot plays a patriot
> Beside Judas Iscariot
> Laval seems all exasperation
> to be on this vacation
> Darnand complains to Jean Luchaire
> That these evictions cost so dear
> Josée Laval now has
> The whim to seduce Marcel Déat
> And Corinne gets up and sings
> In a voice plaintive and touching
>
> Ah! It'll be fine, It'll be fine, It'll be fine
> Pétain Laval to the lantern
> Ah! It'll be fine, It'll be fine, It'll be fine
> Pétain Laval they all will hang

The other, 'Les Neiges de Siegmaringen' – 'The Snows of Siegmaringen', complete with the same misspelling of Sigmaringen a la 'Sieg Heil!' that

Céline sometimes affected, appeared in the February 1945 issue of *Les Lettres françaises*. A parody of François Villon's ballad of lost loves from his *Grand Testament*, it ran:

> Who will blacken all my trash
> Alas Massis Alas Maurras
> All my inkwells are inkless
> Drieu left without a trace
> Ajabert fled to the bush
> Céline is hid in piles of ash
> Lesdain so soft Béraud so tender
> Laubreaux always up for tender

Luchaire recruited one of the fugitive journalists, Jacques Bouly de Lesdain, diplomat, travel writer, and anti-Semitic columnist under the Occupation, as director of Radio-La-France, with the title Director-General of Radiodiffusion of Sigmaringen, as well as a contributor to *La France*. Jean Hérold-Paquis, himself a radio veteran from Radio-Paris, viciously portrayed him in his memoirs, sucking a lozenge or working his jaws so as not to lose his false teeth. Céline likewise in a letter to Charles Deshayes dated 24 August 1948:

> Lesdain... arrived in Baden-Baden with 400 kilos of baggage. He occupied an apartment at the Hotel Bären in Sigmaringen, furious all along at not being able to reside in the Castle. His German wife was engaged, he adds, in a very active black market... an absolutely filthy character, an infinite scoundrel, an old Prussian saintly official. Never... have I seen or come near such a frenzied pro-Boche propagandist.

Vindictive as ever, Céline may have been seeking payback for a scathing review of his novel *Guignol's Band*, published by Lesdain in the magazine *Aspects* on 2 June 1944, where Lesdain berated Céline for not portraying the "horrors" perpetrated by the Resistance, and criticized the writer's "kaleidoscope of painful, often filthy images" and his "world of rascals, pitiful companions of the dregs of humanity."[4]

A typical day of radio programming for Luchaire's Radio-La-France, running from 7.30 to 9.00 pm, consisted of a quarter-hour of classical music, followed by a quarter-hour news bulletin, another fifteen-minute classical interlude, fifteen minutes entitled 'The French Milice speaks to you', another fifteen-minute news and editorial bulletin, and a fifteen-minute program of film songs, followed by the close. For those who were so inclined, Sigmaringen Castle also contained a magnificent library of some 80,000 volumes, including many manuscripts in French and German from the mid-nineteenth century. Abel Bonnard was a regular habitue of the library; the Marshal himself reportedly resorted often to its French volumes.

Otherwise, the higher echelons of Sigmaringen society had little to occupy themselves with, trapped effectively in a prison without bars, in an atmosphere of stultifying boredom punctuated by moments of irrational hope or mortal terror, picking over the slightest incident or piece of news to fill the time. As Schillemans noted:

> All of them seemed sad, idle and above all suspicious. Some, perhaps to make an impression or to fill their boredom, immersed themselves in reading the newspapers, knowing in advance that the news they reported was more or less fallacious. They resembled travellers, waiting in a station buffet for a problematic or very late train. Others debated in low voices, sometimes as if arguing, some assessed their chances of getting out of this mess; finally a few boasted, launching jokes very loudly that, for the most part, fell flat... These people seemed afraid of their own shadows, and even amongst themselves, appeared ill at ease. Everything rang false in this ambiance, the artificiality it exuded hit you in the face, so hard that it became painful.

To some extent, a parody of everyday life went on at Sigmaringen to accompany the parody of political life. As well as appeals for information on prisoners of war and workers in Germany, the small ads column of *La France* bore such notices as: 'I would like to buy a young German Shepherd dog' and 'Will exchange gold Omega bracelet watch, silver Omega pocket watch, black cover, for Contaxlet, Contax or Leica [camera]'. The Governmental Commission formed an Association for War Cripples and Work Invalids of French Nationality in Germany, announced in the 2 January issue of *La France*, to address 'the material and morale interests of members, in particular anything concerning their problems with pensions, medical needs, orthopedic equipment, etc.'

The persistent fantasies of German victory in Sigmaringen might partly be attributed to the same atmosphere of desperate hope still prevalent in Germany, or to the self-deceptions of a tightly knit, isolated refugee community who had nothing to hope for if they faced the real situation. One opinion can be summed up in a remark by Déat: 'Since the Germans resist like they do, either they must be mad, or they must be keeping a secret army in reserve. Now, no one believes they are demented.' Clearly, assessment of the state of mind of the Nazi hierarchy has moved on since Déat's day.

The refugee community was haunted by fears for the future as the cruel prospect of German defeat became ever more unavoidable. The actor Robert Le Vigan shared his hopes and anxieties in his letters to Paul Bonny, a Swiss right-wing journalist and translator, asking Brinon to intervene to assist with their plans to escape to Switzerland:

He will know if there is a chance for Switzerland. But if there is, his approach needs to be lightning fast, so that we have time to pack and get there. Sigmaringen won't last for ever for us either!... I hope that Switzerland's response will be favourable... unless Switzerland, advised by England, refuses categorically... We are so depressed... far from our own people, the music of the language, the tone of thought, the mental climate is more necessary than bread. We can't go on, we can't rebuild our lives; that's for thirty-year-olds, and there's no question of it, since we're condemned and without hope.... Ferdinand [Céline] will only join if we can assure him that the French caravan will be headed towards your country.[5]

Chapter 7

Exodus from the Enclave

Sigmaringen turned out to be a particularly sticky tar pit for the dinosaurs of French collaborationism. Almost every prominent figure subsequently tried for collaboration passed through its gates. By March 1945, high or low, they were desperate to escape the trap, and flee, to Switzerland, or Italy, or Spain – anywhere to evade the vengeful Allies, especially the dreaded Russians.

The situation – and the panic – was complicated and worsened by the new waves of refugees flooding into the region from the front lines, particularly the east. As French forces advanced through the Black Forest and towards Baden-Baden, locals came fleeing from the north, joined by other refugees from Berlin. Bizarre rumours, including deliverance by the much-vaunted 'wonder-weapons', continued to circulate until the last minute. Abetz, resident in the Black Forest since his demotion, wrote subsequently, as recorded by Cointet, that Ribbentrop wanted him:

> if the enemy succeeded in crossing the Rhine and if Germany lost the front, to charge me with forming a maquis in the Black Forest behind French lines. He also thought of using me, if necessary, in peace proposals via political personalities from neutral countries. Finally, he could perhaps use my services, he told me, to settle the questions posed by French political refugees.

Déat's journal gives a fairly concise account of the last days of Sigmaringen. As highlighted by Cointet, the first mention of departure came on 19 March 1945. On 28 March, he wrote, 'the most direct and most urgent questions will soon be posed for everyone'. By 1 April, he was making his first actual preparations to leave. By 5 April, he declared that 'we can pack everything up in one hour'. On 9 April, he wrote 'preparations must go on, and those who are asleep must be shaken out of their torpor'. On 18 April, he stated 'we will leave with a delay of eight hours'.

Céline had already started to plan his flight from Sigmaringen well before the conclusion of the Battle of the Bulge and the death of his onetime idol Doriot. Cointet records his approach to the Swiss consulate in Stuttgart in a letter dated 22 January 1945:

> I have the honour to solicit an entry visa to Switzerland for myself and my wife. Currently a refugee in Sigmaringen, doctor of medicine from the faculty of Paris and 75% war invalid, writer under the name of L.-F. Céline.
>
> This name is perhaps known to you and will explain to you why I must leave France where I would almost certainly be immediately condemned to death. I have no intention to stay in Switzerland longer than the usual time for political appeasement, for example for the duration of one year.
>
> I have with me gold pieces and jewels to the value of around 12,000 Swiss francs. It would also be easy for me to obtain in addition, after my arrival in Switzerland, three times that sum from Spain, courtesy of friends to whom I have entrusted significant sums in gold.

Despite these inducements, Switzerland declined to grant him a visa. Céline fled Sigmaringen on 11 March 1945 with his dependents and baggage, having finally received a permit to enter Denmark.

Meanwhile, the French combatants of the Charlemagne Division were being almost wiped out on the Eastern Front. The advancing Russian forces had split the unit into three pockets, and proceeded to destroy them in detail. Puaud, the nominal French commander, was last reported on 5 March 1945 near Bialogard (Belgard) in Middle Pomerania, either killed with his men or taken prisoner by the Russians. With two out of three of the pockets destroyed, Krukenberg managed to escape with the remainder of the division, some 700 men, evacuated from the Baltic coast to Denmark. He detached some of them to form a heavy construction battalion, and with the last survivors, some 350 men, departed for Berlin on 23 April. Progressively whittled away during the defence of the Reich Chancellery and the Führerbunker, the last remnants of the French collaborationist units fought alongside other German and pro-Axis SS formations until 1 May, when Krukenberg ordered them to separate into small groups and do their best to escape. Most of the thirty or so survivors surrendered to Soviet troops; a few escaped further west to face trial and punishment in France.

Separated from his former Milice fellow combatants, Darnand told Bout de l'An on 8 March 1945 that he had decided to leave Sigmaringen for Italy:

> It's over. I'm fed up with this nonsense. I'm leaving for Italy with the battalion at Heuberg. You will rejoin me later. I signed up for the Liberation Committee. I'll leave you my membership, which you can do what you want with, and a delegation of powers to represent me on the Governmental Commission. Me, I'm fed up with it.

With the 500 or so Milice judged unfit for field service and left behind at Heuberg for ceremonial and other duties, some 200 of them under 20 years of age, he received authorization from the Germans and departed on 12 March for the Valtelline, the proposed last redoubt for the Germans and their fascist allies in northern Italy.

Abel Bonnard lost his mother on 4 March 1945, and buried her in the cemetery at Sigmaringen. He then began to make his own plans for escaping the enclave, looking initially to flee to Portugal, then Spain, but eventually joining the Lavals in their plans.

At the end of March, French forces began their push into Germany, posing a direct threat to the Black Forest region, and Sigmaringen. Negotiations were still under way in the Allied camp to decide what area of Germany and Austria – if any – France should exercise control over after the final defeat, de Gaulle decided, with tacit Allied approval, to create facts on the ground:

> The fate of the left bank of the Rhine interests France directly... While waiting for the question of the occupation of German territories to be agreed between Washington, London, Moscow and Paris, we must

ourselves occupy and take under our own authority the fraction of territories on the left bank of the Rhine where our troops are at present.[1]

General Jacob Devers, commander of the Allied Sixth Army Group, which included General Jean de Lattre de Tassigny's French First Army, gave his assent on 30 March, and the next day, French forces crossed the Rhine. Attaining Sigmaringen before the Americans was a key priority for de Gaulle and the French high command, for national political purposes. No matter that the United States had finally extended the long-delayed recognition to the new government in Paris; de Gaulle did not want the added complication of having Pétain and the rest of the collaborationist rump fall into American hands. By 12 April, the French forces had reached Baden-Baden, the former way-station on the way to Sigmaringen, and the fall of the enclave itself was only a matter of time.

The reestablished French government in Paris appears to have been well informed on the situation in Sigmaringen this late in the war. A report from the new French embassy in Switzerland to the Ministry of Foreign Affairs in Paris, dated 18 April 1945 and entitled 'Note sur l'activité des émigrés français à Sigmaringen', gave very detailed and systematic information on the key events and personalities in the enclave from September 1944 to March 1945, with considerable input from an observer onsite. Such comprehensive, almost daily reporting implies the presence of a mole in the Sigmaringen enclave, although to date, no details have emerged to confirm this.

Until the last moment, Laval lived in the shadow of German plans to transfer him to the supposed Nazi redoubts in the east. On 19 April 1945, he wrote the following appeal to the former Spanish ambassador in Vichy and Spanish Minister of Foreign Affairs, José Félix de Lequerica y Erquiza:

It is in the memory of the long days passed together that I send you this message. It is not the statesman nor the friend who asks you for aid and assistance, just the man. Germany has put me on notice to leave its territory, menaced by the Allied advances, and it is to you that I address myself. I ask you in my own name, as well as that of my wife and my faithful friend, Maurice Gabolde, for the authorization to be

able to enter Spain, to await better times. Today it is an old man, tired
and worn out, who writes to you. In the memory of our long friendship,
I thank you in advance.[2]

Brinon's wife arrived in Sigmaringen from Constance in mid-April 1945.
Apparently, she had remained apart from him throughout his entire sojourn in
Sigmaringen, only arriving at the last minute, although few details survive on
how or why. Brinon now had a wife and two secretaries to take care of during
his escape. The Germans moved slowly to organize evacuation arrangements
for their French guests. Finally on 16 April the first outline arrangements were
made: the Sigmaringen collaborationists were to be put aboard special carriages
and taken by train to the east or south, through Bavaria towards Innsbruck, but
without a definite destination. On 18 April, the destination was designated as
Feldkirch, the westernmost point of Austria, on the border with Switzerland
and Liechtenstein. The same day, the 'German embassy' to the Sigmaringen
enclave closed its doors. On 21 April 1945, the general evacuation began.

Pétain was of course the most important 'evacuee' – or hostage – and his
evacuation proceeded according to its own separate arrangements. Alongside
Laval, he was the only prominent resident of the Sigmaringen enclave who
actively sought repatriation to France to face judgment for his past actions.
Pétain wrote the following *note verbale* to protest, ten days before Hitler's
death in Berlin:

Marshal Pétain
Sigmaringen, 20 April 1945

Note verbale

Ever since my departure from Vichy on 20 August 1944, I have not
ceased to express my wish to return to France.

I emphasized this wish in my letter of 5 April.

I have now been notified that measures are being taken to transfer
me to a zone further east. I am obliged to consider that this decision
does not have the effect of favouring my return to France, as I have
requested, a return which I consider as the accomplishment of a duty.

I therefore insist on receiving a response to my letter of 5 April.

Philippe Pétain

After his return to France to face trial, Pétain's wife submitted the following account on 8 June 1945 of the Marshal's removal from Sigmaringen and the German attempts to convey him eastwards[3]:

The Account of Madam Marshal Pétain

On 5 April 1945, the Marshal, having heard over the radio that his trial in absentia must begin on 24 April, immediately wrote to Hitler to demand a return to France to defend his honour. This letter never received a response.

On 19 April, we learned with joy that the French were in the Black Forest and advancing towards Sigmaringen. The Marshal and our group awaited them impatiently.

On 20 April, in the evening, Minister Reinebeck (who had replaced Abetz) and Tangstein (replacing von Renthe-Fink) came to say that he must leave Sigmaringen. The Marshal protested and said that he wanted to await the French army. The others insisted, demanded, etc... Impossible to resist, the whole Gestapo was there and their chief, Biemelburg (who had been in Vichy and who had said "if we have to put handcuffs on the Marshal, I'll do it") was ready for anything.

The departure was required on 21 April at 4 hours in the morning towards Voralberg, they said, arguing that we would be passing closer to Switzerland and talking of going to Feldkirch.

The Marshal, General Debeney, Admiral Bléhaut and myself were all very worried, convinced that they wanted to take us to Bavaria towards the Redoubt.

Departure therefore took place at 4.30 am. There were two Gestapo cars in front, then the car with the Marshal and me, then General Debeney, then the Admiral and his second-in-command, Commandant Sacy, then a car with our luggage. The Marshal protested in a letter and demanded to return to France.

The staff, seven men, were in our four cars. Then Reinebeck, and all of them intermingled in the Gestapo cars with machine guns.

We were going, it seemed, to Wangen, and afterwards, they said, "we will see". So, by the road to Mengen (where Doriot had been killed by an airplane and many other French afterwards).

We arrived at Wangen at 9 in the morning, having made 120 kilometres in four and a half hours, at first in darkness and along a road encumbered with German convoys which fled eastwards in disorder. From time to time, airplanes spotted in the sky obliged us to stop. It was amazing that we weren't machine-gunned.

At Wangen, no order had been given, no one had been warned. It was intensely cold. They took us into the town hall, among the telephonists. The mayor (Landsrat) arrived, distraught. He greeted the Marshal with respect and appeared sorry at this welcome.

The whole population had gathered in the square and looked at us like strange beasts. Suddenly, the "pre-alarm" sirens, and then, three minutes later, the "alarm", which forced everyone to go home or to the shelters. I learned later that there were no planes, but that the mayor had only found this way to get rid of the citizens. He then took us to his house, where his wife and daughters gave us coffee and bread with sausages. And then what were they going to do with us?

We saw very well that there were discussions. They consulted amongst themselves. After an hour, they told us that they were taking us to the Castle of Zeill (home of the Prince of Waldburg) for a day and a night. And we saw on the map that the castle was 35 kilometers to the north of Wangen – while Switzerland was to the south of this town – and that they were therefore taking us further from the frontier.

Nonetheless, we were received at this castle by very agreeable people, where 114 had found refuge (convents, 45 orphans, parents), extremely Catholic and anti-Hitlerian (I was told this at the moment of departure, as they already had difficulties with the Gestapo). This region lived in terror, like all Germany.

They put us up as best they could: one room for the Marshal and me, next to General Debeney and then the Admiral, I don't know where, in the immense quadrilateral of that castle. Our men were put on mattresses in a room, but three came and laid down in a great corridor outside our door, despite the cold.

We were so tired that we slept well the first night.

Next day, 22 April, we learned that Ulm had been taken and the Americans were advancing. We rejoiced, and asked ourselves who will arrive first to deliver us.

But on the evening of the 22nd, around 11 pm, von Tangstein called for General Debeney and announced that we must leave.

The General warned the Marshal, who answered that there was nothing to do, that he would not leave.

At *midnight*, Tangstein demanded to see the Marshal. He told him that time pressed, etc… The Marshal went to General Debeney's room, right beside ours. Through the door, I heard the whole scene which unfolded, *for three hours*, in that room.

Tangstein – Marshal, the military situation requires that you leave here. I have come to ask you.

Marshal – No, I refuse to leave.

Tangstein – That is not possible, Marshal, we need to ensure the security of your person, we must leave.

Marshal – No, I will wait here for the French troops or the Americans. My safety is not at risk.

Tangstein – Marshal, I must obey. I beg you.

The discussion grew more heated, the Marshal's voice grew hard.

Marshal – It is useless. You have only lied to me since Vichy. Where do you want to take me?

Tangstein – But towards the Swiss frontier.

Marshal – I don't believe you. Have you had assurances from the Swiss that they will let me enter to return to France?

Tangstein, embarrassed – No, but we can ask them from here.

Marshal – I have no confidence. You are taking me eastwards. You have always deceived me. Your Renthe-Fink always lied. I am staying here.

Tangstein – But that was not me, Marshal. I assure you that I am telling you the truth.

Tangstein grew angry. The discussion went on for an hour on this theme. The Marshal called Admiral Bléhaut. He, with his habitual frankness, but with cold correctness, repeated to Tangstein that it was impossible to believe what he said – that they were taking us northwards rather than to the south, towards Switzerland, and that it certainly was to take us towards the Redoubt.

The situation grew violent. Our men, in the corridor, heard everything. The Marshal still resisted. It was 2 hours in the morning. At 2 hours 15, I entered the room and said to Tangstein:

"You are wearing the Marshal out, this has already gone on for two hours. You can see that he will not leave, leave him alone."

Tangstein, addressing himself to me – Madame, I beg you, help me. I can only obey, I must ensure the Marshal's safety. I am in earnest. We will go towards Switzerland.

Me – Very hard to believe you. Let the Marshal rest.

Still talking, we went out into the corridor it was 2.30. Tangstein was still going on. It was clear that he did not know what more to say. In the course of this discussion, he said to me:

"You know well that we have orders to take you to Bavaria. We will not do it."

Me – But what will your government say?

Him – There is no more government… we are acting for ourselves.

At that moment the Prince de Waldburg arrived, announcing that he had just heard by telephone that the tanks were 20 kilometres from Zeill.

At that, the Marshal, seized with a new energy, cried out: "Leave me in peace. I will wait for them, I'm going to bed."

And he went back into our room.

Tangstein, distraught, said: "We must leave at six. I will go and find Minister Reinebeck. It will be like Vichy if needed [use of force]."

The Marshal undressed and went to bed. He even slept.

At 5.45, Reinebeck and Tangstein arrived in our room.

The scene resumed.

We must leave!

No!

The Marshal curled up in his bed. "Leave me in peace, I'm tired, I can't do any more – at my age, you can't put up with such a strain. I refuse to get up, etc... And still you do not have the Swiss agreement to let me enter in transit. If I was sure of that, perhaps I would believe you."

Tangstein jumped on that idea and said: "The Swiss minister is twenty minutes from here, I will go and see him – we can ask Switzerland if they accept this – you will see that I am in good faith."

And then, the Marshal said, I will not leave unless a Swiss diplomat accompanies me to the frontier.

Reinebeck and Tangstein left.

Meanwhile, the Prince de Waldburg, who was certainly in good faith, told us at three in the morning that the tanks were not in the vicinity, but that they were German tanks that the inhabitants had mistaken for American tanks.

We waited for the answer of the Swiss. We should have it around 17 hours. It came towards 19 hours. It was favourable. The Federal Consul was coming and would open the frontier to the Marshal and everyone who accompanied him. Joy for us, still mixed with a little disquiet, but the chargé d'affaires would accompany him.

Departure was fixed for 22 hours, as in the day, Allied aircraft were bombing the roads. At 22 hours 30, we left Zeill for Bregenz, with around 80 kilometres to go. We did not arrive at Bregenz until 3 in the morning, roads clogged with escapees, with disorderly convoys where three or four lorries pulled by a tractor were mixed in with horses, foot travellers, bicycles. At Bregenz, a glacial cold. They gave us a room in a little hotel. The Marshal slept.

I did not sleep; I knew that the French tanks were at Friedrischafen, 30 kilometres away, and I kept listening...

We had to leave Bregenz at 9 in the morning to be at the Swiss frontier at 9.30.

At 8 in the morning, the planes arrived – intense bombardment of Bregenz. We escaped that danger. At 9.30, we left. There were

10 kilometres to make to reach Sainte-Marguerite, the crossing point into Switzerland. Would the planes come back, would we be? No. At 10.00 am, the barrier was raised. We passed through.

We were in Switzerland.

Pétain and his party had headed south-east from Sigmaringen, circumventing Lake Constance to reach Switzerland through territory that is now in western Austria. Doubt persists even now over whether the Alpine Redoubt in the Bavarian Alps ever actually existed; Joseph Goebbels is usually credited with a successful propaganda campaign started in January 1945 to convince the Allies of its existence. The Marshal and his party clearly believed in it; and if it had existed, they would have been taken further east to reach it, rather than south or north.

Madame Pétain continued:

Friendly faces approached us – soldiers, customs officials, civilians. One said: "Happy birthday, Marshal."

And the Marshal replied: "The best present that anyone could give me for this birthday is this: my arrival in Switzerland."

In fact, we had reached 24 April, birthday of the Marshal, who was 89 years old and now entered on his ninetieth year.

At this moment, Tangstein arrived, very moved: "Marshal, I take my leave of you."

The Marshal said to him: "You were in good faith – you have proved it – I thank you."

Reinebeck arrived next.. The Marshal, very coldly, said to him: "Minister, I have seen that you have not deceived me."

The entrance formalities lasted an hour, during which they brought us flowers, chocolates, friendly words. We had the impression of deliverance. We then left the Swiss chargé d'affaires in Germany who had accompanied us and who had been admirable. We learned that the day before, in coming to the frontier for us, he had been shot up, his car had been destroyed, and he had barely escaped the bombs. By sheer good fortune, he had been able to continue his efforts and lead us here. We thanked him warmly. We had to go to Wessen on the shore of the Wallensee in a restful place, surrounded by mountains, until the French government, alerted, would make known its response for our return to France.

Pétain stayed in Switzerland until 26 April, when he surrendered himself to French authorities at Vallorbe at 7.00 pm. The next day, he was imprisoned in Fort de Montrouge, alongside General Debeney.

For the others, the expected trains did not arrive. The rest of the Sigmaringen exiles, including the former members of the Commission, lower priorities for the Germans, were essentially left to fend for themselves. Those with money or connections, or simply able to gain access to a car, made best use of them. Those without were simply left behind in Sigmaringen to await the Allied forces.

Marcel Déat evoked the last moments of the Sigmaringen enclave in his memoirs, cited by Cointet:

> The dull murmur of the Danube rises up to us. The little town is deathly in its silence, and we do not know whether, behind its walls, people are awake, or if they are thinking, and about what. If there were a psychic barometer to measure the pressure of tragedy on this immensity of shadows, at what fantastic gradation would the needle stop? There has perhaps never been a denser and heavier hour since the start. However, we are here at once carried on by an irresistible current and immobile, as if outside time and on the outside of the adventure.

Laval was blacklisted by the Swiss authorities as complicit in Axis war crimes. His efforts to leave the enclave may have stemmed from the same fears of abduction to the 'Redoubt' that apparently infested Pétain and his party, and some sources speak of his wish to secure an adequate interval to prepare his defence, rather than to evade French justice entirely. In any event, he proceeded with his earlier plans to seek refuge in Spain. He made his way by car over back roads to Wangen, where he was reunited with Déat, Luchaire, and the rest of the French political and diplomatic contingent.

At Wangen, he was approached by the Germans with a proposal to follow them, but as per Rousso's account, his wife burst out: 'No! No! No! We will not follow you! That's enough! You've deceived us from the start, now that's enough!'

Laval and his wife drove on towards Feldkirch. Refused entry to Switzerland on 23 April 1945, he addressed a long appeal to Walter Stucki, the Swiss diplomat who had witnessed Pétain's enforced removal from Vichy in August 1944. As quoted by Cointet, it reads:

I presented myself yesterday at your border post at Tisis [Schaanwald]. I informed the officer on duty of my intention to request entry into Switzerland, among with those colleagues who accompanied me, and I asked him to let me know what response would be made by your government. Within two hours, I learned that I had to make a request for transit. Switzerland is for me, in this case, the only route that could allow me to retrace the path by which I was taken to Germany. I would need a respite to finalize all the elements of the presentation that I will make upon my arrival in France. The role that I played in my country, in Geneva and elsewhere, obliges me to defend a policy that, in my opinion, would have preserved France and Europe from war and its misfortunes. This is personal work that I could not accomplish in Germany and that, without doubt, I could not accomplish at present in France. I must, while observing the discretion and reserve that hospitality imposes, be free in a neutral country. If the information given to me yesterday evening, on your part, from the officer on duty, were confirmed, I would no longer have this possibility.

I do not know therefore if I could still ask you for an asylum which would allow me to wait and to find a justice which was one of the new virtues of my country, because I cannot believe that yours has renounced its generous tradition of hospitality.

I have never thought, Minister, of establishing my residence abroad. I can only live in my country. It is for it alone and for peace that I have always worked. I am eager to submit my actions to its judgment, as I do not doubt that it will understand, once passions have cooled, my position during the unhappy period which it has just experienced. It is therefore up to you, Minister, to assess whether it is possible for you to take this situation into account when making your decision.

If you judge otherwise, and following the indication that you will give, I formalize my request for a transit with the approval of the German authorities which I have not obtained until now, and which I am not yet sure of being able to obtain.

I hope and have no doubt that you will be kind enough, if it must be carried out, not to allow biased publicity whereby public opinion might be mistaken about my feelings or about the conditions in which you were able to take your decision.

The Swiss granted him no more than a twenty-four-hour transit period, which Laval judged insufficient to prepare his defence. Temporarily ensconced at the hotel Zum Löwen in Feldkirch, along with the Déats, he obtained permission to enter Spain – once again, on condition that he would be in transit, for eventual return to the French authorities. A Junkers Ju 88 flew him and his wife, plus a handful of acolytes, from Feldkirch to Barcelona on 2 May, delivering him to the Spanish authorities for three months of confinement prior to his return to France.

Once in Feldkirch, Déat decided to leave as soon as he heard of Laval's departure by plane. With his wife, driver and servant, he drove from Feldkirch to Sankt Anton am Arlberg, accompanied by Luchaire and his entourage, then proceeded independently to Tösens, and by 3 May 1945 had crossed the border at the Reschen Pass, one of the main historic crossing points from Austria to Italy. Evading American convoys, the Déat party drove via Glurns (Glorenza) and Schlanders (Silandro) – ironically, some of the most Germanophone communities in Italy – to Naturns (Naturno), where they abandoned their car on the advice of the local priest. After three weeks of rest in the mountain village, they walked overnight to Merano, historic resort for artists and intellectuals, then moved to Bolzano, capital of Italian South Tyrol, assisted by other Italian priests. Subsequently, they took refuge in Milan.

Darnand, having arrived in the Valtelline with his rag-tag dregs of Milice followers, was engaged from 25 April in fierce fighting against Italian partisans. Giolitto repeated Darnand's personal account of the events:

The 25th, at five in the morning, general attack, after a mortar bombardment which hit home every time. Defence organized: the windows manned with machine-guns, submachine guns and rifles. Loopholes are created using sandbags, mattresses and benches. Suppressive fire from our side but, from ten onwards, the fire from the partisans, with automatic weapons, was getting very close to us. The entire population shooting from neighbouring buildings...

The situation worsens hour by hour. I ask myself how all this is going to end. The officers have decided to defend themselves and die. I go around everyone and comfort the hesitant. Distribution of tobacco, songs and music...

Towards 16.00, a spokesperson appears. I agree to talk.

The surviving Milice received guarantees of mercy and safe conduct to Switzerland. They had suffered twenty-five dead and some sixty wounded. Darnand secured for them 'the honours of war' and arranged that they need only give up their arms:

We will leave with our archives, our baggage and our funds... At ten hours, the battalion is assembled in the square. I speak to the men before the partisans and the population. Intense emotion. Many of our comrades cry. The wounded are there on stretchers. Then comes the parade and the handing over of arms. Everything is finished, the battalion, the Milice are dead.

Darnand's remaining followers marched to Switzerland, where they were treated as prisoners of war rather than refugees, before being handed over to the French authorities. Two days later, on 28 April, Benito Mussolini, his mistress Clara Petacci, and a trio of followers were shot by Italian partisans, and their bodies taken to Milan, where they were hung up next day, to be stoned and spat on by partisans and populace alike.

Darnand himself sought to escape separately, taking refuge in the monastery of Notre-Dame in Tirano where he dressed as a monk. He was able to hide the Milice treasury – some 7 million German marks, 40,000 French francs, and a few kilos of gold, totalling some 200 million French francs – in a cave. After a couple of months of cloistered seclusion, he was finally arrested on 25 June 1945 by agents of the British First Special Service, who were seeking for other Italian Fascist fugitives.

Rumours around the treasure of the Milice inflated its volume to some 2 tons in weight, with four trucks needed to transfer the cash boxes, marked with the initials of the Bank of France. According to reports of Darnand's interrogation, he resisted for several hours before finally offering to give up the location of the treasure, if transported there in person with an officer out of uniform. Darnand's interrogator received permission to travel with him in civilian clothing. Driven to Tirano, and escorted by one of his interrogators and two French gendarmes, Darnand revealed that the banknotes were locked in a box hidden in the room of one of the monks, and the gold was in a chest hidden under the chapel organ. The Father Superior and other monks were hostile at first, pretending ignorance even in the face of threats to have the monastery searched from top to bottom, until Darnand said, 'May Our Lady of Puy and Our Lady of Tirano bless you!' At this point, the monks revealed that they had removed the goods and had buried them in the monastery cellar for safe keeping. The interrogating officer recorded the recovery of a carboy of banknotes, a chest filled with gold and Darnand's leather coat with gold coins sewn into the lining. The Milice treasury was transferred to Paris by special plane on 28 June, but rumours and conspiracy theories have circulated ever since, alleging that the sum recovered was only part of the whole, and that other troves still await discovery.

Brinon left the enclave bound for the Republic of Salò, in a convoy of four cars, with his wife, his two secretaries, and some servants. He arrived at the Swiss frontier near Innsbruck on 24 April, and over the next few days, made repeated applications to cross into Switzerland, all of them refused. Once American troops arrived in the vicinity in early May, he presented himself to them as a prisoner, but only on 9 May, with French troops already at Lake Constance, was he finally arrested by US military police, with a French officer in attendance.

For Luchaire, Italy was also an obvious choice. Born in Siena, with a legal claim to Italian nationality, he was optimistic about seeking refuge there.

Corinne Luchaire recalled the family's departure from Sigmaringen. 'We had to watch day and night over the vehicle, because the Milice or Doriot's men were ready to seize it. So we left one day at dawn, ingloriously, from Sigmaringen.' After parting company with the Déats, Luchaire crossed over into Italy on 4 May with his family, having obtained papers without difficulty. Also taking refuge in Merano, he was able to evade arrest after the arrival of the Americans, until a French military security officer, recruited by the Americans to screen French nationals, he and his family were finally identified and arrested on 18 May. The security officer who identified him, a Lieutenant Gallon, was a former agent for the Gestapo, acting on information provided by two other French agents of the Gestapo who had been active in Sigmaringen, Le Can and Talleu. All were later arrested in turn by French military security, and Gallon was condemned to death in 1947.

After his crossing into Denmark at the end of March Céline resided in Copenhagen for the remainder of the German occupation. In December 1945 he was incarcerated in Vestry Prison by the Danish authorities, pending the outcome of extradition proceedings launched against him by the French government.

Sundry other former Sigmaringen residents found refuge, or fell into the hands of the Allies. Admiral Bléhaut and General Debeney followed their Marshal into Switzerland and captivity in France. Bernard Ménétrel, the Marshal's faithful attending physician, was liberated by American troops from confinement in Castle Eisenberg [Jezeří] in Bohemia on 7 May 1945, but imprisoned in France on his return to the metropole on 21 May. Eugène Bridoux was taken prisoner by American forces in Germany in May 1945. By his own account, Jacques Bouly de Lesdain fled on 23 April 1945 with his wife, in a Citroen II procured for him by friends, in a convoy of seven vehicles. He fled to Italy, where he lived after the war. Jean Hérold-Paquis fled to Switzerland but was handed back to France on 8 July 1945. Lucien Rebatet was taken prisoner at Feldkirch on 8 May 1945. Gaston Bruneton, during the last days of the fall of Berlin, surrendered to an action committee of former deportees on 29 April 1945. Alphonse de Châteaubriant, the onetime crafter of spiritual superweapons, was able to escape to a monastery near Kitzbühel. Francis Bout de l'An was another refugee in Bolzano, and was able to remain there undiscovered. Marcel Bucard was arrested in Merano in June 1945 while attempting to flee to Spain. Simon Sabiani successfully absconded to Spain via Italy. Victor Barthélemy was arrested in Milan on 2 May 1945.

The French forces had laid their plans for the investiture of Sigmaringen, which fell to France's celebrated First Army thanks to de Gaulle's decision on 31 March 1945 to order it over the Rhine. 'At Sigmaringen, shut everything down – take it in hand – put a steady, hardline boss in charge of it, with someone beside him who will shut down the "politicos" at once, and keep everything quiet till I arrive', General Jean de Lattre de Tassigny wrote to General Antoine Béthouart, commander of the First Army's First Corps, on 21 April 1945. The French Third Regiment of Zouaves and the second squadron of the Second Regiment of Cuirassiers reached Sigmaringen on the morning of 22 April 1945, finding all the notable occupants fled, and only a few Milice members still in residence. After overcoming the last feeble resistance from the sentries, Charles Vallin, a former Vichy official who had transferred his allegiance to the Free French in 1942, approached the castle, together with Captain André, one of the unit commanders. According to the account later published in de Lattre's *Reconquérir*, the two officers rang the bell at the postern gate around 11.20 am. The heavy ironbound door finally swung open, revealing around five or six functionaries in stiff collars and black costumes. Vallin asked the most imposing:

"Do you speak French?"
The man nodded.
"Are you the proprietor of the Castle?"
"No, Sir," he replied, in a heavy Teutonic accent. "I am Marshal Pétain's valet de chambre..."
"Where is Marshal Pétain?"
"I do not know."
In the courtyard, Vallin and André ran into one of the ladies of the Princess Hohenzollern's household, dressed in black, who asked them, with all the authority of her status:
"Where are you going?"
"We want to visit the Castle," Vallon replied, impatiently.

The maid in waiting then presented His Royal Highness the Prince of Saxe, brother of the Prince of Hohenzollern, who commenced a long genealogical explanation. Vallin interrupted to order his officers to organize the defence of the town, place guards on all the exits from the castle, and to fly the French flag from the highest tower. Preceded by the Prince of Saxe, the former valet de chambre, and other members of the princely household, Vallin then inspected the Marshal's office, still in disorder after his hasty flight. The Germans believed that the Marshal had been killed after leaving the town, and that all the other French occupying the Castle had left well before him. Pétain's relics, left behind in the office, included the internal telephone numbers for his fellow occupants, including Laval, de Brinon and Madame Pétain.

Later, the Princess Hohenzollern herself, a blonde young woman, reportedly proposed to Vallin to prepare the Marshal's bedchamber for him.

"No, madame, I will not sleep in the Castle."

"And why not?"

"I don't like ghosts."[4]

Chapter 8

The Post-War Record

The exodus to Sigmaringen in 1944 did at least save the collaborationists there from the bloodiest episodes of the *épuration sauvage* – the ferocious settling of scores in France in the wake of the Axis withdrawal, which included some 10,000-15,000 summary executions of Milice and other collaborators by Resistance forces and vengeful local populations. Contemporary estimates quoted figures for the number of executions as much as ten times higher. The GPRF had planned from the start to minimize such anarchic bloodletting as part of its agenda to reestablish Republican legitimacy in metropolitan France, and already had a Commission d'Epuration established by its predecessor, the CFLN in August 1943. The *épuration légale* that followed the Liberation was the formal procedure for the punishments meted out to the collaborators at the end of and after the war. Most of the former inhabitants of the Sigmaringen enclave who had not escaped into more permanent exile went through it.

The vengefulness of the Liberation had its roots in popular anger, but also in the spirit of many of the Resistance militants. 'In effect, the French now had been engaged in a civil war that by 1944 had lasted eight years, and the participants on the winning side were led by the force of their own experience to rethink their commitments and to state them in ever starker forms. The absence of any possibility of compromise (and, later, of any need for it) encouraged the emergence of a political and moral vocabulary keyed to absolutes – the absolute defeat of one's adversaries, the non-negotiable demands of one's own side.'[1] The footsoldiers of the Milice and the other collaborationist factions may have been the stooges rather than the instigators of this process, but they had emphatically picked their sides in the civil war, and suffered accordingly.

Perhaps fortunately for its occupants, the Sigmaringen enclave only fell when the structure of judicial punishment had already been put into place.

Full implementation of the *épuration légale* had been delayed by the fractured condition of France immediately after Liberation, and the slow process of reestablishing central government authority over areas frequently controlled by local Maquis units. Other impediments included the large number of legal professionals who had sworn loyalty to the Vichy regime: all but one of the country's judges had pledged fealty to the figurehead who they were now about to prosecute. Also, as de Gaulle emphasized later in his memoirs, in view of the institutional situation in France, and the types of offences being tried, it was necessary to innovate, with new judicial structures that still preserved justice.

Accused collaborationists awaiting trial were held in the detention camps formerly used by the Vichy regime and the Germans. Many of the Sigmaringen contingent, including Laval, Darnand, and Corinne Luchaire, were held in Fresnes Prison, the major penitentiary just to the south of Paris, which had previously housed many Resistance fighters and Allied agents. Some, including Darnand, Luchaire and Jean Hérold-Paquis, were eventually executed in the Fort de Châtillon, also to the south of Paris. Pétain was held separately at the Fort de Montrouge.

To try the collaborators, three types of court were instituted: the High Court of Justice, the Courts of Justice, and the Civil Chambers. Many were tried by these courts, but few suffered the worst penalties: as per the title of an article by Jean-Paul Cointet, there were '400,000 dossiers, less than 800 deaths'. Many collaborationists were convicted of *indignité nationale*, an offence instituted on 26 August 1944 to cover activities that fell short of actual treason or murder, with the corresponding penalty of *dégradation nationale* – exclusion from political and professional activities, and confiscation of property. A fair number of fugitive exiles were condemned *in absentia*, including Marcel Déat, condemned to death in June 1945.[2] The first round of major cases were held under pressure to conclude before the 21 October 1945 constituent assembly elections, and the concurrent referendum on France's new governing institutions.

Pétain was tried by the High Court of Justice, in a process beginning on 23 July 1945 and concluded on 15 August. All three of the presiding judges had previously sworn loyalty to him. Pétain claimed from the first day of the trial that he had always been a covert ally of de Gaulle, and that he was answerable only to the French people, not the High Court. The irregularities of the trial were remarked on at the time and subsequently, but were not enough to derail the process. Pétain was condemned to death for intelligence with the enemy and high treason, but de Gaulle, as provisional head of the Republic, commuted his sentence to life imprisonment on 17 August 1945. Pétain was first held in the remote mountain fortress of Portalet in the French Pyrenees, then on 16 November 1945 was transferred to the Île d'Yeu, off the coast of northwest France just south of Saint-Nazaire, where he died on 23 July 1951, at the age of 95, despite numerous appeals for his release.

Post-war apologetics for Pétain and his behaviour during the war grew so voluminous that they attracted their own catchphrase, the 'sword and buckler thesis' (*thèse du bouclier et de l'épée*). These elaborated on Pétain's own remarks that if he could not be the sword of the French people, he had tried to be their shield, and enlarged on the actions that he had supposedly undertaken to protect France from rapacious Nazi demands. They also frequently picked up the argument that Pétain had played a 'double game' and had secretly worked to undermine the Axis position and facilitate the Liberation all along. The writer Robert Aron made a particularly influential articulation of this thesis in his *Histoire de Vichy* (1954), minimizing the active complicity of the Vichy state in the repression and atrocities of the Occupation era. Proponents of the thesis often cast blame for the Vichy regime's most reprehensible policies on Laval rather than Pétain.

All these revisionist theses were comprehensively undermined by the publication in 1972 of Robert O. Paxton's *Vichy France: Old Guard and New Order, 1940-1944*. This analysis exploded the post-war French consensus typified by Robert Aron and set off an explosive controversy in France following the publication of a French translation in 1973. Paxton's analysis of just how far the Vichy regime had been Pétain's active project from start to finish, and how complicit it had been in such Axis atrocities as the roundup of Jews in France and their transportation to the death camps, attracted virulent protest from pro-Vichy apologists. Nonetheless, his reassessment has now essentially become the new post-war consensus – despite the continuing activities of organizations such as the Association pour défendre la mémoire du Maréchal Pétain.

Pierre Laval was given up by Spain under French pressure ninety days after his flight to Barcelona, and was flown back to Innsbruck in the American Austrian occupation zone. After a failed attempt to seek sanctuary in Liechtenstein, he was transferred to France and imprisoned in the Fresnes Prison on 2 August 1945. Pending his own trial, he was called as a witness in Pétain's on 3 August, where he did his own case no good by turning his appearance into a diatribe in favour of his own wartime policies. His own process began on 4 October 1945, in proceedings that lasted only four days, marked by numerous judicial shortcomings, including death threats from the blatantly partial jury. Despite the deficiencies in the trial, de Gaulle refused to allow a second one. Condemned to death on 9 October 1945 on charges of high treason and plotting against the internal security of the state, Laval attempted to commit suicide by swallowing cyanide, but recovered under medical treatment. On 15 October 1945, he was shot at Fresnes, and was initially buried in a common grave, before his relatives had him reinterred in Montparnasse cemetery. Many subsequent appeals were made for his rehabilitation on the basis of the faults in his trial, and in favour of his own justification that he had always acted in good faith in what he saw as the best interests of France, but to date none has succeeded.

Incarcerated at Fresnes, Joseph Darnand was tried by the High Court at the same time as Laval, in a process which began on 3 October 1945 and concluded the same evening with a death sentence. As per his statement in the Archives Nationales, he declared:

> I do not regret my position in these last few years. I always acted in good faith, in the interest, as it seemed to me, of my country. I did it with the greatest impartiality and I am ready to appear without fear before the justice of my country to prove my faith and the purity of my ideal.

During the trial, while making no conspicuous effort to avoid personal blame, he emphasized the collective responsibility of the Vichy regime for the creation of the Milice and for its crimes. After his arrest, he declared:

> The Milice was created by a law and with the approbation of the Council of Ministers. Furthermore, my activity at the head of the

Milice was always approved and encouraged by Marshal Pétain and Laval... During a meeting of the Council of Ministers, concerning the operation of the courts martial, the Head of State congratulated me in front of all the ministers and urged me to continue my activity with even greater energy.[3]

Notwithstanding his insistence on shared responsibility for the crimes of the Vichy regime, Darnand maintained to the last his devotion to the ideal of a revolution intended to reinstate the grandeur of France. An appeal for clemency, made without his consent, was rejected by de Gaulle on 7 October. He was shot on 10 October 1945 at the Fort de Châtillon.

Fernand de Brinon was kept in detention at Fresnes for almost two years following his arrest and return to France on 20 May 1945, due to interruptions in his trial, and health issues which required removal of his prostate. He was finally put on trial before the High Court on 4 March 1947, on charges of being a spy for the enemy as well as high treason. On 6 March 1947 he was condemned to death and was shot at the Fort de Montrouge on 15 April 1947. According to contemporary news reports, he met his death with relative courage, refusing a blindfold.

Jean Luchaire tried and failed to obtain asylum in Liechtenstein and Switzerland. Arrested by the Americans in Merano in the Italian Alps in mid-May 1945, he was returned to France and charged with collaboration with the enemy. He appeared before the High Court in January 1946. Accounts of the proceedings state that he made a poor impression in the dock, smiling perpetually at the judge, and prattling incessantly. He claimed that the articles written by himself and his underlings for *Les Nouveaux Temps* had 'a double meaning' – a pretty obscure one at the time. 'My articles were written, from 1943, to allow me to defend, with sufficient weight, the populations for which I was responsible,' he claimed. 'I would have written anything.'[4] On 24 January 1946, he was condemned to death. '"Mr President", as he was respectfully termed by the members of his "corporation", was nothing more than a second-rate traitor, a cynical and malicious pleasure-seeker for whom any means was good to procure the money he needed. A bohemian of treason.'[5] He was shot at the Fort de Châtillon on 22 February 1946.

Eugène Bridoux, the least active and visible member of the Commission, was returned to France by the Americans after his capture in Germany in May 1945. Incarcerated in the Fort de Montrouge, he was hospitalized for rheumatoid arthritis in the military hospital Val-de-Grâce in Paris, from where he escaped on 8 June 1947, fleeing to exile in Spain.[6] Condemned to death *in absentia* by the High Court, he died in Spain on 6 June 1955.

Marcel Déat, the highest-ranking escapee from Sigmaringen, remained in hiding in Italy, condemned to death *in absentia* by the High Court, eventually installing himself with his wife in Turin. His trial *in absentia* focused heavily on his activities as a journalist and propagandist as much as his actual ministerial duties. 'Remember the merciless and justified punishment that has befallen the Brasillachs, the Paul Chacks,' the prosecutor declared during the process:

Déat was more guilty than they were, because he had more talent and, in any case, more authority. Remember the merciless but justified punishment that has befallen the Milice, the members of the LVF. [Déat] is even more guilty than they were, because they only followed his counsels. Finally, remember the long years of terror and oppression. Remember, when an article by Déat fell before our eyes, when a speech by Déat struck our ears, remember how we clenched our fists, with anger, justice, disgust, indignation, so hard so that our nails dug into the flesh, thinking: the wretch! How slow is the hour of justice in coming! At last it has struck. I ask you, Gentlemen, to pronounce the only punishment proportionate to the magnitude of the crime: the supreme punishment.[7]

In exile, Déat composed his memoirs, eventually published by Denoël, Céline's publisher, in 1989. One review of a new edition of his memoirs described them as the 'memoirs of a megalomaniac schizophrenic'.[8] The introduction to the same edition described it as 'one of the most important in the political and intellectual history of the 20th century in France'. Déat died in Turin on 5 January 1955.

Bernard Ménétrel, Pétain's faithful physician, was liberated by the Americans on 7 May 1945 from confinement in the castle of Jezeří (or

Eisenberg) in Czechoslovakia. Later that month, he was imprisoned in France on suspicion of intelligence with the enemy, but was given a conditional release for health reasons on 15 January 1946. Interrogated on 8 June 1945 by the High Court's Commission of Instruction, Pétain claimed that Dr Ménétrel 'had never played any political role alongside me', but had been removed due to German suspicions of his role. Benefiting from a *nolle prosequi* decision, on the grounds of his evident anti-German sentiments, he was set at liberty, but died on 31 March 1947 in a traffic accident.

Jean Hérold-Paquis, having given up his place on the plane which carried Laval to Spain to Abel Bonnard, former Vichy Minister of National Education, succeeded in reaching Switzerland, but was extradited to France on 8 July 1945. Imprisoned at Fresnes, he was judged and condemned to death on 17 September 1945. Before his execution, he was able to compose a volume of memoirs, *Des Illusions… Désillusions*, giving his own account of the last days of the collaborationist milieu. Hérold-Paquis was shot on 11 October 1945. Louis-Ferdinand Céline cited the event in his 1960 autobiographical novel *Nord*: 'Hérold Paqui went to the stake, crying, dejectedly "they didn't shoot Céline!"'

Hérold-Paquis, however, wrote just before his death:

Having taken refuge in Sigmaringen, Céline had foreseen the German defeat, after the failure of the Ardennes. From then on, he disowned himself. He said that *L'Ecole des Cadavres* [*sic*], *Bagatelles pour un massacre, Les Beaux Draps*, were only personal notes that he had not wanted given to the public, but that Denoël had literally torn out the handwritten pages of his three books. Yes, L.-F. Céline, carried to the heights by the elite of collaboration, Céline, with whose letter *Je Suis Partout* opened its first page, Céline, the god of the anti-Jews, the messiah of the New Order, Céline whose torrential language had impressed the crowd, Céline who was the "prophet", "the Evangelist", everything, in a word, Céline disavowed the author of *Bagatelles pour un massacre, L'Ecole des Cadavres and Les Beaux Draps*. He cast these three books into the fire of his cowardice; he rejected these three books, spurned them with his foot. Céline himself, in this German city, in front of a few thousand French people, made the "Journey to the end of shame". Then, one day, he disappeared.[9]

Céline himself, as this suggests, avoided sharing Hérold-Paquis' fate. After an initial eighteen months in prison in Denmark, he moved into a small cottage where he spent the next three years. On 20 February 1950, he was condemned *in absentia* by the Civic Chamber of the Paris Court of Justice for collaboration under Article 83 of the penal code – not the dreaded Article 75 – suffering penalties including one year in prison (effectively served in Denmark) and *indignité national*. On 20 April 1951, he was amnestied and permitted to return to France, although ambiguity persists regarding this amnesty, with some claims that it was a forgery of public documents. Céline returned to France in the summer of 1951, settling in Meudon in the suburbs of Paris, where he remained until his death on 1 July 1961.

Céline's post-war writing on his wartime experiences, notably *Castle to Castle*, has been characterized as:

> a vengeful accounting of all the evils and thefts supposedly suffered by the narrator of the German trilogy and by its author. It establishes the simultaneous dimension of a plea for rehabilitation and an indictment against all of Céline's "enemies", a characteristic dimension of these last works. In other words, hatred feeds memory: "I want to remember!... I want to be left!... there! all the memories!... the circumstances! all that I ask for! I live even more on hatred than noodles!... but the right hatred!"[10]

At times, Céline cast his woes in exile in Sigmaringen seamlessly in the same context as the pains and burdens he had supposedly endured in France from childhood onwards. Guilt or blame or personal responsibility hardly comes into the equation, and when it does, it serves to exonerate the refugees at Sigmaringen, and the collaborationists as a whole, as victims rather than perpetrators. Furthermore, indications are that Céline's avoidance of guilt and relativization of experience was not only personal and self-exculpatory, but also collective and ideological.

In *Castle to Castle*, Céline was still writing as late as 1957, passages like 'Saint Louis, the cow! ... let us expiate for him, I say! ... he the brutal! the torturer! ... he who was beatified, that's it! who had a million children of Israel baptized, by force! ... in our dear South of our dear France! worse than Adolf'. One post-war genre he was almost certainly responsible for pioneering was relativizing the Holocaust. He also benefited fully from earlier applications of Poe's law, where irony is mistaken for sincerity, and the irony defence certainly allowed the get-out clause of evading censure for his sentiments while preserving all the original venom for audiences less sensitive to irony.

Céline's post-war revisionism also included a kind of attempted rehabilitation of Pétain. In *Castle to Castle*, he wrote:

If he had not taken command at the key moment, started the procession, no one would have escaped! There would never have been a High Court! Nor Noguères! I saw it, I can say it, the Marshal saved the High Court!... Without him, without his cold decision, no one would have escaped being wiped out!... Not a minister, not a general...Nor the underlings! It was the end! Without indictments! And without verdicts! Total mess! No need for the Île d'Yeu either!... It was Pétain's decision that saved everyone from being wiped out!... As it was Pétain's character that got the army back in line in '17... I can speak quite freely of him, he loathed me.

Whatever that adds to the myth of Pétain as the saviour of the nation in 1917 and in 1940, it certainly shows how ready Céline was to reinforce that myth post-war, and with it the whole collaborationist enterprise. He certainly did enough to play up the miseries of life in the enclave without particular concern for the sufferings of the countless other victims of the Axis. Throughout *Castle to Castle* and elsewhere, he engaged in what one commentator described as 'a sophism which continues with the denial of any specificity to the Jewish genocide', implicitly or explicitly comparing the sufferings of the collaborationists at Sigmaringen with the sufferings of the Jews in the death camps, the crimes of the Soviets with the crimes of the Nazis, etc., etc.[11]

Nonetheless, Céline's literary star remains in the ascendant. The appearance in 2022 of *Guerre* (*War*), a hitherto unpublished fragmentary account of experience during and just after active service in the First World War written in the mid-1930s and rediscovered in the trove of manuscripts that resurfaced after the death of his widow in 2019,[12] was greeted with all the fanfare that one would expect for a new Gallimard NRF edition. As well as the customary denunciations of his parents for 'their enormous optimistic, insane, rotten idiocy' in the face of 'all the degradations which they didn't even accept since acknowledging them would be to despair a little of the world and of life and they didn't want to despair of anything',[13] the work also helped underline just how much of his stylistic trickery, particularly his famous ellipses, was consciously worked into the prose in the course of writing. Any admirer of Céline who maintains that he is a spontaneous untutored oracle of pure truth writing straight from the shoulder in the heat of events is working from very slender evidence, and even less after *Guerre*. And it also emphasized once again how much of his virulent misanthropy and bitter resentment of his society stemmed from personal roots earlier and deeper than his wartime ordeal. His congenitally enlarged spleen may have fuelled his style, but it certainly poisoned his social criticism.

Lucien Rebatet fled to Austria, and was arrested at Feldkirch on 8 May 1945. He was returned to France, and condemned to death on 18 November 1946, but his sentence was commuted to hard labour in perpetuity on 12 April 1947, after a petition campaign organized by numerous notable writers. While in prison, he completed the novel *Les Deux Étendards*, published in 1952 by Gallimard. He was released under house arrest on 16 July 1952 and by 1954 was at liberty and resumed his journalistic career.

Rebatet never renounced his fascist stance, although he expressed support on several occasions for Israel's position in the Middle East. As late as 1962, after a meeting with George Steiner, he wrote:

> No reconciliation is possible with them, even on the highest peaks, even with this one, one of the freest, one of the most intelligent. Each word of theirs confirms all the theses of our anti-Semitism, that they will remain forever the infernal race of the Bible. Nothing to answer him. The arguments jostle in my head: that it is the unanimity of Judaism against France that made me anti-Semitic, its unanimity for the war

that pushed this anti-Semitism to the limit; that if the Jews paid cruelly, terribly, it was an expiation for the fury of their warmongering... They, and even more so their "Christian slaves", who I will not even do the honour of treating as enemy Jews worthy of me.[14]

He also made repeated efforts 'to submit his case on appeal before history, by repeatedly trying to justify his collaborationist past in order to present it as a simple biographical parenthesis, by playing on the fact that one should distinguish the politician in him from the writer he had become after the war, by considering that his pamphlet had made more noise than harm.'[15]

Jean Luchaire's daughter Corinne, arrested with him, was released from prison in October 1945, but condemned in 1945 to ten years of *indignité nationale*. In 1949, she published her autobiography, *Ma drôle de vie*. She died the following year from tuberculosis, on 22 January, aged 28.

Abel Bonnard escaped to Spain aboard the same plane as Laval, but was incarcerated in Montjuïc Castle in Barcelona for arriving without a passport. He was condemned to death *in absentia* in July 1945. Freed from custody in Barcelona in January 1946, he was granted political asylum in Spain and settled there, supporting himself with journalism and translation work. In July 1958, he returned to France to face the judgment of the High Court of Justice in one of the last processes dealing with leading Vichy collaborators. Briefly imprisoned at Fresnes, then granted provisional liberty for medical reasons, he was finally tried in March 1960. Found guilty, he was condemned to ten years of banishment, effective from 20 May 1945, and consequently already served; however, he decided to return to Spain, stating that the sentence of banishment 'signifies to me, and I say it with the greatest regret, that my place is no longer in the France of today'. Installed once again in Madrid, he received many visitors, including Jean-Marie Le Pen, and died there on 31 May 1968.

Doriot's PPF subordinate and storekeeper in Sigmaringen, Simon Sabiani, fled to Italy, then Argentina, and finally to Spain. Condemned to death *in absentia*, he died in Barcelona on 29 September 1956. Paul Marion, former Vichy Secretary of State from 1944, was arrested in Austria in July 1945 and returned to France. He was condemned to ten years in prison on 14 December 1948, but was released on medical grounds in 1953, and died a year later, on 2 March 1954. Francis Bout de l'An, perpetrator of several Milice atrocities during 1944, took refuge in Bolzano in northern Italy, and was able to remain there despite his condemnation to death *in absentia*, dying there on 7 September 1977.

Jacques Bouly de Lesdain lived and worked in Italy until the 1970s, working as a teacher of French and for the Vatican's official local daily, condemned to death *in absentia* on 6 February 1950. Alphonse de Châteaubriant, the proponent of a 'spiritual bomb', fled from Sigmaringen to Austria, where he took refuge in a monastery in Kitzbühel, under the name Dr Alfred Wolf. He was condemned *in absentia* to death and *indignité nationale* on 25 October 1948, but the arrest warrant did not reach him before his death on 2 May 1951.

Otto Abetz, the collaborationists' ever-present counterparty, took refuge in the Black Forest after the collapse of the Sigmaringen enclave, where he was arrested at Todtmoos in October 1945 by French occupation forces. Taken to France, he was condemned in July 1949 to twenty years of hard labour for war crimes, specifically for facilitating the deportation of Jews to the death camps. Benefiting from an act of clemency by the then president of the Fourth Republic, René Coty, he was released on 17 April 1954. Abetz died just four years later, on 5 May 1958, burned to death in a car accident near Langenfeld. Suspicions linger that he may have been killed in revenge for his acts during the Holocaust. Cécil von Renthe-Fink, his colleague in Sigmaringen, was interned by American occupation authorities, and transferred to Denmark in May 1946 to serve as a witness in war crimes trials. He was not charged with any crimes himself, but was held in custody until the completion of his denazification in 1949. Returning to Germany, he never held a professional position again, and died in Munich in 1964.

Charles Maurras was arrested in Lyon in September 1944, reportedly while calling a press conference for American journalists.[16] On 24 January 1945 he was put on trial in Lyon, and three days later, was condemned for a process of demoralization and for intelligence with the enemy, with extenuating circumstances that disallowed the death penalty. 'Such is the Charles Maurras of the occupation years. Cut off from the march of time, overtaken by events that he did not fully understand, locked in his outdated vision, prisoner of his hatreds, frozen in his certainties, for four years he had no other beacon than the figure of the Marshal, to whom he clung blindly. Thus, at the opening of his trial, he wore the Francisque on the lapel of his jacket. Some saw it as a provocation. For him, it was the symbol of a loyalty that had never been denied.'[17] The court condemned him to perpetual confinement and *dégradation nationale*. It was at this point that he came out with his famous remark 'It's the revenge of Dreyfus!' ('*C'est la revanche de Dreyfus!*'). As one source observed, 'the formula above all expressed the Academician's conviction that he was paying more for the hatred expressed over the past half-century than for his commitment to the occupier over the past four years.'[18] Maurras was imprisoned in Clairvaux, and in 1952 was transferred on medical grounds to a clinic in Saint-Symphorien-lès-Tours. Having returned to Catholicism, he died there on 16 November 1952.

As for Maurras:

> Action Française attracted many individuals eager for direct political action, and that it was led by a man who conceived his role as similar to that of being dean of a political science institute. When Maurras thought of action he seemed to think of it in terms of words, which, in turn, would generate acts.[19]

This attitude may have saved him from even deeper disgrace through active participation in the Vichy regime and collaboration, but it hardly excuses his stubborn adherence to the regime even after its effective fall in 1942 and the worsening German-led repression:

> The reasons for Maurras's refusal to shift his position are certainly not simple ones. They are partly psychological, having to do with old age, increased isolation due to a worsening deafness, and partly intellectual, traceable to an insufficient grasp of economics and modern forces of history. He was also a man whose political responses were shaped by the Dreyfus case, nearly half a century before, who kept fighting so many of the same battles over and over again until the lonely end, tainting so much of his prose with a distasteful anti-Semitism.[20]

And Sigmaringen itself? The town is now a fairly remote and unspoilt historic backwater deep in south-western Baden-Württemberg, still very much in the shadow of its castle; peaceful, provincial, picturesque. One of its most notable current residents, Winfried Kretschmann, is Minister-President of Baden-Württemberg, for the Alliance 90/The Greens party. Local pageantry and tourist paraphernalia are mostly focused on the centuries-long heritage of the princely house of Hohenzollern-Sigmaringen. There is hardly a trace left behind either of Nazism or of the French enclave. Black and white Hohenzollern-Sigmaringen blazonry is everywhere. The Schön pâtisserie still serves coffee and cakes; the shell of the hotel Zum Löwen is now a shuttered steak bar.

Chapter 9

Conclusions

This has been a work of popular history, animated by a purpose. It has borrowed from the forensic discipline of true historical research, which I stand in awe of. I would not make any great claim of major capabilities or original research in that direction. As usual, I stood on the shoulders of giants. All the judgments in this section are my own, however much built on the evidence. They may be wrong, but I make no apologies for making them.

The sorry story of the Sigmaringen enclave obviously invites judgment. It certainly received the judgment of history by collapsing as ignominiously as it did. I do want to qualify and expand on that judgment just a little, to shed light on some of its terms.

Pétain's vanity, his saviour complex, his constant self-reinforcing overcompensation for the slights he had supposedly suffered during the First World War, certainly fitted him well to be an autocrat. It also made him very much a man of his time, a fellow sufferer along with Hitler and Mussolini and their followers, exhibiting the same overcompensation for the wounds to their self-esteem sustained during the war. His pretensions to sovereignty, so often rearticulated, appealed less to the tenuous thread of legitimacy he had inherited from the Third Republic than to that inner need to see himself as the prophet in exile, the sole true saviour of France. Perhaps the Germans and de Gaulle never did Pétain a greater kindness than to enable him to play the martyr until the bitter end.

As for Laval, perhaps the best thing he ever did for his country was to do nothing. His aspirations to be a power-broker and mastermind repeatedly left him the creature and tool of others. His sojourn in Sigmaringen was more of an interlude and a rest period between his last days in government and his trial, made more poignant by his preparation of entirely the wrong defence.

Faithful to his commitment to resign his functions, he was sidelined by the active collaborationists and the Germans, both of whom knew where the true prize of legitimacy lay. His failure to measure up to the challenges of his times invites comparison with Stanley Baldwin or Neville Chamberlain, but his moral myopia was far more conspicuous. De Gaulle judged him conclusively in his memoirs:

> Naturally inclined, accustomed by the regime, to approach affairs from below, Laval believed that, whatever happened, it was important to be in power, that a certain degree of astuteness always mastered the situation, that there was no event that could not be turned around, no man who could not be manipulated. He had felt the country's misfortune in the catastrophe, but also the opportunity to take the reins and apply on a vast scale his capacity to deal with anything. But the victorious Reich was an uncompromising partner. In order for the field to open up for Pierre Laval in spite of everything, he had to embrace France's disaster. He accepted the condition. He judged that it was possible to take advantage of the worst, to use even servitude, to associate even with the invader, to make an asset of the most dreadful repression. To carry out his policy, he renounced the honour of the country, the independence of the state and national pride. And yet, these elements reappeared alive and pressing as the enemy weakened.

Laval's former subordinates and colleagues in Sigmaringen perhaps behaved just as expected in the depths of their cynical timeserving, but their petty egotisms in the face of defeat are extraordinary – and perhaps, diagnostic. Brinon, Luchaire, Déat shared the same hunger for personal power and penchant for fief-building as Himmler, Bormann, Ribbentrop, and the other luminaries of National Socialism, but the concentrated, congested environment of Sigmaringen robbed that impulse of any delusive grandeur or flattering pageantry. What is remarkable is how far they deviated from the supposed amoral clarity of vision commonly associated with Machiavellian *realpolitik*. Instead of looking events square in the face, without illusions, they indulged in extraordinary flights of self-delusion, entertaining fantasies of wonder-weapons or incredible strategic turnarounds in the face of all the material evidence. Even a pragmatic and personally courageous figure like Darnand, as these accounts have shown, was ready to believe at the eleventh hour in preposterous overestimation of his own capabilities and chances. Perhaps the Commission represents best the final disintegration of vanity and timeserving into an utter nihilistic divorce from reality, where no truth or fact, like no maxim or moral, has any value when set against the demands of selfish egotism.

Doriot's death has often been presented as one of the last great what-ifs in the Liberation of France. If he had survived, at such a late stage in the war, could he actually have done anything? The Battle of Remagen and the first Allied Rhine crossings came just weeks after his death on 22 February. Barring a few isolated enclaves, metropolitan France was already entirely cleared of Nazi and Vichy presence, and so traumatized by close-up contact with the SS, the Gestapo and the Milice as to never be ready to accept them back except at gunpoint. Nazi hopes of making Doriot into some kind of counter-de Gaulle ignored the absolute absence of any basis of popular support in France – although for the likes of Darnand, force rather than acceptance was always the preferred option. Doriot's own paltry efforts to organize anti-Gaullist insurgency in France were pitifully ineffective, and his plans, such as launching false-flag operations in liberated France to discredit the Communists and provoke civil war, were as fanciful as they were irresponsible.

Furthermore, as with Mussolini and Hitler, Doriot's charisma and posthumous myth appear to obscure basic questions of competence. Pétain's genuine personal appeal was almost certainly non-transferrable to Doriot, even if the Marshal had ever been ready to endorse him. As well as its shadow of legitimacy, Pétain bore the Vichy regime's only personal popularity. However successful as a demagogue among certain limited lower-class constituencies in France, Doriot had little to recommend him to France as a whole at any stage, let alone in the final months of the war. A reasonably capable organizer of subversive fringe political groups, he lacked anything like de Gaulle's strategic vision or aptitude for military command. All through his political career, he had borrowed ideas from his more intellectual peers; at its end, he borrowed them from the Gaullists. And would the Nazis have tolerated co-existence with a revived France led by a French Führer? Doriot's posthumous reputation probably benefits from never having to face the answers to those questions.

The disproportionate representation of writers, journalists and intellectuals in the Sigmaringen enclave, and in Doriot's rival entourage, may seem surprising at first. It certainly underlines the importance of propaganda for totalitarian ideologies. It also exemplifies G.K. Chesterton's 'aristocracy of weak nerves' – the coterie of fastidious literati who parlayed their fear and distaste towards the common ruck of ordinary *bourgeois* humanity into some kind of self-flattering caste virtue. A few, like Charles Maurras, Alphonse de Châteaubriant and Abel Bonnard, were actual relics left over from the aesthetic 1890s, the era of pseudo-nobility and waxed moustaches; many more were literary and intellectual descendants. Chesterton again:

This shrinking from the brutal vivacity and brutal variety of common men is a perfectly reasonable and excusable thing as long as it does not pretend to any point of superiority. It is when it calls itself aristocracy or aestheticism or a superiority to the *bourgeoisie* that its inherent weakness has in justice to be pointed out. Fastidiousness is the most pardonable of vices; but it is the most unpardonable of virtues.

Sigmaringen, like all fascist regimes, was jam-packed with pretenders to the paper crown of supposed racial or spiritual or class superiority. They made a pretty poor contrast to the actual contemporary practitioners of both thought and action, like Marc Bloch or Jean Moulin, or Charles de Gaulle.

If I have placed a disproportionate emphasis on the case of Céline, it is partly because he was such a highly regarded witness to events at Sigmaringen, but also because he exemplifies character traits prevalent throughout the collaborationist milieu: above all, malignant narcissism, ever vengeful against the supposed slights and ingratitude inflicted by the world, ever careful of its own pains, ever ready to project narcissistic injury onto any convenient scapegoat. Pétain was another representative case of the same syndrome, overcompensating for the injury to his dignity suffered during the First World War, pathologically convinced of his own saviour status. It's a shame that France, and French Jews in particular, had to suffer as the butts of such psychopathology; it is absolutely no surprise to find it prevalent in the leading circles of fascism.

Céline's own credibility as a reliable narrator of the events at Sigmaringen – and furthermore, their historical context – hardly needs remarking on. Hallucinatory delirium and deranged stream-of-consciousness may be a really fitting narrative mode for portraying the nadir of fascism, but they hardly can support simultaneous insistence on the truth, reliability, and authority of their representations. And Céline insisted constantly on the primacy of his own version of events, stressing his record as a war veteran, his presence on the ground, his readiness to report statements from those who detested him, etc. There is no reason to doubt some of his direct accounts of goings-on in the enclave, but that leeway does not extend into his relativization of the suffering of other groups, his trivialization of the Holocaust, his equation of the Axis with the Allies, and so on. Always a consciously artful writer, appearances notwithstanding, Céline went well beyond mere self-justification in his post-war writing, and seems to have disguised and muted, but never abandoned, his pre-war and wartime position.

The history of French collaborationism and its Sigmaringen coda offers plenty of validation for George Orwell's thesis from 'Notes on Nationalism' of the fundamental qualities and easy transferability of nationalism:

> The nationalist does not go on the principle of simply ganging up with the strongest side. On the contrary, having picked his side, he persuades himself that it is the strongest, and is able to stick to his belief even when the facts are overwhelmingly against him. Nationalism is power hunger tempered by self-deception. Every nationalist is capable of the most flagrant dishonesty, but he is also – since he is conscious of serving something bigger than himself – unshakeably certain of being in the right.

It also provides plenty of fodder for exponents of the horseshoe theory of political extremism – 'Fascist movements were largely recruited from among Communists... What remains constant in the nationalist is his own state of mind: the object of his feelings is changeable, and may be imaginary', as Orwell put it. Laval, Déat and Doriot all switched camps from socialism, or even

Communism, to fascism, along with many of their followers, and these three at least all seem to have been motivated by personal ambition and personal antipathy, plus eagerness to be on the winning side.

A different kind of horseshoe effect might give a better explanation for the French right-wing writers and intellectuals who flocked to the collaborationist camp, and so many of whom ended up in Sigmaringen and similar enclaves. Beyond the positive imbecilities of Maurrasianism, or Drumont's rants, or Nazi race theory, so many of them seem to have started their ideological pilgrimage from a purely negative hatred of ordinary life and ordinary humanity, the frustration and exasperation that Céline indulged and wallowed in. Democratic politics and the Third Republic, the political expression of everyday human society and ordinary human compromises, naturally attracted their ire. The literary end of French politics, or political end of French literature, had nourished such impulses since 1870. It's significant that the key work of Abel Bonnard, poet, PPF member, pro-German collaborationist and Vichy Minister of National Education under Laval, was *Les Modérés* (1936), an attack on the very principle of moderation and democracy.

Céline's patients in the enclave, and the other more obscure refugees at Sigmaringen and its satellite camps, certainly suffered far more and died more neglected than their more famous fellow exiles. They probably deserve more sympathy, especially the women and children. But the movement that got them there in the first place deserves no posthumous tragic glamour or aura of martyrdom. The Milice were hated and despised by the broad sweep of French society, with reason. Their brutality and indiscipline was not accidental excess: it was absolutely inherent to their ideology and their purpose within the Vichy regime. The National Revolution ultimately could only be sustained by revolutionary levels of violence and repression. Darnand was right to call out Pétain's eleventh-hour protests against Milice excesses; these simply brought home the actual cost of sustaining the Vichy project. Pétain was lucky enough to get away with two years of relative domestic calm and limited repression, but the conditions that had allowed the Vichy state to come into existence in the first place could not permit that to continue for too long. And if the Milice were the enablers and stooges of Nazi conquest and atrocity? They were exactly what the Vichy state had been from day one, only a little more blunt and open about it.

Joseph Darnand himself looks to be a sympathetic, even tragic, figure compared to his venal, self-serving Sigmaringen contemporaries. His honesty, his consistency, his courage are not in doubt. Even his temporary flirtation with the idea of changing sides in July 1943 looks to be a readiness to serve France in one way or another. But his pre-war activities, his involvement in Action Française, the Croix-de-Feu, the PPF, and the treasonous terrorist activities of the Cagoule, all count against him. The Third Republic had ample justification to arrest and imprison him well before the war, and deserved better from him than constant subversion just because it was not grand enough to satisfy his ideals. Also, a self-professed leader of men and devotee of action could have seen perfectly well the kind of people he was recruiting for his Milice, and how hard it would be during the Occupation to keep them in line, and restrain their more brutal and vindictive tendencies. His exoneration of them and himself in post-war testimony does not stand up, and the only mitigation was that Pétain and Laval and the entire Vichy regime were ultimately as responsible for Milice brutality as he was.

Less immediately brutal but just as disgraceful was Vichy France's homegrown Maurassian policy of anti-Semitic, anti-Masonic, anti-Enlightenment 'integral nationalism' – a creed fully implemented in Vichy, and perpetuated past the war into some French right-wing ideologies today. France was the nursery of some of the most virulent expressions of modern anti-Semitism, often indulged with a reprehensible level of intellectual respectability in a republic built on the principles of Reason and the Rights of Man. Conservative France's ideologues may have been unable to find any better scapegoats for the consequences of modernization and industrialization, but by delving back past the heritage of rights and reason, they unearthed toxins whose consequences would only come home to roost later in a less stable, less forgiving time. And the Vichy experience was not enough to discredit integral nationalism. Pétain's apologists were on hand from his conviction onwards to whitewash his record and perpetuate the ideology he enforced under the Nazi aegis. Even now, Éric Zemmour – himself Jewish – and other far-right French nationalists are still throwing shade on Dreyfus' innocence, while branding French Muslims as the modern incarnation of Maurras' *métèques*. Action Française still exists in France as a royalist, nationalist, patriotic organization, but hardly exerts much influence on national politics, with membership in the low thousands, yet its modern successors enjoy far more popularity.

Sigmaringen's character and eventual collapse can also stand as symbolic of the collapse of fascism as a whole. As Pierre Milza concluded:

> Already partially marginalized on the eve of war, French fascism thus discovered the logical conclusion of the disenchanted choice which had led many of its adepts to see no possible salvation for the West except in the great upheaval of a return to barbarism. National-Socialist Germany having missed its rendezvous with History, all that remained was to disappear with it. With no other hope than that of destruction, perhaps the inescapable prologue to the birth of a new world. "What is the point of writing literature," wrote Drieu two days before killing himself: "I am waiting for the Huns".[1]

Unfortunately, that's not the end of the story. As elsewhere in the world, certain sectors of French opinion and their political enablers are showing dangerous tendencies to flirt with exactly the ideas that once before brought France nothing but disaster, disgrace and horror. Céline's modern-day literary successors are being lionized by the French cultural establishment with the same indulgence once extended to anti-Semites. At the time of writing, election posters warn of the dangers to French civilization in terms that would have warmed the heart of Maurras, or Darnand. At least one French politician has publicly endorsed the replacement of '*Liberté, Egalité*, Fraternité' by the Vichy slogans '*Travail, Famille, Patrie*'. France has already gone down this road, and the legacy speaks for itself. There lies the serious purpose behind this chronicle of a farcical, ludicrous, marginal little coda to a national tragedy.

The Sigmaringen enclave certainly never succeeded in being a perfect fascist society in miniature, but it succeeded all too well in being an unflattering microcosm of fascism in actuality: the petty feuds and turf wars, the cannibalistic hierarchy where some gorged while others starved, the atavistic decor of feudal totems and relics, the popinjay parade of insignia and uniforms, the arbitrary whimsy and inconsistency masquerading as force of will, the verbose cult of strength contrasted with physical cowardice, the grinding collisions of fanaticisms of varying degrees of delusional insanity, the melange of deranged conviction and cynical timeserving. As a community and a government-in-exile, it was no more phantasmal and delusional than fascism itself. And at least it does a good job of discrediting the ideology it embodied.

Acknowledgements

Awork of this length and type does not get written without a huge debt to a plethora of historians and researchers, many of them transformative influences on their fields of study. In particular, I'd like to acknowledge the French chroniclers of Vichy and its downfall, Jean-Paul Cointet, Pierre Giolitto, Pierre Milza, Louis Noguères, Henry Rousso, and others whose work is the basis for the historical core of this volume. If I've failed to acknowledge any citation from or reference to them, and to their peers, I apologize, but readers should have no doubt where many of the facts and arguments in this history originally stem from. In English, Robert O. Paxton and Robert A. Doughty deserve similar acknowledgement. Extended translations of contemporary documents and statements, except where indicated, are as reproduced by Louis Noguères. The translations from all French sources, except where indicated, and any resulting mistakes or mistranslations, are entirely my own.

I'd like to make a personal acknowledgment of a different kind to Louis-Ferdinand Céline. I owe him some thanks for perpetuating and amplifying the bizarre fascination of the Sigmaringen enclave, and for making it possible to publish this book in the first place. I owe him more thanks for providing an ideal test case for my personal thesis that the obsessive focus which creates great art can be fuelled by the grubbiest, most sordid, most toxic and pathetic private flaws in the smallest and sickest of minds. Like Gabriele D'Annunzio, fascism's choreographer, he is an ideal corrective to Percy Bysshe Shelley's claim that 'poets are the unacknowledged legislators of the world'.

My thanks to the Tourismus und Stadtmarketing service of Sigmaringen, and the town's other hospitable citizens. My eternal gratitude for the irreplaceably valuable online services of Gallica at the Bibliothèque nationale de France. My undying gratitude also to Trinity College, Cambridge, and to Cambridge University for starting me down this road that it took so long to come back to. My thanks also to my editors and publisher – in fact, to all my publishers. My thanks to Clan Mackintosh, and the great historical and literary heritage of Scotland. My thanks to France, my second home and saviour from the imbecility of Brexit. And as always, my thanks to my parents and my family; to Rae Gee, Krys, Aina and Bahashty for their belief and support; and to my daughters Diana and Esther for providing the best reasons to remain in the world and try to make it better.

Bibliography

Amouroux, Henri, *La Grande Histoire des Français après l'Occupation*, Robert Laffont, 1999

Arendt, Hannah, *The Origins of Totalitarianism*, Schocken Books, 1951

Bechtel, Guy, *Laval vingt ans apres*, Robert Laffont, 1963

Bloch, Marc, *L'Etrange Défaite*, Folio, 1946

Bloy, Léon, *Sueur de Sang*, Éditions Dentu, 1893

Bourdrel, Philippe, *Les Cagoulards dans la guerre*, Albin Michel, 2009

Burin, Philippe, *France Under the Germans: Collaboration and Compromise*, New Press, 1997

Carroll, David, *French Literary Fascism: Nationalism, Anti-Semitism, and the Ideology of Culture*, Princeton University Press, 1994

Céline, Louis-Ferdinand, *D'un château l'autre*, Éditions Gallimard, Paris, 1957 (published in English as *Castle to Castle*, tr. Ralph Mannheim, Delacorte Press, 1968)

Céline, Louis-Ferdinand, *War*, translated by Charlotte Mandell, New Directions, 2024

Cointet, Jean-Paul, *Sigmaringen: Une France en Allemagne (septembre 1944 – avril 1945)*, Perrin, 2003

Coniez, Hugo, *La Mort de la IIIe République, 10 mai–10 juillet 1940: de la défaite au coup d'État*, Perrin, 2024

Dard, Olivier, *Charles Maurras*, Dunod, 2013

Doughty, Robert A., *The Seeds of Disaster: The Development of French Army Doctrine, 1919–39*, Stackpole Military History Series, 2023

Epstein, Simon, *Les Dreyfusards sous l'Occupation*, Albin Michel, 2001

Giolitto, Pierre, *Histoire de la Milice*, Perrin, 1997

Hérold-Paquis, Jean, *Des illusions... désillusions! Mémoires 15 août 1944 – 15 août 1945*, Bourgoin, 1948

Jackson, Julian, *France: The Dark Years, 1940–1944*, Oxford University Press, 2001

Jauneaud, Jean-Henri, with Chérasse, Jean A., *J'accuse le maréchal Pétain*, Pygmalion, 1949

Lacouture, Jean, *Charles de Gaulle, I. Le rebelle 1890-1944*, Le Seuil, 1984

Luchaire, Corinne, *Ma drôle de vie*, Editions Sun, 1949

Maurras, Charles, *Dictionnaire politique et critique*, 5 volumes, Artheme Fayard, 1932-34

Maurras, Charles, *Enquête sur la monarchie*, Gazette de France, 1900

Maurras, Charles, *Trois idees politiques: Chateaubriand, Michelet, Sainte-Beuve*, Champion, 1898

Meletta, Cédric, *Jean Luchaire, L'enfant perdu des années sombres*, Perrin, 2013

Meltz, Renaud, *Pierre Laval*, Perrin, 2018

Milza, Pierre, *Fascisme français: passé et présent*, Flammarion, 1987

Miot, Claire, *La Première Armée française. De la Provence à l'Allemagne 1944-1945*, Perrin, 2021

Noguères, Louis, *La dernière étape, Sigmaringen*, Fayard, 1956

Ogé, Frédéric, *Le journal « L'Action française » et la politique intérieure du Gouvernement de Vichy*, Institut d'études politiques, Toulouse, 1984

Paul-Boncour, Joseph, *Entre deux guerres. Souvenirs de la IIIe République*, Plon, 1946

Paxton, Robert O., *Vichy France: Old Guard and New Order, 1940-1944*, Knopf, 1972

Quétel, Claude, *Vichy, vérités et légendes*, Perrin, 2024

Rebatet, Lucien, *Les Memoires d'un fasciste*, Vol. 2, 1941-1947, Jean-Jacques Pauvert, 1976

Le Robert Dictionnaire des grands ecrivains de la langue francais, Robert, 2000

Rousso, Henry, *Pétain et la fin de la Collaboration: Sigmaringen 1944-1945*, Complexe, 1984

Rousso, Henry, *The Vichy Syndrome*, Harvard University Press, 1994

Rousso, Henry, *Le Régime de Vichy*, Presses Universitaires de France, 2012

Scapini, Georges, *Mission sans gloire*, Morgan, 1960

Schillemans, Gérard-Trinité, *Philippe Pétain: Le prisonnier de Sigmaringen*, Editions M.P., 1965

Stucki, Walter, *La fin du régime de Vichy*, Oreste Zeléditeur, 1947

Veneer, Dominique, *Histoire de la Collaboration*, Pygmalion, 2000

Vergez-Chaignon, Bénédicte, *Les secrets de Vichy*, Perrin, 2015

Weber, Eugen, *L'Action française*, Hachette Littératures, 1985

Notes

Introduction

1. Céline, Louis-Ferdinand, *D'un château l'autre*, Éditions Gallimard, 1957, pp. 102-03
2. Jackson, Julian, *France: The Dark Years, 1940-1944*, Oxford University Press, 2001, p. 568
3. Watts, Phillip, 'The Ghosts of Sigmaringen', *Studies in 20th & 21st Century Literature*, Vol. 23, 1999
4. Rousso, Henry, 'Histoire et mémoire des années noires', *Histoire, Institut d'études politiques de Paris*, Sciences Po, 2000

Chapter 1

1. Sutton, Michael, 'Nationalism, Positivism and Catholicism: The Politics of Charles Maurras and French Catholics 1890–1914', *Cambridge Studies in the History and Theory of Politics*, Cambridge University Press, 1982, p. 51
2. Byrnes, Robert F., 'Antisemitism in France before the Dreyfus Affair', *Jewish Social Studies*, 11, no. 1, 1949, pp. 49–68
3. Weber, Eugen, 'Fascism(s) and Some Harbingers', *The Journal of Modern History*, 54, no. 4, 1982, pp. 746–65
4. Epstein, Simon, *Les Dreyfusards sous l'Occupation*, Albin Michel, 2001, p. 197
5. Gilbert, Bentley B., and Bernard, Paul P., 'The French Army Mutinies of 1917', *Historian*, Vol. 22#1, 1959, pp. 24–41
6. 'Hero of Verdun: Marshal Henri Philippe Pétain', *Warfare History Network*, 15 July 2021
7. Ambron, André, 'Pétain's Political Ambition', *The American Scholar*, Vol. 21, no. 1, 1951, pp. 81–89
8. Amouroux, Henri, *La Grande Histoire des Français après l'Occupation*, Paris, 1999, p. 954

9. Johnson, Douglas, 'Léon Blum and the Popular Front', *History*, Vol. 55, no. 184, 1970, p. 200

10. Allardyce, Gilbert, and Picard, Andrée R., 'Jacques Doriot et l'esprit fasciste en France', *Revue d'histoire de La Deuxième Guerre Mondiale*, Vol. 25, no. 97, 1975, pp. 31–44

11. Carroll, David, *French Literary Fascism: Nationalism, Anti-Semitism, and the Ideology of Culture*, Princeton, 1994, p. 7

12. *Le Robert Dictionnaire des grands ecrivains de la langue francais*, Robert, Paris, 2000, p. 238

13. Hewitt, Nicholas, 'Céline: The Success of the "Monstre Sacré" in Postwar France', *SubStance*, Vol. 32, no. 3, 2003, pp. 29–42

14. Carroll, op. cit., pp. 11-12

15. Carroll, op. cit., p. 13

16. Belot, Robert, 'Lucien Rebatet De l'intellectuel Fasciste', *Esprit* (1940-), Vol. 201, (5), 1994, pp. 65–94

17. Milza, op. cit., p. 159

18. Rossiter, Adrian, 'Popular Front Economic Policy and the Matignon Negotiations', *The Historical Journal*, Vol. 30, no. 3. 1987, pp. 663–84

19. Irvine, William D., 'Domestic Politics and the Fall of France in 1940', *Historical Reflections/Réflexions Historiques*, Vol. 22, no. 1, 1996, pp. 77–90

20. Johnson, op. cit., p. 184

21. Judt, Tony, '"We Have Discovered History": Defeat, Resistance, and the Intellectuals in France,' *The Journal of Modern History*, Vol. 64, 1992, S147–72

Chapter 2

1. Coniez, Hugo, *La Mort de la IIIe République, 10 mai-10 juillet 1940: de la défaite au coup d'État*, Perrin, Paris, 2024, p. 6

2. Ambron, op. cit.

3. Coniez, op. cit., p. 7

4. Irvine, op. cit.

5. Irvine, ibid.

6. Blatt, Joel, 'The French Defeat of 1940: Reassessments: Introduction', *Historical Reflections/Réflexions Historiques*, Vol. 22, no. 1, 1996, pp. 1–10

7. Alexander, Martin S., 'After Dunkirk: The French Army's Performance against "Case Red", 25 May to 25 June 1940', *War in History*, Vol. 14, no. 2. 2007, pp. 219–64

8. Alexander, ibid.

9. Bankwitz, Philip C.F., 'Maxime Weygand and the Fall of France: A Study in Civil-Military Relations', *The Journal of Modern History*, Vol. 31, no. 3, 1959, pp. 225–4

10. Bankwitz, ibid.

11. Ambron, op. cit.

12. Paul-Boncour, Joseph, *Entre deux guerres. Souvenirs de la IIIe République*, Plon, 1946, Vol. 3, p. 274

13. UK National Archives, https://blog.nationalarchives.gov.uk/battle-heavy-water/

14. Schillemans, op. cit.

15. Quoted in Eugen Weber, *L'Action française*, Hachette Littératures, 1985, p. 517

16. Rousso, Henry, *Le Régime de Vichy*, Presses Universitaires de France, Paris, 2012, pp. 3-4

17. Rousso, ibid., pp. 4-5

18. Sutton, Michael, 'Jews and Christians in Vichy France: New and Renewed Perspectives', *French Politics, Culture & Society*, Vol. 35, no. 3, 2017, pp. 105–28

19. Ambron, op. cit.

20. Belot, Robert, 'Lucien Rebatet: De l'intellectuel Fasciste', *Esprit* (1940-), no. 201, 1994, pp. 65–94

21. Belot, ibid.

Chapter 3

1. Jordan, Nicole, 'Strategy and Scapegoatism: Reflections on the French National Catastrophe, 1940', *Historical Reflections/Réflexions Historiques*, Vol. 22, no. 1, 1996, pp. 11–3

2. Meltz, Renaud, 'Laval, antisémite qui s'ignore et persécuteur cynique', *Revue d'Histoire de la Shoah*, no. 212, 2020, pp. 121-151

3. Barthélemy, Victor, *Du communisme au fascisme*, Paris, Albin Michel, 1978, p. 342

4. Ogé, Frédéric, *Le journal « L'Action française » et la politique intérieure du Gouvernement de Vichy*, Toulouse, Institut d'études politiques, 1984, p. 483

5. Lacouture, Jean, *Charles de Gaulle, I. Le rebelle 1890-1944*, Paris, Le Seuil, 1984, p. 757

6. Amouroux, op. cit., pp. 954-55

7. Dard, Olivier, *Charles Maurras*, Paris, 2013, p. 207

8. Les 1502 jours du chef de l'Etat français, https://www.etat-francais.fr/

9. Azéma, op. cit.

Chapter 4

1. https://www.lemonde.fr/livres/article/2021/08/04/lettres-manuscrits-photos-inedites-les-archives-retrouvees-de-celine-constituent-une-decouverte-extraordinaire_6090545_3260.html

2. Vergez-Chaignon, op. cit., pp. 914-15

3. Meltz, Renaud, *Pierre Laval*, Perrin, Paris, 2018

4. Azéma, op. cit.

5. Rousso, Henry, 'L'Organisation industrielle de Vichy', *Revue d'Histoire de la Seconde Guerre mondiale*, no. 116, 1979

6. https://www.etat-francais.fr/07-aout-1944/

7. Quoted in Vergez-Chaignon, op. cit., p. 956

8. Quoted in Noguères, Louis, *La dernière étape, Sigmaringen*, Fayard, 1956, pp. 160-61

9. Hérold-Paquis, Jean, *Des illusions... désillusions! Mémoires 15 août 1944 – 15 août 1945*, Paris, 1948, pp. 28-30

10. Milza, op cit., p. 263

11. https://gallica.bnf.fr/ark:/12148/bpt6k33596291/f23.item

12. Marguerat, Philippe, and Roulet, Louis-Edouard (ed.), *Diplomatic Documents of Switzerland*, Vol. 15, doc. 213, Bern, 1992, dodis.ch/47817

Chapter 5

1. Rebatet, Lucien, *Les Memoires d'un fasciste*, Vol. 2, 1941-1947, Paris, 1976, p. 215

2. Amouroux, op. cit., p. 834

3. Rapporté par un émissaire des Renseignements généraux, envoyé par le gouvernement provisoire de la Libération, à Sigmaringen: Activités des émigrés français à Sigmaringen, Paris, Sûreté nationale

4. Peyrefitte, Alain, *C'était de Gaulle*, Vol. 2, Paris, 1997
5. Hérold-Paquis, Jean, *Des Illusions... Désillusions*, Paris, Bourgoin, 1948, pp. 119-122
6. https://presseillustree.home.blog/2019/04/10/jacques-de-lesdain-itineraires-dun-collaborateur-5eme-partie-1944-1945-de-paris-a-sigmaringen/
7. Amouroux, op. cit., p. 814
8. Les Proces de Collaboration: Brinon, Luchaire, Darnand, pp. 477-478

Chapter 6

1. Luchaire, Corinne, *Ma drôle de vie*, Paris, 1949, p. 205
2. Scapini, Georges, *Mission sans gloire*, Morgan, Paris, 1960, pp. 257-58
3. Sigmaringen, *l'ultime trahison*, *Documentaire Historique de Laurent*, Perrin, 1996
4. https://presseillustree.home.blog/2019/04/10/jacques-de-lesdain-itineraires-dun-collaborateur-5eme-partie-1944-1945-de-paris-a-sigmaringen/
5. https://www.tessier-sarrou.com/lot/9634/1882679?npp=10000&

Chapter 7

1. Telegram from Charles de Gaulle to General de Lattre, quoted in Miot
2. Letter quoted in Bechtel, Guy, *Laval vingt ans apres*, Robert Laffont, 1963
3. Annexe to the interrogation of Marshal Pétain by the High Court on 8 June 1945; quoted in Noguères, op. cit., pp. 328-35
4. Amouroux, op.cit., pp. 807-809

Chapter 8

1. Judt, Tony, '"We Have Discovered History": Defeat, Resistance, and the Intellectuals in France', *The Journal of Modern History*, Vol. 64, 1992, S147–72
2. https://www.historia.fr/guerres-conflits-contemporains/2eme-guerre-mondiale/epuration-legale-400-000-dossiers-moins-de-800-morts-2054808
3. Interrogation of Joseph Darnand, 3 July 1945, quoted in Vergez-Chaignon, op. cit., p. 750

4. https://gallica.bnf.fr/ark:/12148/bpt6k6821302v/
5. https://gallica.bnf.fr/ark:/12148/bpt6k6821304p/
6. https://www.lemonde.fr/archives/article/1947/06/10/le-general-bridoux-s-evade-du-val-de-grace_1892676_1819218.html
7. Statement of the prosecutor at Marcel Déat's trial in absentia, quoted in Vergez-Chaignon, op. cit., p. 766
8. Marcot, François, 'Déat: les mémoires d'un schizophrène mégalomane', *Guerres Mondiales et Conflits Contemporains*, no. 159, 1990, pp. 110–15
9. Hérold-Paquis, op. cit., pp. 125-126
10. Hartmann, Marie, 'Celine et la Seconde Guerre Mondiale: La Presentation des "collaborateurs" en victime de guerre', in *Actes du XVIe colloque international* L.-F. Céline: *Céline et la guerre*, Paris, 2007, pp. 172-176
11. Hartmann, op. cit., p. 179
12. https://lareviewofbooks.org/article/the-moral-delusions-of-patriotism-on-louis-ferdinand-celines-war/
13. Céline, Louis-Ferdinand, *War*, translated by Charlotte Mandell, New Directions, New York, 2024
14. Quoted in Mongin, Olivier, 'L'Antisémitisme, Rebatet et Maritain', *Esprit* (1940-), no. 299, 11, 2003, pp. 179–81
15. Belot, Robert, 'Lucien Rebatet: De l'intellectuel Fasciste', *Esprit* (1940-), no. 201, (5), 1994, pp. 65–94
16. https://www.retronews.fr/journal/ce-soir/13-septembre-1944/19/1177429/1
17. https://www.lhistoire.fr/maurras-prisonnier-de-ses-haines
18. https://www.lhistoire.fr/maurras-prisonnier-de-ses-haines
19. Roudiez, Leon S., Review of Maurras and the Action Française in Historical Perspective, by Edward R. Tannenbaum and Eugen Weber, *The Modern Language Journal*, Vol. 49, no. 7, 1965, pp. 443–46
20. Roudiez, ibid.

Chapter 9

1. Milza, op. cit., p. 275

Index